Get Online

Get Online

TIME LIFE BOOKS

Time-Life is a trademark of Time Warner Inc., USA

ISBN: 0 7054 3085 5

Designed and edited by Eaglemoss Publications Ltd
in association with VNU Business Publications Ltd

CIP Date is available from the British Library

Printed in Singapore

1 0 9 8 7 6 5 4 3 2

Contents

What's the Net?

The Internet is a collection of computers that spans the world, linked together by a high-speed communications system. You can become part of the Net by linking your computer to it with a modem. All the computers pass information on to each other, so a connection to the Net at one point allows you to access computers anywhere else, just like an ordinary phone allows you to connect to any other telephone in the rest of the world. The Internet, like the phone system, routes your requests to the appropriate place.

There are many things modern computers can be used for, and with the Internet you can do almost anything you want, anywhere in the world. You can keep in contact with people, save money on shopping, catch up on the news, look up a history project, or play online games. It's like a cross between a giant library, a shopping center, and an amusement park, all available from your own home.

The Web and the Superhighway?

When people talk about the Internet, they often also talk about two other things: the World Wide Web and the Information Superhighway. You might think they are the same, but they're not.

The Internet is a network of networks, millions of computers exchanging information around the world. It supports electronic mail, or email, discussion groups, files you can download to your computer, and pages of information on the World Wide Web, often simply referred to as the Web.

The Web is just one of the things you can access on the Internet; it is the pages full of links that take you to other pages, rather like clicking the highlighted words in a Windows Help file. Because the Web is so easy to use, it's the most public face of the Internet. Most Web browsers also allow you to access other features of the Internet, like email and downloading files to your computer, so it's not surprising the two things are often confused.

The Information Superhighway is a creation of the politicians intended to expresses the idea of how the world will be when everyone can connect, share information, and find out what's happening. While this concept doesn't rely on the Internet, the Net is the best way of making that information available now — even though sometimes the speed seems more like a horse and cart than a superhighway.

As computers and the links between them become faster, however, and more information is available at the click of a button, the Internet, or something very like it, will one day truly become the Information Superhighway.

Viruses

A word of warning should be given at the start. Before downloading any document or file to your computer — from the Web or any other source — check for viruses. There are people who find it amusing to introduce viruses into the system deliberately, which, if downloaded, will affect your machine and may destroy your files. Install software which will do this automatically. Make sure the software is active whenever you log on to the Internet.

1

Internet Basics

Get connected to the Internet and the World Wide Web and the whole world comes to your screen.

It's out there, and it's hard to ignore. Even institutions as traditional as the Royal Family are on the Internet. You can hardly turn on the television or pick up a magazine without seeing something about it, even if it's just the address of a Web page at the bottom of a car ad, or on the bag your groceries were packed in.

The Net is described as a library, a newspaper, a chat line, a shop and just about everything else. Since it started to become popular a few years ago, it's grown tremendously, and there's no doubt that, whatever your needs and interests, there's information on the Internet that you'll find useful.

A global link

The Internet is a collection of computers spanning the world, linked together by a complex network of phone lines, high-speed computer networks, dedicated undersea cables, and just about any other type of communication you can imagine. The one thing that all the computers have in common is a shared protocol or language, which means that any of them can exchange information with any other.

Something for everyone

Information makes the Internet special. You can find lengthy technical details about the Space Shuttle or how to repair your old car. There are clips of the latest singles and videos from top artists; guides to your legal rights; competitions for you and your children; fan club magazines; mutual support groups for everything under the sun; and electronic banking. You could even order up a box of chocolates or a bottle of wine. It's all simple to get to, just a few clicks of the mouse away, and for only a small amount of money each month. So what are you waiting for?

You will need

ESSENTIAL

Software To browse the Internet you need a program called an Internet browser. If you use Windows 95 or Windows 98, you'll already have a browser called Microsoft Internet Explorer, which is represented by an icon of a globe or of the letter e on the Desktop. If you don't have a browser, your Internet service provider should supply one, such as Netscape Navigator, when you open an account (see below). A browser displays pages retrieved from the Internet and presents them in a form you can understand, usually combining text, graphics and sound.

Hardware A modem.

Other An account with an Internet service provider, or ISP. For a small monthly fee, an account with an ISP gives you unlimited access to the Internet, and you just pay the cost of a local telephone call while you're connected. An ISP account also gives you access to email.

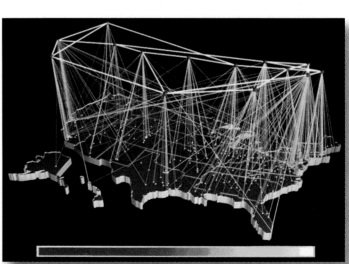

A map of the Internet over America as visualized on the Atlas of Cyberspace World Wide Web page.

How to connect

Jargon buster

Surf To spend time wandering around the World Wide Web looking at Web sites. People who do this are called surfers.

Which modem?

The speed of a modem is measured in bits per second (bps). The higher the number, the faster the modem will transfer data to and from your PC. Modem speeds are a maximum speed under perfect conditions — conditions that rarely occur. Your location, telephone line quality and even the time of day can affect your modem's performance.

56,000bps Also known as V.90, x2, 56K and K56flex. These can receive information at speeds up to 56,000bps but can only send it at 36,600bps. There are two different types of 56K modems — x2 and K56flex; a new modem standard called V.90 combines the two. When buying an x2 or K56flex modem, check that it is upgradable to V.90.

33,600bps Also known as 33K6, V.34, and 33.6Kbps. These have come down in price as 56K has become the standard, so they may still represent an economic solution if you sometimes use the Internet but don't require maximum speed.

28,000bps Sometimes called 28K or V.34 modems, these have all but been replaced by the slightly quicker 33,600bps models. If you can still find one, 28,000bps modems are a good budget option for occasional use.

14,400bps Also known as V.32bis. A few years ago this was the top speed. Although this modem is comparatively slow now, it may still be worth considering buying one if you only use the Internet very occasionally, but wish to send faxes from your computer.

All you need to get on to the Net is a modem and an account with an Internet service provider.

Connecting to the Internet is much easier than it used to be, and it needn't cost you too much money. If your PC runs Windows, you already have most of the software you need. All you have to do is add a modem — short for MOdulator/DEModulator. This is a small unit that converts the digital information stored inside your PC into a series of noises that can be sent along the phone line.

As well as a modem, you'll need an account with an Internet service provider (ISP). You can find out more about them on pages 10–11. The ISP is the company which lets you have a unique email address, so that anyone else in the world can send a message to you. It also provides the telephone lines that you dial to access the rest of the Internet, and links to the rest of the world.

International access

What happens when you want to access information somewhere else? A common misconception about the Net is that it costs more to access PCs overseas, just like making an international phone call. That couldn't be further from the truth. No matter where you are in the country, you can access the Internet by making a local call. Apart from the charges made by the Internet provider — usually a flat monthly fee — the local phone bill is all you'll pay. When you want to access information on a computer in Japan from the UK, your PC is still only connected to the local phone number you dialled. From your Internet provider, data travels over international links, through Internet Exchanges where all the different providers connect together, until it finally reaches a link to the Japanese computer. Best of all, it all happens invisibly. You don't need to know anything except the email address of the person or the address of the Web site that you want to access.

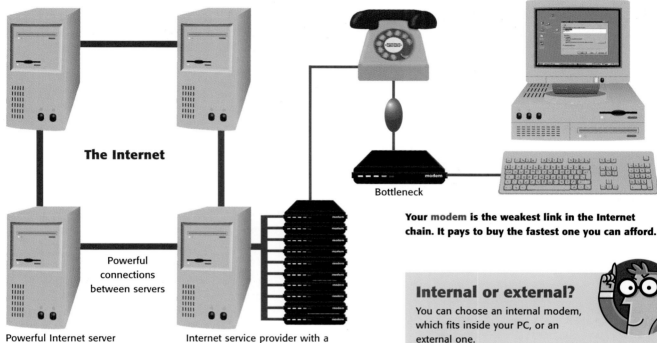

The Internet

Powerful connections between servers

Powerful Internet server

Internet service provider with a powerful bank of modems

Bottleneck

Your modem is the weakest link in the Internet chain. It pays to buy the fastest one you can afford.

Modems, the missing link

For most people, the easiest way to connect to the Internet is via a modem, which converts the 1s and 0s that your computer understands to squeals, squawks and other noises that can be sent along the phone line. At the ISP, other modems convert the information back into a digital format, so that it can continue its journey over the Internet.

Since the bulk of the Internet is made up of very fast links between high-powered computers, the slowest point on a connection is almost always the modem on your computer. So it makes sense to choose the right one.

Face the fax

You should also look at other features when you choose a modem. Almost every modem that you buy can be used to send and receive faxes, turning your PC into a fax machine. Some have voice features, which means that they can turn your PC into an answering machine, or even a voicemail system, so you sound like a big company when people call you.

When you buy a modem, you'll need to consider how fast it is. The faster the modem, the less time you'll spend faxing, thus saving money. Decide whether to buy an internal or external modem, and take into account any extras that are offered. Shop around and you might even find a modem that comes with up to a month's free Internet trial.

Internal or external?

You can choose an internal modem, which fits inside your PC, or an external one.

INTERNAL
Good points Internal modems take up no desk space. They don't need to be connected to a wall outlet, and they leave your second serial port free.
Bad points You have to take the PC apart, and they don't have status lights to monitor activity.

EXTERNAL
Good points External modems can be installed by plugging them into the PC. Their status lights show what is going on with your modem.
Bad points External modems need desk space and occupy your second serial port.

A modem brings the world to your door.

Service providers

A typical ISP offers you access to the Net only, with no bells or whistles. Until you change it, your browser will always start with its own Web site e.g. Netscape, Net Center. This will get you started but then it's up to you to decide where to go and what to do.

Choose the right Internet service provider to ensure trouble-free and cost-effective surfing.

The Internet service provider (ISP) is your gateway to the Internet. Think of an ISP as providing a service in much the same way as a telephone company. Just as a new telephone is useless unless you have an account with a telephone company, so your PC and modem combination can't get on to the Internet unless an ISP provides the connection.

What to ask

Choosing an ISP can be a daunting task. Hundreds of companies are competing for your attention. Many will offer free trials of their services for a month, so you can try before you buy. Knowing the right questions to ask before you sign on the dotted line and commit yourself is by far the best tactic. Here is a list of five questions for your ISP.

Do you support my operating system?

There is no point going any further if the ISP doesn't provide support for the platform version (e.g. Windows 95 or 98) of any software they supply, depending on which OS your computer runs on.

Using an online service provider usually means a much more interesting way of accessing the Internet, as you can see here with CompuServe. There's lots to do and see, yet it's very easy to use, even if it's your first time online.

Online tip

The easiest way to speed up surfing is to take account of differing world time zones. Avoid peak times in the US between 9am and 11am (3–5pm in the UK) when businesses wake up and connect to the Net.

Can I connect at a local phone rate?

Most ISPs will have a local rate phone number for access which reduces your costs. It's worth making sure, especially if you live in a remote area.

How much do you charge?

Some ISPs charge a flat monthly subscription fee on an all-you-can-surf basis with no time restrictions. Others charge by the minute or hour, while yet others allow you a few hours each month for a set fee, with any extra time being charged by the hour. Check if there is a one-time joining fee to cover administration costs. A growing number of ISPs offer Internet access for free, but the quality of service might not be as good as more established ISPs.

What do I get for my money?

Check the number of email addresses you get — more than one is useful. Ask about free Web space to enable you to have your own home page. Ask about software too. Does the ISP supply a free browser or other Internet software?

What technical support can you offer me?

If things go wrong, you'll want to know where to get help. Find out if the ISP offers 24-hour telephone support — not via email because it may be your email you are having problems with.

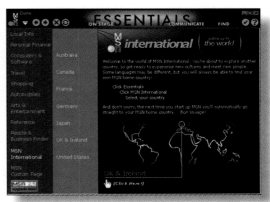

The Microsoft Network offers an international feel, with gateways to different parts of the world.

Which system?

There are three types of ISP that you may come across. All have their own particular strengths and weaknesses.

● **Dial-up ISPs** These are the most common type of service provider, so called because you use a modem and phone line to dial up and connect to the Net. They typically charge a monthly fee which includes as much surfing time as you like, with just the additional cost of phone calls to budget for. The weakness is that you only get Internet access and basic amenities, such as free Web space and email. Examples include Netcom, Pipex Dial and Demon Internet.

● **Online service providers** OSPs tend to have millions of customers and offer additional services over and above Internet access. You get a complete package: easy-to-use software and lots of value-added content such as discussion groups, databases, and online games only available to members. The OSPs charge a flat fee for a few hours each month, with additional time spent online being charged for by the hour or minute. Examples include the Microsoft Network (MSN), CompuServe and AOL.

● **Cyber cafés** Cyber cafés are coffee shops with computers to access the Internet. They are a particularly convenient way to try out the Internet to see if you like it, without having to buy a modem and ISP account. On the other hand, if you do get a taste for surfing, they are expensive and you can't use them from home.

AOL draws on its reputation as a family-oriented access provider by making the interface colourful and fun, with clearly marked routes for kids to explore.

Bandwidth

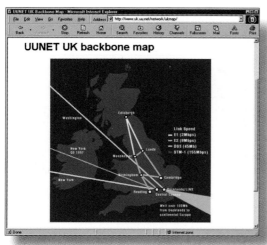

UUNET UK backbone map

UUNET is one of the biggest Internet backbone providers. Here you can see how it connects globally with ultra high-speed backbone pipes.

Speed tips

Don't slow down your Internet connection by buying a cheap but slow modem. A modern fast modem (33.6Kbps minimum, preferably a 56Kbps model) will eliminate a bottleneck of information between your ISP and your PC. This is the only part of the bandwidth equation you can do something about from home, so make the most of it.

The larger your ISP's connection to the Internet, the quicker it will be able to pipe information to your PC.

Imagine your connection to the Internet across the phone network as about the size of a drinking straw. The ISP is connected to the Internet via an upstream provider, which rents part of a bigger pipe to the ISP. This connection can be thought of as being the size of a drainpipe. The upstream provider, or backbone provider, is much bigger and has a much larger connection to the Internet.

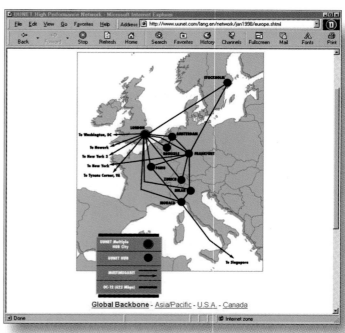

Global Backbone - Asia/Pacific - U.S.A. - Canada

Here is a broad picture of how UUNET connects the UK to the rest of Europe and beyond. These backbone pipes are the railway tunnels, each with hundreds of smaller drainpipes connected to them.

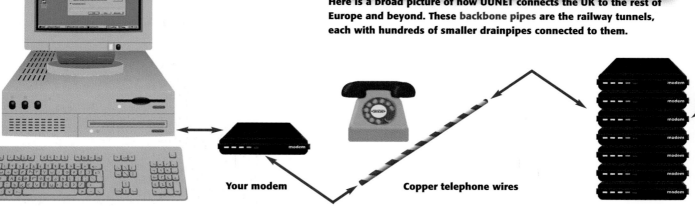

Your computer   **Your modem**   **Copper telephone wires**   **Internet service provider**

Jargon buster

Bandwidth The capacity of the Internet connection to deliver data. Your ISP will be connected directly to the Internet by way of a leased line fibre optic cable. The bigger the line the more bandwidth it will have and the faster information will be able to travel by way of that Internet connection.

Backbones vary in size according to the size of providers and the amount of money they have to invest. Think of Internet backbones as being the size of anything from a main drainpipe right through to a railway tunnel. When you want to look at a Web page for example, you send a request for that information from your PC via the modem through the telephone line straw to your ISP, then it travels through the drainpipe to the backbone provider where it's moved out on to the Internet by way of the railway tunnel.

Traffic jams

It travels through a number more tunnels and drainpipes before reaching the Web server that holds the Web page you want — and then has to find its way back to you. Thousands of people are also using these same pipes to move information at the same time as you, so it's not surprising that things slow down.

Squeeze it through

The amount of information that can fit into any pipe at any one time is known as the available bandwidth. If your ISP has a 64Kbps (kilobits per second) pipe to the Net and 64 people are using it at the same time, then the available bandwidth is a lot less than when just one person is using it.

The less available bandwidth, the slower your Internet connection becomes as more information is squeezed into the pipe. Even if your ISP has plenty of available bandwidth, you may still find it slow going when you try to access certain popular Web sites. This is because thousands of people are all asking that server for information at the same time.

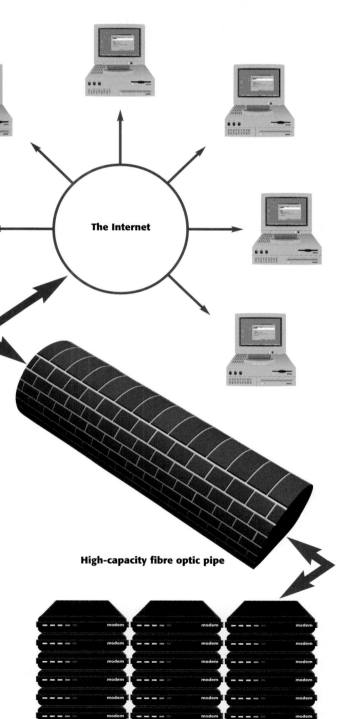

The Internet

High-capacity fibre optic pipe

Low-capacity fibre optic pipe

Upstream backbone provider

World Wide Web

Search tips

There's so much on the Web that it can be hard to find what you're looking for. Help is at hand in the form of directories and search engines, which catalogue as many pages as they can. Directories put everything into categories. You start with broad headings like sports, then work down to outdoor sports, then mountaineering, for example. Search engines let you type in a word and search for pages that contain it.

Two popular search systems are AltaVista and Yahoo!. AltaVista is a search engine, Yahoo! is a directory. You can submit your URL to be placed in a Yahoo! category (e.g. http://dir.yahoo.com/Arts/Art_History/Art_Historians/) and traditionally

a member of Yahoo!'s staff will inspect your site before including it. It's best to start looking in a directory, and use a search engine if you're still finding it hard to track down what you want.

The World Wide Web brings colourful, musical and informative pages straight to your PC.

The World Wide Web is just one of the many ways that information can be accessed on the Internet. Often called just the Web, or WWW, it's the best place to start when you're starting on the Internet.

No place like home

The Web is made up of Web servers which contain pages of information. You tell your browser which server you want to look at by typing in its address. You then see the server's home page. Click on a link and you'll see another page. Think of it as an advanced version of Windows' Help system, where clicking can take you half way across the world.

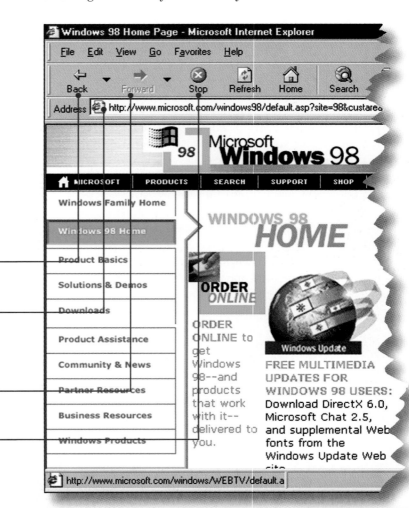

Click on Back to step back through the pages you've visited recently.

This is the URL (name) of the page that you're viewing. If you click in this area, you can type in a URL that you want to visit. Press Enter and the browser will get it for you.

After you've used the Back button, Forward will move in the opposite direction.

Microsoft Internet Explorer's Favorites menu is called Bookmarks on the popular Netscape Navigator browser. If you like a page, a quick mouse click will add it to this menu so you can visit it again easily and quickly.

A unique name

Each page on the Web has a unique name called a URL, which tells your browser its location. You'll often see them starting http://. This tells your Web browser how to ask the server for the page. For example, http://www.timelife.com/ will display the home page of the company that publishes this book. Typing http://www.microsoft.com/windows into your browser will display the first page about Windows on the server called www.microsoft.com.

Some pages have pictures or movie clips. Others are like forms, where you fill in the blanks to order some flowers or take part in a survey. There's no limit to what can be put on a Web page. You'll find weather maps, live TV, comment areas and games. Just about anything that can be done on a PC can appear on the Web, although the more graphics there are on a page, the longer it'll take to appear.

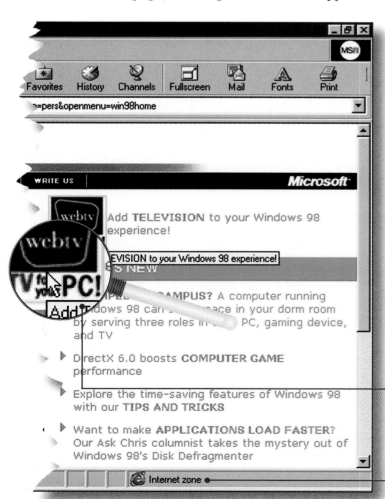

Watch out!

One of the worries that many people have about the Internet is that there's some material on it that they'd rather not see, or rather their children didn't see. Fortunately, with a modern Web browser, you can set options to control whether you'll see pages that contain violent or explicit language. The screen below shows Internet Explorer's rating features.

In Microsoft Internet Explorer version 5 choose Tools, then click on Internet Options. Select Content, click on Enable and you can then make your own adjustments within the Content Advisor section. If you are using MSIE4, you will find Internet Options on the View menu.

Jargon buster

URL Stands for Uniform Resource Locator. A standard way of naming Web pages used for linking pages together on the World Wide Web.

HTTP Stands for Hypertext Transfer Protocol, and is the way in which World Wide Web pages are transferred over the Internet.

Server A computer that provides a service to other computers, called clients, on a network.

When you move the mouse pointer over a link, it will change. Click on it to follow the link to a new page. Wherever text is underlined you can also click to go to a new page.

Messages from the browser can appear on the Status bar, sometimes telling you what will happen when you click on the link that the mouse is over.

Email

Jargon buster

AOL Stands for **A**merica **O**n**L**ine. It is an online service that provides a multitude of services in addition to Internet access. You can make travel reservations, shop and access chat groups using AOL.

Jargon buster

Microsoft Network Sometimes called MSN, this is an online service that provides Internet access as well as services like email, magazines, chat groups, car buying and so on.

The Internet provides a quick and easy way to send messages or pictures anywhere in the world.

Electronic mail or email is very simple to use. You just type a letter as if you were using a word processor, then tell your PC the address that you want to send the message to, and click on Send.

There in a flash

In a matter of seconds, the message will be sent from your computer to your Internet service provider, where it begins its journey across the Internet, sometimes passing through several computers on the way. Finally, it reaches the Internet service provider used by the recipient, where it's stored until he or she logs on to collect it. In minutes, your message can be on the other side of the world, all for the cost of a local phone call.

Click on the **send icon** to place the message in your email Outbox.

This is where you type the **email address** of the person you're sending the message to.

Just as with a paper document, you can send a **carbon copy (cc)** of an email message to someone else.

Send a **blind carbon copy (bcc)** of a message to someone and he or she can't see who else it has been sent to.

This line is to give a brief description of the **subject** of your message.

This is where you type the **body** of your message. Some email programs let you format your message with different fonts but most just use plain text.

When you click **Send and Receive**, all mail in your Outbox is sent and any new mail that you have been sent appears in your Inbox.

The **Attach button** lets you attach a file to an email, just like stapling an extra page to a memo. You can send any type of file but it will usually take longer to send and receive.

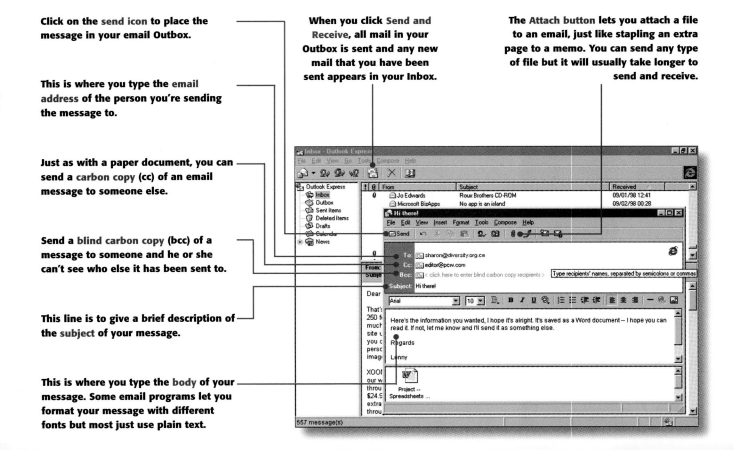

Email can do more than just send messages. You can attach all kinds of files to an email message. Why not create a birthday card for someone with a desktop publishing program and email it? Or you could send work you've done at home to the office, so you don't have to carry floppy disks around.

It's good to talk

You can even take part in discussions with other people via email, using systems called mailing lists. Messages sent to a special address are automatically passed on to hundreds or even thousands of others. There are lists for general chat, for discussing different types of music, or special diets, and even for mutual support. It can be a great way to make friends all around the world. You can send a note to friends inviting them to a party, fill in a job application or ask for emotional support on a mailing list. They are also cheap, since you can connect to the Internet, send and receive your messages, then disconnect again, all in a few minutes.

Finding tips

With tens of millions of people accessible via Internet email, it can be hard finding an address for someone that you want to get in touch with. That's where directories come in. Two of the biggest are called Bigfoot and Four11. You can visit them both on the Web and search for names or other details about people. Bigfoot also offers users a free permanent email address for life. If you have an email program like Microsoft Outlook Express or Netscape Messenger, you can even search for a name and automatically copy the address into a new message.

- Visit Bigfoot at http://www.bigfoot.com/
- Visit Four11 at http://www.four11.com/

Anatomy of an email address

The format of email addresses on the Internet is pretty standard. They take the form of someone@somewhere. The part to the left of the @ symbol (pronounced 'at') identifies the person on a computer, while the part to the right specifies the computer where their email is received. It's made up of a number of words, each separated by a full stop. For example:

sharon@diversity.org.uk

This is the name of the user of a computer. There can only be one user with a particular name on each computer.

The name of an organization. Sometimes there might be extra levels, such as departments within an organization.

The type of organization, in this case, 'not for profit.' Other common types are edu for educational, com or co for commercial, and ac for academic.

The country. Most countries use a two letter abbreviation at the end, but international addresses may just end in a domain like edu, com or mil for the US Military.

File transfer protocol

Jargon buster

Shareware Programs that are available for people to download and try out on the understanding that if they decide to keep and use the program they will send a specified small fee to the shareware provider.

File transfer

FTP Stands for File Transfer Protocol. A method of transferring files from one computer to another over the Internet. An FTP server is a computer on the Internet that stores files for transmission by FTP.

You can download files using your Web browser, or alternatively a dedicated FTP program, like WS Archie, that looks just like the Windows Explorer.

The FTP servers of the Internet are a great way to keep your system up to date, by downloading new drivers for things like sound and video cards too; if you find that your computer behaves in an unexpected way, it can usually be traced to a faulty driver for one of the add-on cards. For Windows users, Frank Condron's World O'Windows at http://www.conitech.com/windows/ is one of the best places to look for information about the latest versions that you'll need on your system.

There are thousands of free or shareware programs on the Net just waiting for you to download them.

Imagine a huge record store where you can wander in, pick up a CD, take it home and listen to it. If you like it, you can pay for it later, and if you don't you can simply throw it away. Sadly this doesn't yet apply to CDs, but it does work with a certain type of software called shareware.

Shareware is try-before-you-buy software, usually written by enthusiastic amateurs or benevolent professionals. Most shareware software is disabled in some way to encourage you to pay for an original. If you like the software, a small fee fully activates it and you may even get a manual to go with it, together with a free upgrade to the next version.

Keep up to date

You can find shareware, movie trailers, sound files, and updates for your PC's programs on the Net. In many cases, you don't even need to know where to look. You can use Web search engines designed to find the files that you want from the Internet's many servers. Often you'll see a description and a review of the file that you want. Good places to visit are www.winfiles.com and Download.Com at www.download.com/.

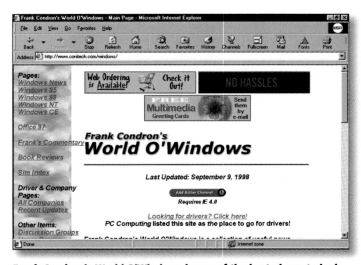

Frank Condron's World O'Windows is one of the best places to look for updates to your system and its drivers.

Chat

The Internet is a great channel for making new friends with similar interests, all over the world.

If you want a chat with people, the best thing to do is to pick up the phone. The Internet Relay Chat (IRC) system is a close second for some. It provides areas dedicated to topics such as cars or sports, where people interested in the same thing can join in using a program like Comic Chat.

Type a message and it's sent to everyone using the channel in seconds. You can send a private message to another person or send a file, like a picture. There are thousands of channels, covering most interests. All you need to take part is an IRC program, which most ISPs supply.

Join a group

Other ways to exchange views are News or Usenet. They are like email in that you write your message, post it, and then check the server for replies. But you don't send your messages to a specific person; instead, you choose groups that interest you.

The group rec.sports.soccer is all about the game of football, while soc.culture.bangladesh is for discussions about the culture of that country. You don't need any special software to visit a newsgroup; your Web browser should already have it built in. In Internet Explorer, for example, choose News from the Go menu.

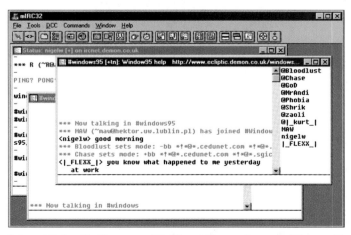

Internet Relay Chat is a way of talking with people around the world instantly. After you have signed up and logged in with the chatroom, select an area to begin your chat.

Forums

Some Internet service providers, such as AOL and MSN, provide their own chat areas. Since services such as these often make you use their own software, you may find that there are more features in their chat systems. The disadvantage is that you'll often have to stay connected to read the messages, whereas Internet newsgroups can be transferred to your PC and read later, with the phone hung up.

Emoticons

Many users on the Internet use symbols or 'Emoticons' to express emotions.

:-) I am happy, smiling (tilt your head to to see it).

:-(I am sad.

BTW By the way.

IMHO In my humble opinion.

l8r (See you) later.

SO Significant other (boy/girlfriend).

LOL Laughing out loud.

Netiquette

It pays to watch your manners when you surf the Internet, just as in any other social situation.

The Internet is often referred to as the Information Superhighway. And just like a real road, you should know the basic rules before you set out on a journey. You might have heard stories about how people on the Internet can be hostile to newcomers, or how you'll receive junk mail, or the weird jargon that's being used. But it's all straightforward. The most important thing is to keep an open mind, and watch to see how things are done before telling people to do them your way instead.

The Highway Code

The Internet's rules of the road are called Netiquette. They're mostly common sense, and if you stick to them you shouldn't have any problems. You'll usually find people more than willing to help you, although some of their Web help pages may be bigger and much more commercial than they used to be. Most people on the Internet are still happy to give time and help you out.

It may feel a bit bewildering at first, taking your first steps into a community of millions of people. But the global village is a reality on the Internet. So get online, and find out what all the fuss is about.

Jargon buster

FAQ Stands for Frequently Asked Questions. A file or page that answers questions that come up a lot. Many newsgroups have FAQs that are posted regularly.

Rules of the road

GENERAL
● In a discussion area, watch and see how people get on, and what questions keep coming up, before joining in. Different areas may have different rules.

● If you can, check for an FAQ area (frequently asked questions) in a site before you ask questions. People don't like answering the same thing all the time.

● Don't say something to someone on the Internet that you wouldn't say face to face.

It's easy to get carried away when you're just typing words into your computer, but they can still hurt to read.

EMAIL
● Don't send unsolicited messages to people, especially if you are trying to sell them something.

● Always check files you receive via email to make sure they don't contain viruses.

● Don't pass on chain messages.

● If you receive junk email, just delete it. Replying confirms that your address works, and is unlikely to get your name off any lists.

NEWSGROUPS
● Think before sending your message, and check that you are only sending it to appropriate groups.

● Don't send messages with files attached to groups unless they're specifically intended for sending out files.

2

Equipment & Software

To use the Internet you will need a modem. Here's how they work and what to look for when you buy.

All you need to turn your PC into a complete communications system is a small plastic box that plugs into the back. A modem takes the digital information stored in your PC and turns it into a series of beeps that can be sent along the phone line to another modem, which turns them back into digital information so that the receiving computer can use the information you've sent.

Setting up your modem

Modems are easy to set up. If you're using Windows, all you have to do is plug the modem into your PC and click on the Modem Control Panel.

Modems allow you to connect to the Internet via an Internet service provider (ISP), such as CompuServe, AOL or Microsoft Network (MSN). ISPs will allot you an email address so you can send messages via the Internet, and give you access to the World Wide Web.

Modems can also be used to send and receive faxes, so you can transmit orders, contact businesses, or just send letters faster than by mail.

Your modem connects to your PC's serial port 2 using the cable supplied, which plugs into the DTE (data terminal equipment) interface at the back of the modem.

To route the phone via the modem, plug it into the phone socket with the adapter lead.

If you have a separate line for your modem, connect the line socket on the modem to your telephone wall socket using the cable supplied.

The power cable plugs into the mains and into the back of your modem.

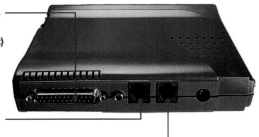

Buying tips

● **V.90** This is the current fastest standard for modems. It combines K56flex and x2 modem speeds into a single technology that gives download speeds of up to 56,000 bits per second.

● **V.34** This modem standard allows data to be sent and received at 28,800 bits per second. Most modems support an extension to V.34 that gives speeds of 33,600 bits per second.

● **14,400bps (bits per second) fax** Not all modems can send faxes at this speed, but if you're connected to another one that can, you'll be sending each page 50 per cent faster.

● **Flash upgradability** Flash memory is a special type of memory that can be reprogrammed by running a program on your PC. A modem with flash memory will be capable of being upgraded to newer standards in the future just by downloading a program from the manufacturer's Web site.

● **Approval**
In the UK, a modem must be approved by BABT (there are similar organizations in other countries).

Without this, the phone company may refuse to repair faults on your line if they think that the modem caused them.

APPROVED
for connection to telecommunications systems specified in the instructions for use subject to the conditions set out in them.
NS/3396/3/P/604258

● **Phone socket** If a modem has a phone socket on the back panel, you can plug a phone into that, rather than using a double adaptor at the wall socket. The advantage is that the modem will disconnect the phone when it's using the line, so you won't get an earful of squawks and beeps if you accidentally pick it up.

Fact file

Modem speeds These are defined by international standards, often called V numbers. The current highest speed standard is V.90 (56,000 bits per second), followed by V.34 (28,800 bits per second).

Hayes compatibility Just about every modem you buy claims to be Hayes compatible or 'Compatible with the AT command set'. That just means that the basic commands for dialling, hanging up the phone and so on are common to all these modems. Advanced features tend to be different from modem to modem, so you should make sure it's supported by Windows if you want to get the best from it.

Make the most of your modem To make a modem perform well, you'll need a high-speed connection from your PC. Most Pentium PCs have a high-speed serial port built in, but if your system is older, it may not have. You can buy one on an add-in card, or choose an internal modem, which includes the serial port.

Top five brands

Whatever your budget, you'll be able to find a modem that suits your needs. A top-of-the-range model will also be suitable for answering the phone 24 hours a day and dealing with your calls.
- **Hayes** 01276 704400
- **Lasat Communications** 01270 886223
- **Motorola** 0118 984 1075
- **Pace** 0990561001
- **3Com** 0118 9228200

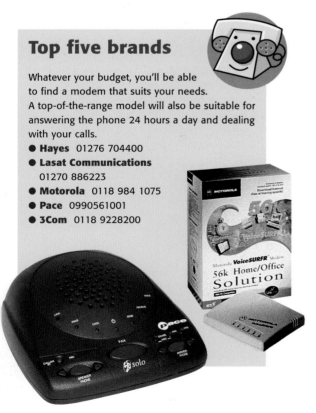

Internet service provider

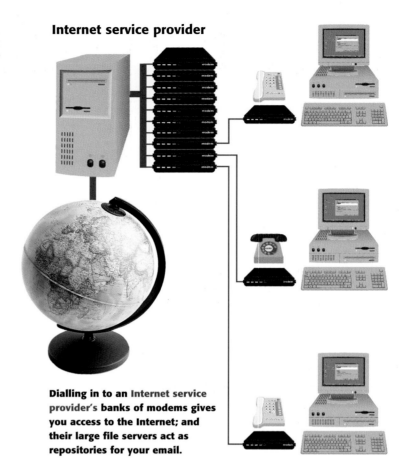

Dialling in to an Internet service provider's banks of modems gives you access to the Internet; and their large file servers act as repositories for your email.

Your personal receptionist

Most modems can be used for voicemail — turning them into glorified answering machines. You can record a series of messages so that you can present a professional appearance to people who call you.

You can choose between internal and external modems. The former are cards that fit inside your computer, which is a neat solution. But if you have more than one computer, it can be inconvenient to have to move between them. External modems mean more wires, but they also have plenty of indicator lights so you can see what's going on. And if, as sometimes happens, the modem needs to be reset, you can do it without shutting down your computer.

Modem speed

The speed of a modem is measured in bits per second or bps. Roughly 10 bits are used to send one letter of the alphabet. That means a 56,000bps modem can send 5,600 letters every second — about an A4 page of text. Slower modems are less expensive, but watch out for the false economy: half the speed means twice as long on the phone!

Just browsing...

A Web browser is your key to the Internet and all it has to offer, so make sure you choose a good one.

The Internet brings together many resources: email, online chat, inexpensive transatlantic telephone links and conferencing systems. But the World Wide Web is the biggest attraction. Initially, the Net was the domain of the written word with no visual content. Even the first incarnations of the Web were text-based, with hypertext links allowing you to jump from one typed page to another. However, Web browsers changed all that, bringing the Net alive with more than words. At first only visual images were used, then sound, then video, and finally the multimedia explosion the Web is today.

Browsing around

Web browsers are now among the most widely distributed applications in the computing world. In the same way that a desktop publishing program will take a plain text document and display it together with images formatted exactly as you want them to appear on the printed page, so a Web browser takes the plain HTML code used to write Web pages and displays them on your PC screen in

The Favorites feature lets you bookmark those pages you visit and find interesting, building into a useful address book of Web sites and keeping online information just a click away.

Fact file

● **Cache** A directory on your hard disk where the browser stores files from World Wide Web pages you have visited for a specified period of time.

● **Client** Another name for the Web browser software on your PC.

● **Cookie** A small text-only file sent by a Web server to your Web browser that records your actions on a Web site and any preferences or information you may have entered, such as login or registration information.

● **Server** A computer system where World Wide Web pages are stored, which serves the information it contains to anyone whose Web browser requests access.

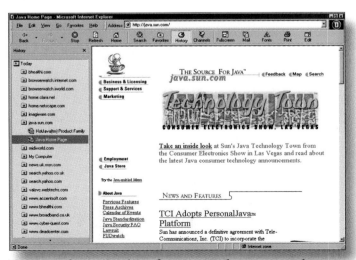

The History feature in Microsoft Internet Explorer uses a cache on your hard disk to store information from Web sites you visit in order to let you browse them again without the need to be online.

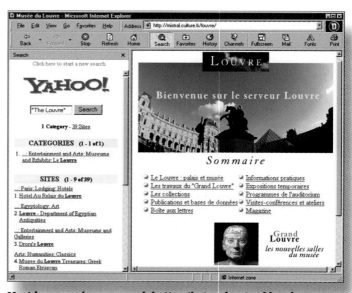

Buying tips

● Make sure that your ISP hasn't supplied you with an out-of-date browser by visiting the developer's Web site where an automatic check for the latest version can be carried out.

● Some of the best browsers cost nothing — Web software is a case of getting what you don't pay for! However, be sure to check the licence agreement on any browser you are using as there may be a requirement to pay money under certain circumstances, for example, if you are using the software for your business.

● Ensure that your browser supports Web standards such as Java, ActiveX, Frames and Tables, otherwise you may find that many Web sites will either be inaccessible or features will be unavailable to you.

● Watch out for bloated browser syndrome where the software comes as part of a hard disk-filling suite of applications that you don't need. Only install additional programs such as HTML editors, video conferencing tools and Internet chat systems if you think you will use them.

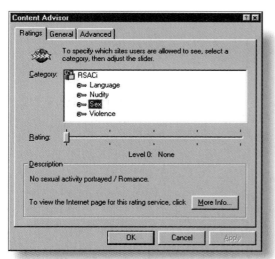

Security options, such as a content advisor, enable parental controls to be easily and quickly established, leading to peace of mind and safer surfing for the whole family.

Top five brands

● **Microsoft Internet Explorer**
  www.microsoft.com
● **Netscape Navigator**
  http://home.netscape.com
● **Opera** www.operasoftware.com
● **HotJava** http://java.sun.com/HotJava
● **NCSA Mosaic** www.ncsa.uiuc.edu

their full intended glory. HTML code is used to provide formatting and display instructions for the browser software, which then knows how and where text and images should appear on the page. It also provides route-map instructions for any hyperlinks on the page. All this complicated translation and display formatting is handled behind the scenes. You just see the final result on screen.

Easy access

Navigating a page is a simple matter of mouse clicking on the scrollbar, and jumping from one page to the next involves nothing more than clicking a hyperlink. When you select a hyperlink, the browser — known as a client — sends a request for that information across the Internet to the computer system that stores the pages in question — known as a server. The server sorts out the relevant files and these are then downloaded by the browser and displayed on your screen.

Windows on the Web

Choosing a Web browser isn't as difficult as you may think. The market is dominated by Netscape's Navigator and Microsoft's Internet Explorer. Both are constantly updated with new features and there isn't a lot of difference between the two. Which you choose comes down to a matter of personal taste or which one your Internet service provider supplies when you sign up. Both have become much more than just a window on to the Web, and will let you send email, participate in online conferences, organize Web site information and even browse the Web offline to save money on phone charges.

Most browsers have a search button that makes tracking down information on the Web easy. Microsoft Internet Explorer is particularly impressive in this area.

Surf the world

Get much more from the World Wide Web using Windows' Internet Explorer.

Microsoft Internet Explorer is an application for browsing Web pages. It is also a suite of programs for using the Internet. These include programs that let you send and receive email, receive and contribute to bulletin board discussions or newsgroups and even join in electronic conferencing over the Net.

Internet Explorer 5, the latest version, is free from Microsoft. You can download it by going to www.microsoft.com/ie/download and following the on-screen instructions. There are three versions: the browser only, which will take around an hour to download, the standard version which includes email and newsgroup reader software and takes about an hour and a half, and the full version which includes conferencing software and will keep you online for about two and a half hours. If you don't want to run up a large phone bill you'll also find it on some PC magazines' cover disks.

How to use Internet Explorer

1 Internet Explorer displays **Web pages**. The toolbar has the same controls you will find on any Web browser. The Back button takes you to the last page you visited. The Forward button takes you to the next page after you have gone back. Stop lets you abandon downloads of files you don't want or that are taking too long to arrive. Refresh downloads the current page again, so you can be sure you have the latest copy. Internet Explorer saves Web pages on your hard disk, so if you have previously visited a site the page you see when you revisit may be the saved copy.

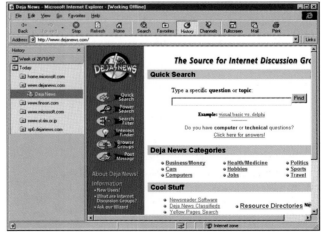

2 Internet Explorer 4's **Fullscreen** option lets you view Web pages full-screen with only a narrow control bar at the top. This is useful if you have a small screen and need to use the scrollbars to view the whole of a page.

Search makes it easy for you to access World Wide Web search engines. Favorites stores shortcuts to your favourite Web sites (just click on the page and choose Add to Favorites to add a site to the list). And History lets you revisit recently accessed sites. Channels are special Web sites containing frequently updated content, which can be delivered to your computer on a regular basis. Internet Explorer 4 presents the results of these four options in a frame on the left of the window.

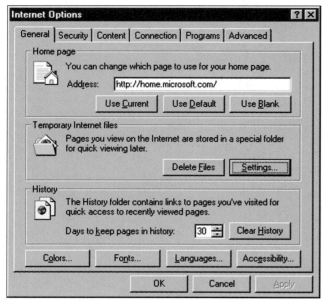

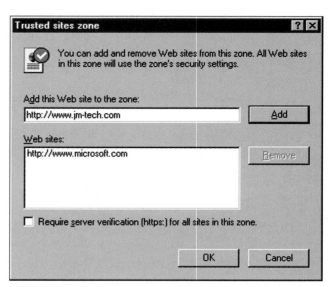

3 Use the **Internet Options** dialogue to customize Internet Explorer. To access it, click View (in Internet Explorer 5, click Tools), then Internet Options. The Home Page option lets you choose the page Internet Explorer displays when on launch. The best way to set this is to go to the page you want, open Internet Options and click Use Current.

Temporary Internet Files is where Internet Explorer saves pages. Click Settings and you can choose when you want Explorer to check if a file has changed. Choose Never and Explorer will always display the saved copy of a page unless you click Refresh. The settings page (above) lets you choose how much of your disk space should be used for saving files. The History folder is a list of pages you've visited recently. You can specify how long pages stay in the list.

5 If you use Internet Explorer's default security settings you will probably receive warnings every time you visit certain sites. After a while this could become tiresome. Web sites run by reputable companies can usually be trusted. You can bypass the warnings for these sites by adding their addresses to a trusted sites list. Click the Zone drop-down list, select **Trusted Sites**, then click Add Sites. You can then type the addresses of the sites you trust into the Add This Web Site to the Zone field, and click Add.

Unless all the sites you want to trust have addresses that start http:, you should clear the Require Server Verification check box before clicking OK to close the dialogue box.

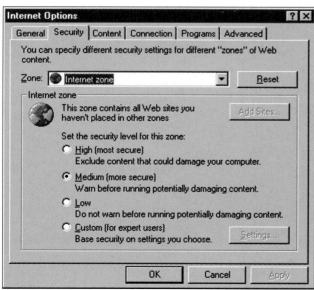

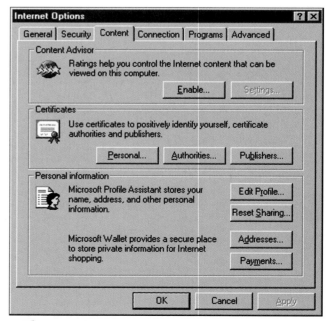

4 The **Security** page lets you change settings that determine what protection Internet Explorer gives you from things like viruses. Files which are automatically downloaded could harm your computer system. You can set up lists of sites that you trust, and lists of sites that you want to treat with caution.

Internet Explorer treats all sites the same way and groups them in a category called the Internet Zone. By default it will warn you before allowing potentially harmful active components to run. This is the best option for most people.

6 **Content Advisor** lets you control the material that can be viewed on your PC using the content ratings present on many sites. If you enable it, Internet Explorer will only let you view inoffensive sites. It will not allow you to view sites which are unrated. You can set up user names for members of the family using the Users icon in Control Panel, and then control the type of content each is allowed to see. To set the content ratings for a user, click the Settings button in the Content Advisor panel. You will need to enter a password. Make a note of this password: you will need it to change the Content Advisor settings in the future.

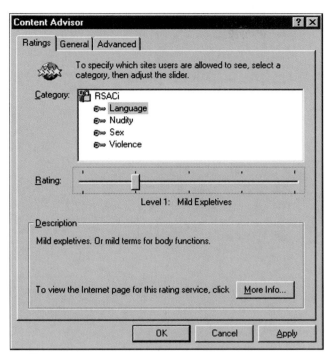

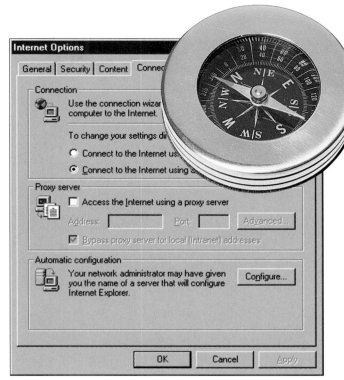

7 The first page of the Content Advisor dialogue box lets you select the limit of bad language, nudity, sex and violence you wish to allow the current user to see. Select a category, then use the slider to set the level.

On the General page you can check a box to allow unrated sites to be viewed. If you do this, you might stumble across sites you find offensive. You are given the option of entering the **supervisor password** to view sites which would otherwise be barred.

9 The Connection page of Internet Options lets you set up your Internet connection. Most of the options on this page will only need to be touched by experts.

If your modem is already installed and working, connecting to the Internet is easy. All you need to do is click Connect to run the **Internet Connection Wizard**. This Wizard will install and set up the software necessary to enable your computer to communicate with the Internet. You should have your Windows CD-ROM handy in case the Wizard needs to install extra files.

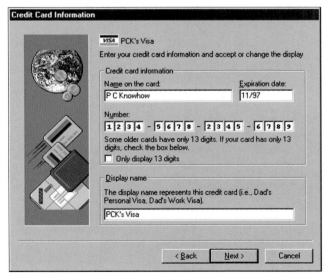

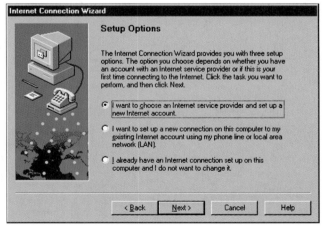

8 The Certificates panel lets you install and use certificates which verify that you, or a Web site you are exchanging sensitive information with, are who you say you are. You probably don't need to worry about this.

The **Profile Assistant** lets you enter information about yourself that can be requested by Web sites that you visit. Click the button and fill in the information if you wish. However, you may soon find yourself receiving a lot of junk mail. Microsoft Wallet lets you store information such as your address and credit card details for use when buying goods and services over the Internet. If the site you are using supports Wallet, it will save you typing in this information.

10 If you don't currently have an account with an Internet access provider, choose the first option offered by the Wizard. The Wizard will start by installing the software needed to allow your computer to communicate with the Internet. Next, it will dial a local rate number to connect you to the **Internet Referral Service**. This is a computer that maintains a list of Internet access providers, with information about the services they offer and the fees they charge. After you sign up with one, the Wizard will set up the software to work with your new access provider.

If you already have an account with an access provider but need to set up Windows to work with it, choose the second option. If you have an account which was set up and working before you installed Internet Explorer, choose the third option.

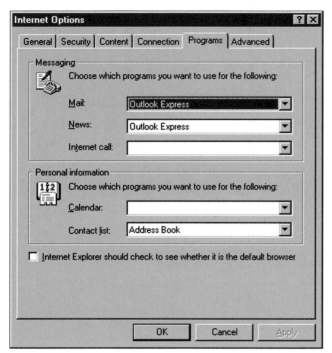

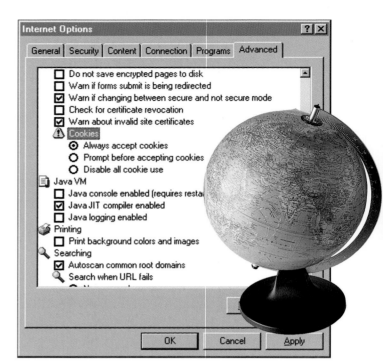

11 On the **Programs page** you choose the programs you want Internet Explorer to use for various functions. In the Messaging panel you choose the email program and newsgroup reader that Explorer will use if you click on an email address or news article reference on a Web page. You can also choose a program to use for voice messaging or conferencing over the Net, and programs such as Address Book for obtaining diary and contact information. The programs you choose appear in Internet Explorer's Go menu.

12 The **Advanced page** of Internet Options allows you to customize various elements of the appearance and behaviour of Internet Explorer. The Advanced page contains a scrolling list of check boxes and buttons. If you want to find out what they all do, click on the question mark button at the top right of the title bar, then move the pointer to the item you are interested in and click again. A tool tip will appear describing what the item does.

What's the difference?

Microsoft Internet Explorer 4 is the most widely used version of Microsoft's Web browsers. What are the differences between it and its predecessor **Internet Explorer 3**? Internet Explorer 4 (and its upgrade to version 5.0) works in the same way as its predecessors, but it is more powerful. It has better support for offline browsing, so you can re-read pages that you've downloaded without having to go back online. And it's easier to use. Functions like Search and History are now displayed in a frame, so the links don't disappear as soon as you click on one of them.

Channels are a major innovation. They are a bit like TV channels: information is sent to you, rather than you having to visit a Web site to get it. In reality, your browser goes and gets the information, and you really need a permanent Internet connection to benefit from it. Subscribe to too much channel content and your PC will be dialling the Net at all hours of the day and night.

The programs which form the Internet Explorer Suite have all been improved. Outlook Express is an integrated email and newsgroup reader program that replaces the Internet Mail and News of version 3. NetMeeting, which allows people to link up over the Net for group collaborations, supports video conferencing, and there is an updated version of Chat. FrontPage Express is an excellent Web page editor, which includes a Home Page Wizard to get you started designing your own Web site. There's also Microsoft Wallet, a technology to make paying for online shopping easier.

One of the most significant updates to Internet Explorer 4 is the Active Desktop. Also a part of Windows 98, the Active Desktop

effectively turns your Windows Desktop into a Web browser: folders look like World Wide Web pages, shortcuts are underlined like Internet hyperlinks and opened with a single click, and you can display World Wide Web pages as Desktop wallpaper. The Active Desktop works only if you have a permanent Internet connection, which most home users don't. Fortunately, you can turn off the Active Desktop and use Windows in the good old-fashioned way.

The Desktop Upgrade replaces Windows Explorer with Internet Explorer and makes your folders look like Web pages.

Email it

Use Outlook Express to send and receive email messages.

Outlook Express is a program for sending and receiving email and newsgroup messages. There are other programs you can use for either or both of these tasks but Outlook Express comes with Microsoft Internet Explorer 4 and 5 and it's included free with Windows 98. It's a powerful program and well worth using even if you're currently using a different mail program or news reader.

In the first chapter, we looked at the Internet and email in general.

Here we will look specifically at Microsoft Outlook Express and see how to set it up and make use of some of its powerful features.

Using Outlook Express

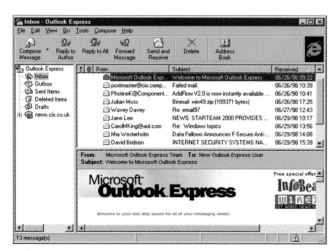

1 You can start Outlook Express from the **Internet Explorer** group on the Start Menu. If you haven't deleted it you should also have an Outlook Express shortcut on your Desktop, and if you are using Windows 98 there will be a button to run the program on the QuickLaunch part of the taskbar.

If you are running Outlook Express for the first time, the Internet Connection Wizard will run. The wizard provides an easy way to set up your Net connection and Outlook Express. When Outlook Express starts, it displays a window with three panes. On the left are your mail and news folders. When you select a folder by clicking on it, the messages inside are listed in the topmost pane on the right. The pane on the lower right is the preview pane. It displays the contents of the message selected in the pane above.

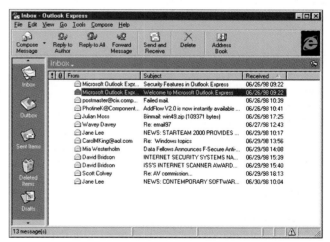

2 You can change the layout of Outlook Express so that it looks the way you want it to look. From the menu, click View, then Layout. The **Window Layout Properties** dialogue box will then appear.

From the Basic panel you can choose whether to have the Explorer-like Folder List in the left-hand pane, the narrower Outlook Bar which just shows icons for the folders, or the Folder Bar which shows the currently selected folder in a horizontal bar and lets you choose other folders by clicking the bar and then selecting one from a drop-down list. These alternatives take up less space, so they are useful if your computer has a small screen.

You can also choose the location of the Preview pane, or not to have it at all. If you don't have the preview pane you will have to judge what a message is from its title in the message list. You will have to open the message before you can see its contents. Experiment with different layouts until you find one that suits you.

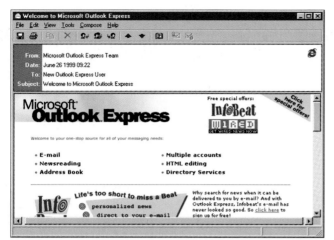

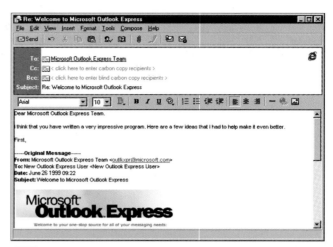

3 The **Preview pane** is intended, as its name suggests, to allow you to read the first few lines of a message only. There's nothing to stop you from reading the whole of a message using the Preview pane, of course. But it is often more convenient to read a message by opening it. When you open a message it is displayed in its own window so you can see more of it. You can open more than one message at a time, each in its own window. You can also use the up and down buttons on the toolbar (or Ctrl+>, Ctrl+<) to browse forward and back through the list of messages. Outlook Express is one of the few mail programs to be able to display messages formatted using HTML, the language used to create Web pages, so messages can use a variety of text styles and graphics.

5 When you reply to a message, Outlook Express opens a new window for you to compose your reply. The new message will be addressed to the original sender. The subject will be RE: followed by the subject line of the original message.

By default, Outlook Express copies the original message into the body of the new message. This is considered a courtesy, so that the recipient can easily see what you are replying to without having to hunt for a copy of the original message. It wouldn't be necessary if mail programs threaded messages so that you could instantly refer back to the message you've had a reply to, but most don't. However you can delete the original message text if you know that the recipient will be using a threaded mail reader. You can change this default behaviour from the **Send Options** dialogue box.

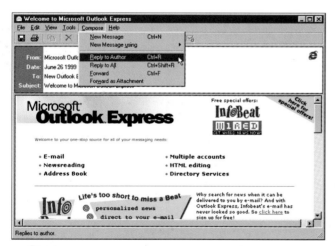

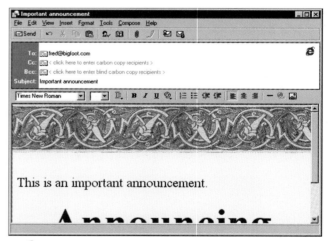

4 You can **reply** to the message selected in the message list by clicking one of the buttons on the toolbar or by right-clicking the message and choosing the option you want from the pop-up menu. If you have opened the message, there are reply buttons on the message window toolbar, or you can choose an option from the Compose menu.

If you choose Reply to Author, your reply will be addressed only to the person who wrote the original message. If you choose Reply to All, it will be addressed to all the people who were listed as recipients. Most often, messages are addressed to only one person, but if a message is sent to several people — members of a committee, for example — it is important to choose the right reply option. You can also forward the message — in other words send it on to someone else.

6 To originate a message (rather than reply to another message) click the **Compose button** on the Outlook Express toolbar, or select Compose, New Message, or use the keyboard shortcut Ctrl+N.

When the new message window opens you must type the address of the recipient into the To: field, or click the address book icon and select a name from your Address Book. You should also enter a subject, then type the body of the text.

If, instead of clicking the Compose button, you click the drop-down button next to it on the toolbar (or select Compose, New Message Using... from the menu), Outlook Express gives you a choice of message stationery which you can use to give your messages greater impact. The example above uses the Formal Announcement stationery.

Voice & fax software

You can turn your computer into an advanced telephone answering system and fax machine.

If you think automated messaging systems (where you press buttons on your phone in response to a menu of choices) is efficient, the good news is that you can now design your own. All you need is a voice modem and the right software. Only very inexpensive new modems are not equipped with voice features.

The big names in voice and fax software are Cheyenne (BitWare Plus) and Symantec (WinFax Pro). But lesser-known companies like Pacific Data (SuperVoice) and Trio (Trio Communications Suite) supply a number of modem makers with software to bundle with their products. Just because a program is supplied with a modem doesn't mean it's any less useful than one sold separately. Apart from the fact that commercial products work with any modem, not just the hardware they're sold with, many of the differences are cosmetic. These include better cover page design utilities, clip art libraries and sound files to use as background music when people are being kept on hold.

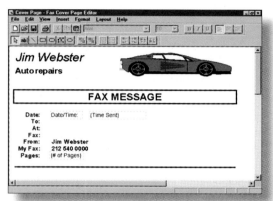

A **cover page editor** is more than just a page designer. It can be used to insert dates, times, names and other information fields that are automatically updated when a fax is transmitted.

The speakerphone in **SuperVoice** is also the central **Control Panel** from which faxes and messages are viewed and played back. More advanced options are hidden from the general user.

Fact file

● **Broadcasting** Sending the same fax to a number of recipients. This is made easier if the names are stored in an address book within the fax program.

● **Caller ID** Identifies the number of the person calling you. It only works if you subscribe to your telephone company's caller identification service. If the calling number is in your address book you'll see the caller's name, if it isn't you'll see just the number.

● **Fax on demand** A way of automatically distributing faxes to people who request them over the phone. Callers listen to a description of the faxes available and choose the ones they want. The fax program then instructs the modem to transmit the selected documents.

● **Fax machines** Faxes can be transmitted and received between ordinary fax machines and PCs. In fact, standalone fax machines can't tell whether they're communicating with a modem or another fax machine.

● **Remote retrieval** This lets you call into your PC from another location to check your messages and faxes. Messages are played over the phone and faxes are redirected to a computer or fax machine near you.

Buying tips

● Heavyweight commercial programs don't work any better than the ones supplied free with modems; they simply offer more features. Typical enhancements are to play music to callers on hold and turn faxes into editable text using optical character recognition.

● The majority of voicemail programs provide a hands-off speakerphone feature, but this only works if your PC has a sound card and microphone. The microphones built into multimedia monitors are not very sensitive and seldom work well in a speakerphone setup.

● Being able to record your telephone conversations so you don't have to scribble notes while talking can be very useful. Not all programs provide this facility.

● Voice and fax programs are seldom able to use existing address books from PIMs and other Windows programs. Names and numbers have to be imported, so check the export options of your address book and match them to the import options of your fax and voice software.

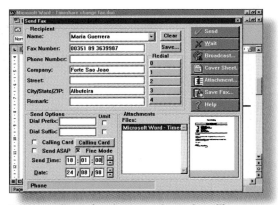

When sending a fax there may be options like broadcasting it to more than one person or attaching additional files to the core document. The fax above has been scheduled for transmission after 6pm when call rates are cheaper.

Top five brands

● **Cheyenne** 0990 134216
● **Microsoft** 0345 002000
● **Pacific Image** 0181 549 1437
● **Quarterdeck** 0645 123521
● **Symantec** 0171 616 5600

Voicemail

In its simplest form, a voicemail system can be used rather like an answering machine on which you record a single message to all callers. This is probably all you need if you're using a computer from home, but for business purposes you can record a number of different messages to be played in response to inputs from push-button phones.

A further refinement enables several users to share the same voicemail system by allocating each of them a separate mailbox. A mailbox is nothing more than a part of a hard disk set aside for one person's messages. The first message that a caller hears asks them to press a button to indicate who the message is for. They then hear a personalized message from the chosen person. Passwords can be allocated to keep shared users from listening to messages in other people's mailboxes.

Keep it secret

You can retrieve your voice messages from any phone by calling up your PC and pressing a secret code number, and you can instruct your voicemail software to call you and let you know there are messages waiting if you have a pager.

There are several ways of faxing from a PC. One is to create a fax within your fax program. You type on to a pre-designed page, supply a fax number and press the Send button. Another way is to create a fax in a word processor or some other program and then 'print to fax'. This is like ordinary printing but when the Print dialogue box appears, you select your fax modem instead of your printer.

Scan to fax

If you have a scanner, you can fax paper documents by scanning them and printing to fax, a task that is made easier by the inclusion of a Scan to Fax feature in many scanner drivers. This starts up your fax software as soon as scanning is complete.

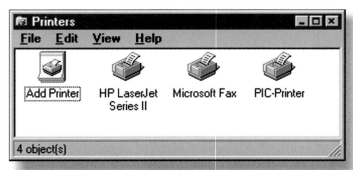

You can send a fax by printing it and selecting a fax driver instead of a real printer. This computer has two fax drivers, Microsoft and PIC, in its Printers panel.

Design online

Creating your own home page on the World Wide Web is easy with the right design software.

Take a look around the World Wide Web and you will notice that there are very good pages and there are truly awful ones. What may surprise you is that some of the best are created at home by ordinary people using Web design software packages, while some of the worst have been designed by agencies with enormous budgets. On the Web anyone can produce superb pages with the right software.

Get an editor

The simplest Web design software is nothing more than a text editor with a few buttons on a toolbar that paste HTML tags into blank documents. These really aren't worth considering; you may as well just use the free copy of Notepad that comes with Windows on your PC and enter the HTML coding manually. However, modern software packages have wysiwyg (What You See Is What You Get) HTML editors, providing an intuitive and graphic work environment. Think of an HTML Editor as being similar to a top-of-the-line word processor or a DTP program and you won't be far wrong.

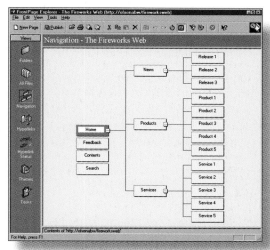

The ability to manage your Web pages from the familiar interface of your design software suite is a great advantage for more complex sites. This **FrontPage Explorer** view shows how all the pages on this site are linked together.

Fact file

● **HTML** HyperText Markup Language, the programming code used to create Web pages.

● **Frames** They divide a Web page into separate windows within the same browser screen, each window containing a Web page in its own right. Used to make Web pages more interactive and easier to navigate — one frame could display an index of the site, while another displays the Web pages as you browse, for example.

● **Java applets** Small programs that can run on your Web page, in the browser of the site visitor. Clocks, counters and animations are all examples.

● **Wysiwyg** What You See Is What You Get is a term applied to software that lets you create something on screen that looks the same as it will when available on the Web itself. Ensure your Web design software is wysiwyg and there should be no unwelcome design surprises when your Web page is published online.

● **Site management** This refers to the ability to maintain your Web pages once you have created them. Things like checking that the hyperlinks to other sites are still working and updating time-sensitive material.

Templates can help create a consistent look to your Web pages by providing ready-made backgrounds, buttons and fonts. FrontPage comes with a selection of templates including this automotive one.

Buying tips

● Buy the software that best suits your needs. By spending less money you may get a package that isn't powerful enough, but at the same time there is no point spending a small fortune on features you will never use. If you are planning to create a home page for yourself, then a simple HTML editor will suffice. If you want to design an impressive and extensive site for your small business or on behalf of a club you belong to, then a powerful design program will be a worthwhile investment.

● Make sure that your software has a preview mode built in so that you can see the progress of your design as you design it. Some packages don't have this ability and will force you to load the HTML file in an external browser every time you want to look at it, which is extremely time consuming and annoying.

● Make sure your Internet service provider supports Web pages created by your Web design package. FrontPage makes creating advanced pages very easy indeed, but not all ISPs support the special codes needed to make use of the more advanced features. Check with your ISP before spending money on a design package.

Wysiwyg Web editors come with an imposing array of toolbars and buttons, ensuring that every conceivable HTML facility is just a mouse click away and that learning to design Web pages is as easy as possible.

Top six brands

● **FrontPage** Microsoft
● **HotMetal Pro** SoftQuad
● **PageMill** Adobe
● **HomePage** Claris
● **HotDog Pro** Fourthnet
● **Dreamweaver** Macromedia

Some programs do more than help you create a Web page; they help you maintain it as well. This is important, because an out-of-date or broken Web page is worse than no Web page at all. If you want to create lots of pages, or your Web site contains material that needs regular updating, these features will come in handy. Software such as Microsoft FrontPage lets you update pages without hassle and checks for broken hyperlinks automatically.

No fuss

All Web design packages have a similar interface consisting of a main document window where your Web page is created, and a number of toolbars and menus containing features to aid that creation process. The simplest software lets you draw tables with the cursor as you would in a word processor, and create frames at the click of a button. You'll also want to be able to drag and drop images on to the page and produce hyperlinks without a problem.

Wizards

Some resources you will need are less obvious. The best software will include a spelling checker to ensure your page isn't full of mistakes, a library of images, bars and buttons to include on your pages, and the ability to add Java applets, scripts and other advanced techniques without the need to learn advanced programming skills. Look for software that includes wizards to guide you through the page creation process, and templates to help give your site a professional look by standardizing backgrounds, fonts and navigation buttons.

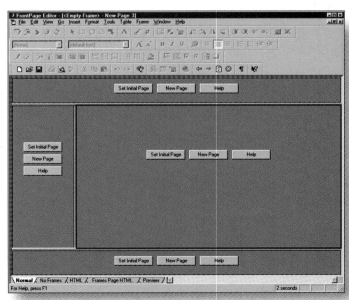

Creating frames in a Web page is as simple as selecting the layout from a template, then editing each frame on the page as a separate window. Wysiwyg HTML editing software makes this easy.

Made for sharing

Shareware is great if you want to try out new software without having to pay lots of money up front.

Shareware programs are just like commercial programs. They have menus and dialogue boxes, windows and icons. They can save your work, print it out, store it on a floppy disk and do everything that more expensive programs can do.

Try before you buy

There are some key differences. First, you won't find shareware programs in shops. Second, they tend to cost a fraction of the price of commercial equivalents. And third, you're allowed to try the programs before you decide whether to buy them.

Shareware started when amateur programmers started to ask for donations to cover their costs. The idea was that if you found a program useful, it was in your interest to donate a small fee to the programmers so they could continue to develop the software.

A bit of a nag

Shareware authors encourage you to pay for their software in a number of ways. Some programs stop working after 30 days; others won't let you save anything; some don't print; and some periodically display a reminder, called a nag screen, to register. Most of these and other limitations are usually included in free-trial evaluation versions and once the program has been registered (and in most cases, purchased), you can then use the fully functional version. Some shareware is fully functional; the authors rely on the honesty of the people using it. If you like a shareware program, you should always pay for it. You'll then get help when you need it, free updates, extra features and so on. Shareware used to be sold by mail order, but these days you're more likely to find it on the Internet or on online services like AOL and CompuServe. The range of programs is much wider and more specialized than you'll find on the shelves of a retailer.

You will need

ESSENTIAL
Software There is a range of programs available for earlier versions of Windows such as 3.1, but new shareware is typically written for Windows 98.
Hardware Shareware programs are less demanding than commercial ones, so any modern PC will do. You'll only need a CD-ROM drive if you intend to buy compilations of shareware on CD. If you want to download shareware from the Internet you'll need a modem and an account with the relevant provider.

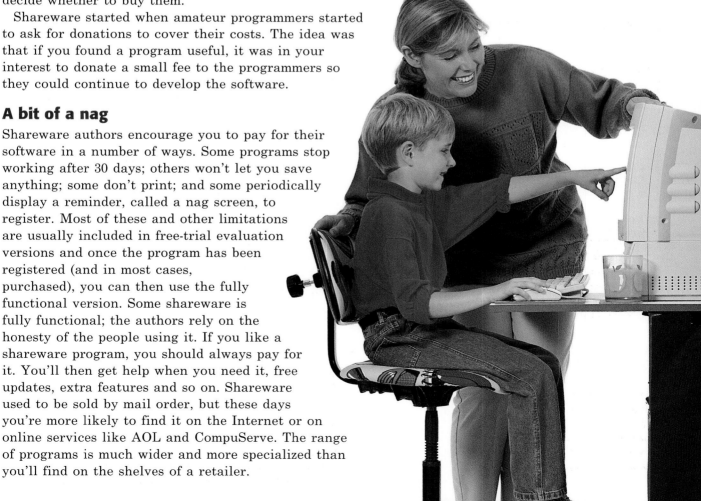

Where to look

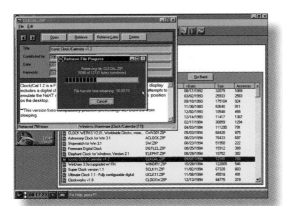

You can download a file from the Windows shareware forum on CompuServe. In the yellow window you can see a list of available files, in front of that is a description of the file downloading and in front of that is the progress bar indicating how far through the download process you are.

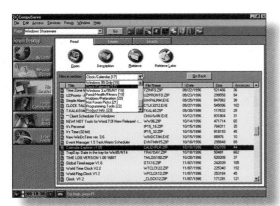

CompuServe's Windows shareware forum divides up its file libraries by categories to make it easier for you to find what you're looking for.

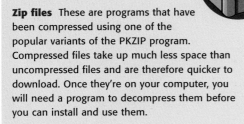

Jargon buster

Zip files These are programs that have been compressed using one of the popular variants of the PKZIP program. Compressed files take up much less space than uncompressed files and are therefore quicker to download. Once they're on your computer, you will need a program to decompress them before you can install and use them.

Downloading The process of copying a program or other kind of computer file from the Internet to the hard disk on your PC using a modem.

Good shareware is easy to track down on the Internet or on free CD-ROMs included with magazines.

The best sources of shareware are the Internet (e.g. www.shareware.com allows a search of over 250,000 files by platform/version and category) or a commercial online service like CompuServe or AOL. You'll find a wide range of programs, usefully divided into categories, which you can either browse through, program by program, or search by keyword (e.g. to find a cassette labelling program, search for the words 'cassette label').

Different sources

Traditionally, commercial online services were the best source of new shareware, but as people come on to the Internet in increasing numbers, you're just as likely to find new programs there. Another thing to remember is that since there's no financial incentive for shareware authors to choose one outlet over another, you're likely to find the same programs available in different places.

You can find out about new programs by visiting different shareware sites. Recently some have set up a free service: they'll email you once a week to let you know what new software has been added to

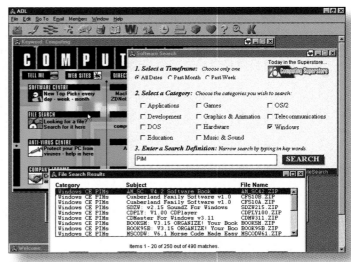

On AOL, go to the Computing section, select search option, then select Windows and type in PIM to find personal information managers. The results are in the window at the bottom.

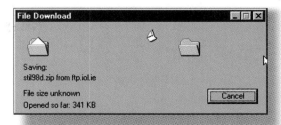

This is the dialogue screen you see when you download a file. The scrap of paper flying between folders shows you that something's being copied, and the figure at the bottom tells you how much has been downloaded so far.

their lists and what programs have been updated. All you have to do is fill in a simple form with your email address when you visit, and they'll send the news direct to your PC. Such sites are usually responsibly run, so you shouldn't find your in-tray clogged up with loads of junk email.

Download times

When you find a program you want to download, the sites make it clear where to click and what to do. Typically, the program will be represented by an icon or blue underlined text, and when you move your cursor over it, the cursor will change into a pointing hand, to indicate that this is a link to something. Click on the link and your browser will ask if you want to copy the program down from the Internet and save it to your hard disk. Once you've said that you do, you'll see a dialogue box with a little progress meter in it which tells you how long the download is going to take.

Computer magazines often include a free CD-ROM with demonstration and shareware programs. A number of mail-order companies specialize in shareware and sell large compilations on CD-ROM. Check the advertisements in various computer magazines for details of these companies.

Download managers

There are now download managers that track your download so that if you lose your Net connection halfway through downloading you don't have to start all over again but can resume from where you left off. This is very useful if, for example, you've downloaded 10Mb of a 12Mb file. You can also pause the download and resume when it suits you. Examples are: GetRight (www.getright.com) and Download Manager (www.download.com).

Which service?

Most shareware is available from the Net or other online services, but how do you get to these services, and which is best?

First, it's important to understand the difference between an **Internet service provider** and a **commercial service**. Both let you send and receive email; both allow access to newsgroups; and both offer software that lets you explore the World Wide Web. But a commercial service like **AOL** will come with a number of extra services that you won't find on the Internet. Often, these are in the form of electronic magazines, travel guides, news services, weather guides and so on.

Commercial services try to look like TV channels and some of them are entertaining and informative. A commercial online service is a bit like going on an all-inclusive package trip to a holiday resort. Everything you need (information, entertainment, other people) is already there, but you can go outside the complex (to the Internet) if you want to explore further. Signing up with an Internet provider is like getting accommodation and flights only; from then on, it's up to you.

You can find out more about AOL by visiting www.aol.com, while **CompuServe**'s home page is www.compuserve.com. You'll find a list of shareware Web sites on the following pages.

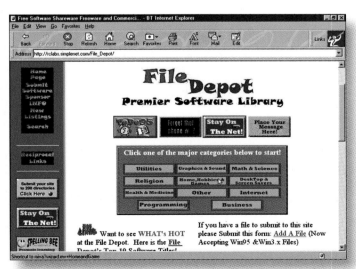

Here's a shareware library on the Internet, called File Depot. There are many large sites like this that categorize software and have indexes. Note the link at the bottom right: shareware authors who want to add software to File Depot click here for instructions.

Office suites

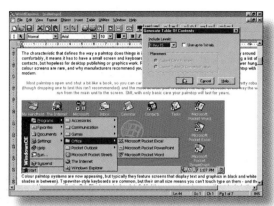

WordExpress is a fully featured word processor that supports graphics, tables, indexing, tables of contents, spell checking and word counts, yet takes up less than 4Mb of disk space.

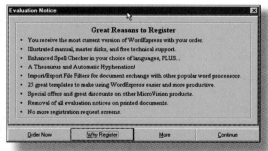

This speaks for itself. Here the authors of the WordExpress word processor try to convince you of the benefits of registering their software.

Where to go

Point your Web browser at these addresses and you'll find thousands of shareware programs. Sign up for their free electronic mail newsletters and they'll tell you when new products arrive. Each site also has a sophisticated search engine.

● **File Depot**
   http://rclabs.simplenet.com/File_Depot/
● **SoftSeek**
   www.softseek.com
● **ZDNet Software Library**
   www.zdnet.com/swlib/
● **shareware.com**
   www.shareware.com/
● **PC World**
   www.pcworld.com/fileworld/

You can put together your own suite of office software using shareware downloaded from the Internet.

There's no point kidding yourself that you'll be able to put together a collection of shareware programs, written by different people at different times, under different conditions, and end up with something as good as Microsoft Office. You will end up with a collection of lean programs that won't take up much disk space and, should you decide to keep them, will cost a fraction of the price.

The Internet is dynamic and ever-changing, so it's possible that the addresses given here may not be valid by the time you read this. If in doubt, go to one of the big search engines like Alta Vista at www.altavista.com and type in a phrase such as Windows Shareware or Shareware Word Processors. Here's an idea of what to expect in each category.

Word processing

For simple text editing of the kind you can do with Word Pad — the program that comes free with Windows 98 — you will have hundreds of choices. For more sophisticated jobs, consider WordExpress (www.softseek.com) or the unusual YeahWrite (www.wordplace.com) which is written by ex-WordPerfect employees.

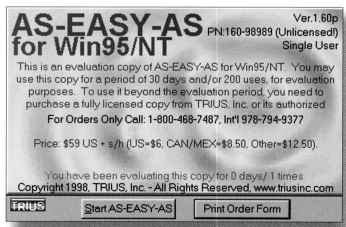

Here's the ordering information for the As-Easy-As shareware spreadsheet. It clearly explains the length of the evaluation period, how the pricing works and lets you print out an order form if you prefer to fax your order.

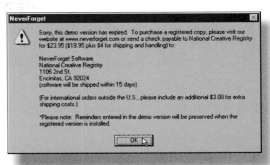

Here's a typical screen from the Never Forget calendar program explaining that your evaluation period has expired and the program will no longer work until you register it. Usefully, any data that you've typed into the calendar is still safe and will be available to use, should you buy the program.

Spreadsheet

For something with real financial muscle, you have to look further afield than Windows' Calculator. The As-Easy-As 30-day free evaluation spreadsheet (www.triusinc.com) is worth considering, as is GS-Calc for Windows 95 and 98 (www.jps-development.com).

Database

Viabase (http://viablesoftware.com) is a simple, good-looking database that can be used with Windows 3.1, 95 and 98, while FileXPress (www.creasoft.com) is for Windows 95 and 98.

Graphics

For drawing, photo manipulation and general image editing, there's little that can beat PaintShop Pro (www.jasc.com). Astound (www.astoundinc.com) is an excellent all-round presentation program which has extensive multimedia features. For general chart drawing, particularly organizational and flow charts, SmartDraw (www.smartdraw.com) is a good shareware choice.

Desktop publishing

Check out PagePlus (www.serif.com), where you'll also find other good graphics programs. It's a full-featured desktop publishing program.

It's not Access, but ViaBase is a good enough database that can store not just text and numbers, but pictures and sounds as well.

Shareware tip

Make sure your shareware programs are able to understand the file formats used by popular programs like MS Word or Excel.

This is the latest version of the excellent image-editing and painting program Paint Shop Pro – probably the best shareware graphics program in the world.

Practical shareware

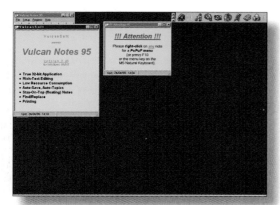

Vulcan Notes is the electronic equivalent of those yellow sticky notes so popular in offices, while ToolBar for Windows 95 (the column down the right of the screen) is a programmable button bar on which you can store commonly used programs.

CD Wizzard is one of many good CD players.

Shareware tips

Some shareware comes in two versions: 16-bit and 32-bit. It's important you pick the right one. 16-bit programs are designed for Windows 3.1; 32-bit ones are for Windows 95 and 98.

There are plenty of useful programs available to make your PC or even your life run more smoothly.

Shareware authors are good at finding the little things that commercial software developers either deliberately left out of their programs or simply forgot to include. Consequently, you will find that the majority of shareware comes under the utilities heading. Here's a rundown of some shareware programs you should consider.

Good to have

You should look for a program to compress and decompress files that you want to send using a modem, or just squeeze on to a floppy disk. WinZip is probably the best available. Sticky note programs are good too and let you quickly write out notes and stick them to your Desktop.

Both Windows 95 and 98 provide an address book, but if you do not find this versatile enough for your purposes, you'll find hundreds of address books are available as shareware, such as Desktop Cardfile at http://www.franklindev.com/dcard.html.

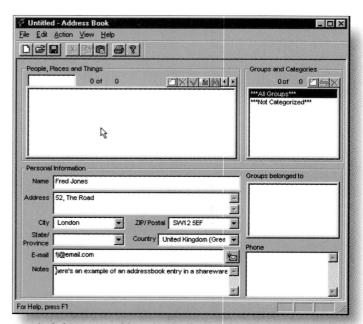

A typical shareware address book allows you to input not just basic details, but also email addresses and notes. This program, Address Book 1.5, allows entries to be grouped into categories.

WinZip is one of the best-loved shareware programs around. It allows you to compress and decompress files that have been squeezed using the popular ZIP format. It has a great interface, it's easy to use and it's invaluable.

Useful

Launch bar utilities are worth a look. They let you create a button bar or a space at the bottom right of the taskbar where you can get to your favourite programs fast or store useful things like a calendar or shortcuts to system utilities. You'll also find label-making software that can print high-quality sleeves for cassettes and CDs. And there is a range of sound editors which have many more features than you get in Windows Sound Recorder.

Fun

You'll find hundreds of fun shareware, from icons and icon editors to wallpaper changers, collections of sounds, screensaver makers, screensavers, CD players and so on. Don't overload your system with too many of these or it will start to slow down.

Look and feel

Some shareware programs can change the way that Windows appears. Some offer 3D icons, others alter the way the scrollbars, menus and windows work. There are even some programs that change the way Windows looks completely.

There are lots of programs that attach to popular commercial software. Many of these are small programs written for Microsoft Office that add features not already found in the software — a Word-based calendar, for example.

Believe it or not, this is Windows. Or rather, it's the LiteStep shell running on top of Windows. As you can see, it transforms the look and feel of Windows 95 and 98. Use programs like this with caution.

Watch out!

● Some shareware programs need extra software to make them work properly. Check their descriptions and see if they need a file called Vbrun. If they do, the authors usually tell you where to find it.

● Some downloads are very big, so authors give you the choice between downloading the whole thing at once, or downloading it in small chunks. If you can, choose the latter. The Net can be unreliable. It's frustrating to spend an hour downloading something, only for it to crash with seconds to go to finish.

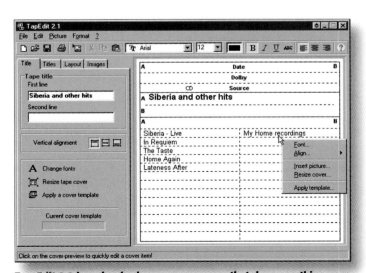

TapeEdit 2.1 is a classic shareware program that does one thing very well. It helps you design and print sleeves for audio cassettes.

Shareware games

This is **Gamespot**, one of many good sites on the Internet for downloading games. Games are categorized by genre and the whole thing has an entertaining, magazine-like feel.

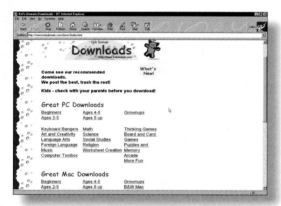

Kids Domain is an Internet site with a range of good shareware programs for kids which have more of an educational theme than your run-of-the-mill entertainment software.

Get extra levels for your favourite games and test the latest releases to see whether they are worth buying.

Shareware gaming was pioneered by a game called Doom, which was distributed as a free program over the Internet. It wasn't the complete game, it was just the first few levels, but it was enough to give potential buyers an idea of whether they were going to like the game. It was a milestone in the games software market and paved the way for the hundreds of playable demos you'll find on the Net.

Because playable demos have become so popular, you'll find examples of nearly every kind of game available for download over the Internet from shoot 'em ups to strategy, board games to simulations, action games to point-and-click adventures.

Where to learn while you play

Those looking for purely educational games are likely to be disappointed. At best, companies have a few token products available. File Depot for example, doesn't even have a games category. However, you will find many games for Windows and DOS (less so for Mac) at www.shareware.com and www.download.com.

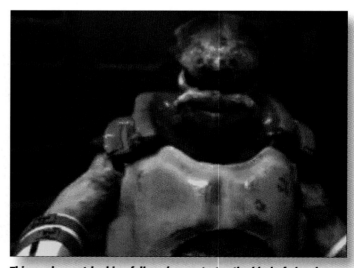

This unpleasant-looking fellow demonstrates the kind of visual quality you can expect from a modern computer game. He's one of the characters from Ion Storm's Dominion: Storm Over Gift 3.

If you scan through the shareware sources listed on page 38 and do the same on CompuServe and AOL, you will find plenty of games that aren't full of blood and guts: these include art and Bible quizzes, jigsaw puzzles based on famous paintings, electronic hangman, word games, crosswords, anagrams, draughts and chess.

If you go outside of the main directories, you can find some that specialize in educational shareware. At Kids Domain (www.kidsdomain.com), there are programs for learning music, foreign languages, PC and keyboard skills, painting and drawing, religion, maths and science. In fact, you may find a number of interesting looking sites just by going to Alta Vista at www.altavista.com, and searching for Educational Shareware.

Games tips

● Games are rated like movies, so before downloading something for your kids, check that the content is suitable.

● Many games need a special Microsoft component called DirectX. For the latest version of this, go to www.microsoft.com.

● Games have a bigger system requirement than most other programs, so before spending a lot of time downloading something, make sure your PC is powerful enough to run it properly.

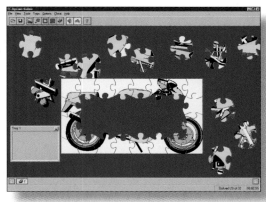

Typical of the more contemplative shareware games you can find, Jigsaws Galore is a terrific puzzle game with lots of different pictures, difficulty levels and sound effects.

Like Doom before it, the violent and funny shoot 'em up, Duke Nuke 'Em 3D was first released as a playable demo over the Internet. This is a screen shot from the Atomic Pack, which adds new levels to the original game.

It's not all death and destruction. Here's FIFA: The Road to the World Cup in action, demonstrating excellent use of 3D figures to produce a lifelike soccer simulation.

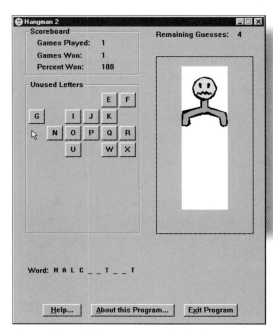

The popular word game Hangman gets a computer twist with this simple but highly enjoyable version.

Freeware

This is WordMagic, an entirely free word processor that may not be as powerful as Microsoft Word, but has more features than the Word Pad word processor that comes free with Windows.

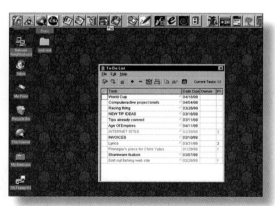

Here are two fine freeware programs in action. In the middle of the screen you can see a simple, clear to-do list of prioritized items, and at the top, there's a freeware button bar for launching your favourite programs.

Shareware tips

● If you're downloading shareware, you should take a couple of precautions. Invest in an anti-virus program and keep it running in the background so it can check that there's nothing unpleasant hidden in the program. Second, get yourself a program that can properly monitor the installation of Windows programs and then remove them properly.

● Invest in the fastest modem available. But make sure it's supported by your provider, because there's no point in you having a 56Kbps modem if you can only communicate with your Internet provider at the slower speed of 33.6Kbps.

Look on the Internet and for CD-ROMs included with magazines and you'll find some software that's free.

It's possible to find lots of programs that are not shareware, but are actually free. It's not a trick. This is fully functioning software usually created by programmers for their own use, then distributed for fun, rather than profit. That's why you'll often see some free programs described as postcardware. If you like one of them, you send the author a postcard instead of paying money for it.

A true free lunch

Freeware tends to be smaller or more specialized than shareware, but not always so. Along with calendars, to-do lists, notepads, clocks and Desktop themes, there are much larger free programs, like the WordMagic word processor available from www.usa7.com or database templates that will work with popular programs like FileMaker Pro and Access. The Netscape Navigator and Internet Explorer Web browsers are also free. But such programs are the exception rather than the rule.

There are a number of good freeware sites organized like the best shareware ones, by category and with a search capability, where you can find excellent programs, like the ones illustrated here.

Pay up or else!

One word of warning. Some programs that are described as free aren't. They are actually shareware that don't contain nag screens to remind you to register, or don't limit the number of times you can start the program or prevent you from saving your work. None of that matters: somewhere the program will tell you that it isn't free, and if you continue to use it, you should respect that, and pay for it.

Where to go

● **Freebiez**
www.bcpl.net/~wnidiffe/free.html
● **Freeware Now.Com**
www.freewarenow.com/

● **Tudogs**
www.tudogs.com/
● **Freeware Archive List**
www.ptf.com/free/archives/

3

Internet Technologies

Understand the technology behind the Internet to make time online more enjoyable and profitable.

The Internet has come a long way since it started, when it was able only to show simple text. Now animation, sound, video, multimedia, menus, and drop-down lists as in any word processor are pretty much the norm on a Web page. Yet the technology behind these advances — Java, Shockwave, ActiveX, streaming audio, DHTML, plug-ins and Push — still remains a mystery to most people.

Increased understanding

These are the technologies that make it all possible, and by understanding what they are, how they work, and when you should use them, you'll soon discover that your time on the Internet can become more enjoyable and more efficient — enjoyable because you'll have access to all the Internet can offer, and efficient because you won't need to interrupt your browsing to download an application, install it, reboot your PC and then return to the Web page just to see a 30-second animation.

Just as important is knowing when not to use these advanced Internet technologies. For instance, turning off Java functionality in your Web browser can speed up your online travels and may even save your PC from the danger of hostile applets. Switching to the latest streaming audio and video systems will result in smoother and faster sound and video on the Web compared with the methods used just a couple of years ago. Downloading and installing a small basic set of plug-ins will enable your browser to deal with just about anything it comes across online.

You will need

ESSENTIAL
Software Internet connection and Web browsing software such as Internet Explorer or Netscape Navigator. To ensure that the advanced applications can run smoothly, you should use version 4 or later of the software. You will also need to download some plug-in software from the Internet. Plug-ins integrate with your Web browser to provide extra functionality. Full download instructions will be given for each application where this is necessary.
Hardware A fast modem, plus a sound card and speakers for audio. Although it's possible to make use of the advanced features of the Internet with just 16Mb of RAM, things run a lot smoother and faster if you have at least 48Mb RAM available.
Other An account with an Internet service provider.

Java jive

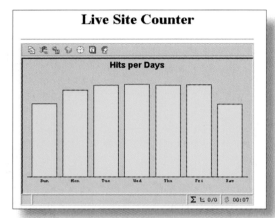

Live Site Counter

Hits per Days

Sun   Mon   Tue   Wed   Thu   Fri   Sat

Σ ≟ 0/0 $ 00:07

Hit counters are the classic Java utility, and this one which can be found at http://javaboutique. internet.com/LiveSiteCounter shows just what is possible using Java to the full.

Java makes it possible for people to swap files no matter which computer system they are using.

Java has revolutionized the way the Web works and the way people use it. Java is a programming language that differs from other languages in that it doesn't matter what computer platform you run the software on. The same Java-programmed software will happily run on a PC or a Mac, or even on a suitably equipped mobile phone, handheld computing device or powerful network server. It does this by using something called the Java Virtual Machine. This is built into your Web browser and acts as a go-between by catching the code as it comes down off the Internet and ensuring that your computer understands what it says.

Hot Java

Java software falls into two categories: applications and applets. Applications are stand-alone programs, such as Web browsers written in Java — they do exist. The best known is called HotJava. However, it's Java applets that are most interesting and it's applets that you will encounter during much of your online browsing time. An applet is a small program that runs inside a Java-enabled Web browser, allowing for interactive resources that can be embedded directly into any World Wide Web page you are viewing.

Applets are one of the most popular methods of providing interactive resources like clocks, visitor counters, animated logos, images that change as you pass the mouse cursor over them, financial spreadsheets that let you calculate payments off the page and so on. One of the surprising uses of Java

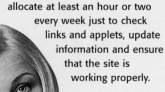

Management tip

Always remember that your Web site will stand or fall according to the amount of effort you are prepared to put into its development and upkeep. Planning and designing the pages is only the beginning; the real fun starts when you begin to manage your site. Try to allocate at least an hour or two every week just to check links and applets, update information and ensure that the site is working properly.

Many people use Java to place a clock on a Web page. This one at www.totem.co.uk/personel/garethe/java takes things a step further by displaying the time in different parts of the world.

has been in the online entertainment business, with sites springing up that contain dozens of interactive games that you play on the Web using nothing more than Java applets.

Small is beautiful

Java runs very quickly as long as the applet isn't too big — most applets are small for this very reason — and the Web page will come alive and be up and running in front of your eyes within just a few seconds. Best of all, you don't need to download any special viewers or plug-ins to be able to use Java since all but the most ancient versions of Internet Explorer and Netscape Navigator have Java support built in.

Java tip

If you are creating a Web page of your own and want to add some Java interactivity, make sure you get it right. That means no animated text, bouncing balls or clever fireworks displays just for the sake of it. Using Java like this will slow down the loading of the page and result in visitors moving elsewhere. Use Java to add to your site, but not at the expense of annoying the very people you are trying to attract. Like all things when it comes to Web design, if you don't go crazy, your visitors won't either.

This golf game, which you can find and play at http://members.aol.com/edhobbs2/applets/cgolf3d, is a Java applet. This small program runs inside the Web page and shows just what fun you can have with Java.

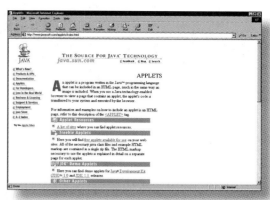

The JavaRama Gallery at www.javasoft.com/applets is a great place to take a look at amazing examples of Java applets in action. If you like what you see, you can download many of them to use on your Web pages.

Watch out!

Most Java applets are harmless little interactive gadgets that add an extra degree of enjoyment to Web pages. But because they are programs that have to be downloaded and run from your hard disk, there is always some risk. Just as some people get kicks by distributing viruses that can damage your PC, so some authors of Java applets have turned to the dark side of programming.

There are some Java programs known as hostile applets that will cause havoc on your computer. Some, like the ghost or whiteboard applets, will paint your Desktop completely white if you are using Internet Explorer with the Active Desktop turned on. The only way back is to reboot your PC. Others will reboot the PC for you whether you want it to or not, and others still will cause your PC to crash.

Most of the programmers of these applets argue that they are just drawing attention to security holes left by developers like Microsoft, but it's the user who suffers if someone includes such applets on their Web page. The majority of Web pages are safe places to visit, but if you want to be sure of not running into a hostile applet, you can disable Java from the options menu of your browser and just turn it on when you are connected to a page which has an applet you want to run.

Jargon buster

Hit A hit is a unit of measurement of Web page activity. One hit equals one page visit, so a single visitor may generate dozens of hits as he or she wanders around your site. The more hits you have, the more popular your Web pages.

Push technology

Subscribing to a channel

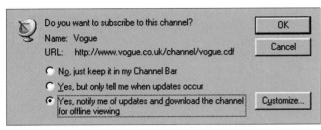

1 When you hit the **Add Active Channel** button, you'll get this window. To subscribe, select the bottom option and then click the Customize button.

2 You can choose to download only the **channel home page** if you want, but that's pointless. Ask for the whole thing and you'll get everything the channel has to offer.

Channel tip

Make sure you configure channels to deliver content manually. Doing this will mean the content updates when you connect to the Net. If you choose the automatic update option, then Internet Explorer will get your modem to dial up and download even when you are not there, which might increase your phone bills.

A number of channels appear here by default. Select the top one for a Microsoft guide to a wide selection of available channels to which you can subscribe.

If you position the mouse over a channel name an information window will pop up giving you a brief description of what the channel is about.

Push technology turns the Net into something like a TV in the way it delivers information.

Push technology brings all the resources of the World Wide Web straight to your desktop. When you browse the Web you have to go and get the information you want, pull it off the Web and into your Web browser. When you watch TV you just tune into a channel and the programs are sent to your screen. The same thing applies to Push technology: you subscribe to a channel and it sends information directly to you over the Net. So you could subscribe to a news service and have news headlines delivered to your desktop at regular intervals, without having to go to a Web page to retrieve them.

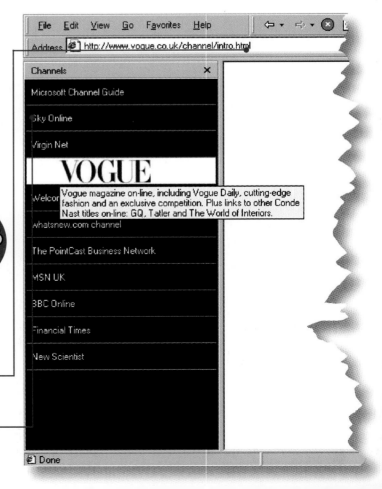

A compromise

These channels are not the same as TV. Signals are not constantly broadcast for anyone with a receiver to pick them up. Instead, it's a compromise between TV and the Web. You have to subscribe to a content provider and tell them that you want their information and when you want it, and they will send it to you accordingly.

Push channels were developed in Internet Explorer 4. Adding an HTML layer to the Windows desktop means it can display Web pages. When you subscribe to such a channel, the content can be delivered straight to your Active Desktop and displayed as if it were a Web page in a browser. This is not as complicated as it sounds. All you have to do is click on a few buttons and select the information you want delivered.

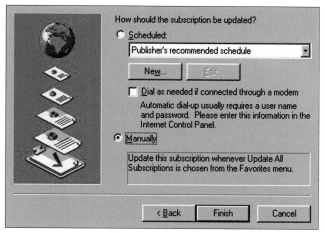

3 If you choose the **Manually** option, the channel content will be updated only when you ask for an update. You can choose to let your modem dial up at scheduled times, without you being there to watch over it, or if you are lucky enough to have a permanent Internet connection, just let the content get pushed to you as required.

4 The final result is the **Vogue Channel**, updated whenever you request it with all the content downloaded to your PC and available for you to read at your leisure offline.

Jargon buster

Push technology A system that delivers content to you automatically from the Web.

Click here to add the Vogue Channel to your desktop

Click on the Channels button in Internet Explorer and a channel navigation frame will appear in the left third of your screen.

A click on the channel entry in the left-hand frame will connect you to the channel site of your choice.

Click the Add Active Channel button if you want to subscribe to the channel shown. This will start off the channel subscription wizard and you then just follow the instructions step by step.

Shock treatment

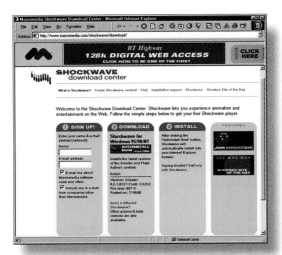

Shockwave players can be downloaded directly from the Macromedia site that developed the software. Just follow the onscreen instructions and the software will auto-install on your PC.

You can send live video to your Web site by using a Webcam.

Visit any impressive multimedia site on the World Wide Web and you could get a bit of a shock.

If you have ever visited the Disney Web site, the Microsoft Network or any Web site where there are impressive multimedia presentations, you will have come across Shockwave files. Shockwave is the name given to multimedia content created using special software and viewed off the page by a Shockwave player plugged into your Web browser. Such content can range from simple buttons that roll over and change as you click on them to video presentations, animations and even games you can play online.

Get shocked

Shockwave is behind the kind of interactive entertainment you can find at the Disney site and other sophisticated multimedia Web sites. It is also used to bring business presentations alive online and for educational and instructional guides.

To view Shockwave content, you need to use a Web browser that has the correct player software installed. Internet Explorer 4 and 5 have Shockwave support built in. If you aren't running this, go to

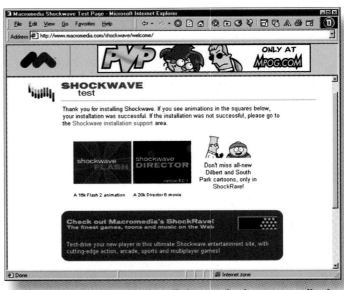

To make sure everything has installed correctly, the Macromedia site lets you test the software by playing a few small animations.

the Macromedia site at www.macromedia.com and download the player. This doesn't take long, and once downloaded it will attach itself to your Web browser seamlessly. Next time you connect to a Shockwaved site you should be able to see the presentation without any problems. More than 40 million free Shockwave players have already been downloaded from the site.

Shockwave automatically downloads presentation files when you connect to a site. You don't need to wait for the whole file to download before you can see an animation or hear a sound. The software uses a buffering technique so you only have to download a small part of a file and can then run it while the rest downloads in the background.

Shocking stuff

You might not realize you are visiting a Shockwave site at all. Everything works smoothly and appears as just another part of the page. But some sites get it all wrong; a common problem is the huge files that designers can produce. If a Web site seems to be taking an age to appear on your screen, just hit the browser stop button and go somewhere else.

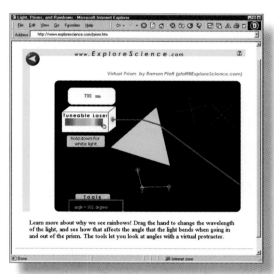

The Explore Science site at www.explorescience.com uses Shockwave to bring simple interactive experiments alive on the Web.

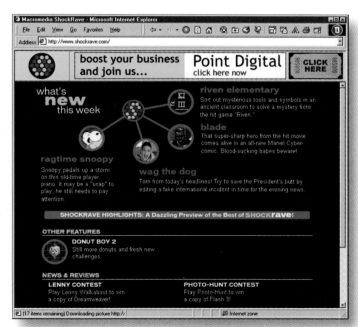

Once installed and running, head straight over to ShockRave (just follow the links from the Macromedia site) for a selection of Shockwave items to try out. You'll find everything from games to cartoon strips and musical extravaganzas.

Audio and video

Download and install the **RealPlayer** and you get a neat but not very exciting application to play with. It sits waiting behind the scenes until you need it.

Businesses are using the **RealAudio** and **Video** software to present training guides, advertisements and online brochures with a difference. It's possible to combine audio, video, animation and text together or any single ingredient as needed.

Plug-in tip

If you use technology on your Web page that requires a plug-in to work, stick to the mainstream resources like Shockwave and RealPlayer. That way the majority of your visitors will be able to see your content and won't wander off after discovering you want them to spend 20 minutes downloading and installing a new piece of software just to see an animation on your page.

You can watch video and listen to music in real time as you download them from the Internet.

Not long ago, if you wanted to listen to some music from a Web page, you would have to first download a large music file then load this into a music player program and play it from there. As well as the lack of true integration between the music and the Web page, the files were often large and you had no choice but to download the whole thing before you could hear the music. If it was not to your taste, you had wasted your time. Then along came a company with a product called RealAudio that revolutionized sound on the World Wide Web simply because it used streaming.

On track

Streaming audio is a simple concept. Instead of you having to download an entire file before hearing a track, special software starts to play back the track as soon as possible. The streaming process makes this possible by downloading an audio file into a

Connect to a Web site with multimedia content produced in the **Real** format, and the software leaps into action – in this case with a multimedia presentation combining audio, images and text.

buffer, and after a short delay it starts to play the music from there. All the while the rest of the file is downloading into the same buffer area, producing an effect like pouring water into a kettle at the same speed as it is coming out of the spout. By employing this buffering technique, a music track can start to play within seconds of you clicking on the link. If you don't like it, you can stop it at any time without downloading the whole thing.

The brains behind RealAudio soon developed a similar technique for video, enabling video images to be played back in the same way, and then produced an application called RealPlayer that handles sound and vision. You will need to download this software from the RealNetworks site at www.real.com and install it on your computer.

The right speed

During the installation process, be sure to choose the right speed at which you connect to the Internet. This is important because it determines how the software buffers the files it downloads. Once installed, whenever you come across a Web page which has audio or video content that has been produced using RealAudio or RealVideo software — the most commonly used for Web page design purposes — you can click on it and the player will launch automatically and start playing the file.

Music videos complete with sound can be played straight from a Web page thanks to RealPlayer software. Many record companies are making demo videos available like this.

Where to Go

Now that you know about all these exciting technologies, you may want to try them out for yourself. You will come across Web pages that use all these things during your travels, but you can get a feel for working examples right away by following these links:

● **Java** The Java Centre at www.java.co.uk contains hundreds of Java applets ranging from office utilities such as calendars and clocks right through to time-wasting but entertaining games.

● **Push** The Microsoft Windows Media Showcase at www.windowsmedia.com/guide includes a searchable channels guide for Internet Explorer.

● **Shockwave** ShockRave at www.shockrave.com features some of the finest examples of Shockwave available on the Web, including animated cartoons and a vast collection of games.

● **DHTML** The Dynamic HTML Zone at www.dhtmlzone.com is a good starting point, with links to lots of DHTML demos and resources.

● **Streaming Audio/Video** RealNetworks at www.real.com is the home of the RealPlayer and birthplace of streaming audio and video on the Web. It is an excellent showcase for the technology, as you might expect.

● **ActiveX** (See page 54.) The Microsoft Network www.msn.com is a great place to see ActiveX components at work — the trick is spotting what they are. Just look how smoothly menus slide out, and how interactive the buttons and toolbars are.

The Microsoft Windows Media Showcase lets you browse by category or search by keyword for the subjects that interest you.

Jargon buster

Streaming A technology that allows you to start listening to a piece of music or watch a piece of video before the whole file has been downloaded over the Internet.

ActiveX

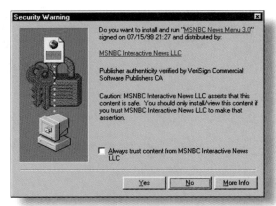

ActiveX **has a security system, so you can be sure you are installing a safe application on your PC before you download an ActiveX component.**

The results can be quite stunning, like these embedded pop-up menus on the MSNBC news site.

You can give all World Wide Web pages a familiar look and feel with Microsoft's ActiveX components.

Microsoft's ActiveX enhances Web browsing with extra interactivity. You only have to download a set of component parts once, and they can then be used by any page that requires them.

The X files

ActiveX makes Web pages look and feel more like Microsoft programs, with familiar buttons, toolbars and menus. If you are using Internet Explorer you don't need any extra software to view ActiveX components because support is built in. If you are using Netscape things are not so easy. Netscape Navigator doesn't support ActiveX, but there is a plug-in at www.ncompasslabs.com. Even with this, some ActiveX enhanced sites don't display properly.

One reason ActiveX is so tightly integrated with Internet Explorer is security. ActiveX components have freedom to operate on your PC once you have installed them. It brings increased functionality compared to technologies like Java, but has no defence against what is known as 'hostile code'. A programmer, if so inclined, could insert malicious or 'hostile' code into an ActiveX component which, when downloaded, might cause minor or major damage to your computer data. To get around this problem, ActiveX developers sign their work with a digital signature. When you download a component a window pops up showing the digital signature, enabling you to identify the author, find out more about the application and choose whether to trust the sender. Internet Explorer has different levels of security built in, with the default warning you every time an ActiveX control is encountered.

ActiveX tip

While ActiveX brings familiarity to Web pages, making them seem more like applications you are already used to by incorporating menus and toolbars and the like, remember that it's a Microsoft invention. This means that to get the best from it you need to be using Internet Explorer, otherwise the chances are it won't work properly.

4

Email

The Net links you and your PC to the rest of the world and can be used to send messages quickly and inexpensively.

Access to the Internet is increasingly one of the main reasons why people buy their first PC. This worldwide network of interconnected computers seems to have caught people's attention and captured their imaginations. The Internet can bring the world into your home thanks to the wonders of digital communication, and it appeals to the whole family from the youngest to the oldest.

Send it

Communication on the Internet for the majority of people means electronic mail, known as email. This is the process of sending messages on a computer network rather than using pen, paper and stamps (a process known to email users as snail mail).

Email can be used to send more than just written messages. You can add pictures, sound and video. You can send PC files by email, so your message can contain a spreadsheet file or a database. And it's very fast. An email message can be sent across the world in a few seconds, without fuss or delay. It's also not expensive; it involves only the cost of a local telephone call to your Internet service provider, no matter where the mail is heading. The equivalent of 100 A4 sheets of paper can be sent to Hong Kong for the cost of a one-minute phone call. Compare that with the rates from your postal service.

Jargon buster

ISP Internet service provider, the company that connects you to the Internet.

OSP Online service provider, a company that connects you to the Internet but also provides its own proprietary services.

Dial-up A common term that simply means connecting to the Internet using your PC, a modem and an ordinary telephone line.

Email client The software program that you use to send and receive electronic mail.

You will need

ESSENTIAL
Software Windows 95 or 98 and an email client (software that lets you send and receive email, such as Outlook Express).
Hardware A modem (look for a speed rating of at least 33.6Kbps, preferably 56Kbps).
Other An account with an Internet service provider (ISP) such as CompuServe, AOL, Microsoft Network or Netcom.

Jargon buster

Attachment Any item that is sent along with email. An attachment may be a PC file, a picture or an audio recording, for example.

Email clients

Sending an email using **Outlook Express** is just a
matter of clicking the Compose button on the
toolbar and filling in the details. You choose whom
to send it to from your address book, and click on
the Send button when you've finished. If you are
not connected to the Internet at the time, the email
software will dial up your ISP, make the connection
and send the message.

Outlook Express comes complete with a selection of
special **stationery** like this party invitation, to jazz
up your email the easy way.

Jargon buster

Blinking Email software that lets you
stack up your replies to received
messages and then sends them all at once,
checking for new mail at the same time. This act
of both sending prepared messages and checking
for new ones simultaneously is known as blinking.

Internet email is only as useful and efficient as the software you use to send and receive it.

Most ISPs supply Netscape Navigator or Microsoft
Internet Explorer as part of their packages. Both of
these come with usable email programs. Internet
Explorer 4 includes Microsoft Outlook Express, an
email client and personal information organizer
blended into one. It's free of charge and does just
about everything you could ask of an email client.

Filtering

Outlook Express will sort email into different
folders according to preferences you set. Known as
filtering, this works by defining a set of rules that
are applied to email as it arrives. Mail from certain
addresses can be sent straight into a personal
folder, for example, while mail with certain words
in the subject field can go to a work folder.

This type of administration makes dealing with
lots of email a pleasure. Outlook Express also lets
you keep an in-depth address book of your contacts
to make addressing new mail much easier.

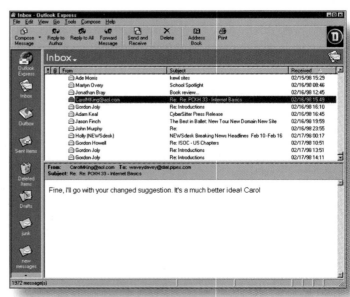

Receiving email is simple in Outlook Express. Hit the **Send/Receive**
button and it connects to your ISP and downloads any waiting mail
to your PC. You can then browse through the inbox entries and
select the messages you want to read.

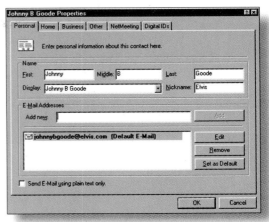

Adding contacts to your address book is easy in Outlook Express. It doubles as a personal organizer with tabs for home and business details and email.

Carbon copy

Both Outlook Express and Eudora (another good email package) allow you to keep carbon copies of mail, format messages using different fonts and colours, and spell check mail before you send it.

Online services such as CompuServe and AOL have their own interfaces, i.e. they have their own email software. These do not have as many features as Outlook Express or Eudora and often sacrifice enhancements for simplicity. They are fine for everyday use, but you may not be enthusiastic about them if you've ever tried a dedicated email client.

Filter tip

If you get lots of junk email, like ads for get-rich-quick schemes, use the filtering capabilities of your mail software to deal with the problem. Create a folder called Junk and set up a filter to move messages from known junk addresses straight to it. Much junk mail comes from a small number of email addresses, so by cutting and pasting these into your filter rules you should be able to reduce the amount of junk you have to read.

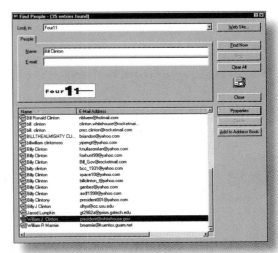

Some email programs include a directory service for finding email addresses when you only know the name of the person. The software connects to an online directory and returns a list of matches. Identifying Bill Clinton at the White House may be easy, but picking the right address is more usually guesswork.

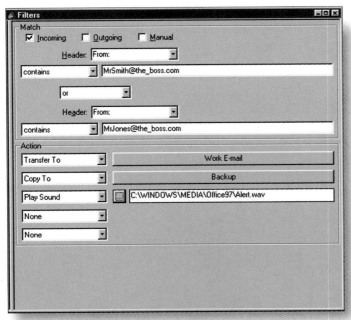

Software such as Eudora lets you apply filters to your incoming email. Here a work mailbox has been created for any important work-related email (as well as a back-up copy for safety), and a sound file has been requested to let you know when it arrives.

Mail software is just part of the CompuServe interface. It's easy to use – a matter of clicking on buttons. However, it does lack some of the power features of Outlook Express and Eudora.

Attachments

1 Outlook Express is used in this example, but most modern mail software works in the same way. First compose your message as you would ordinarily, and then click on the **attachment icon** in the toolbar — in this case a paper clip.

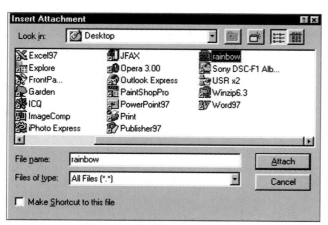

2 Then a **file selection window** pops up. You choose the file you want to attach to the email and click on it.

Jargon buster

MIME Stands for Multipurpose Internet Mail Extensions, the most common system used by email applications to allow the automatic posting and display of email attachments.

UUencode The predecessor to MIME, requiring manual coding and decoding of attachments, and now less popular.

BinHex Another mail attachment coding system, for users of Apple Macintosh computers.

Turn your email messages into a multimedia experience by adding pictures, sound and video.

You can attach files such as pictures, sounds and video clips to your email. Attachments bring interactivity to email, and they are easy to send and receive. Email software takes care of everything except selecting which files to send. But bear in mind that when you attach a file to your email, you are increasing the size of the message being sent, and a sound file can occupy a lot of space.

Reduce the size

There are a number of tools to reduce the size of files, known as compression utilities. The most popular is WinZip, which produces files with a .zip extension. You can use WinZip to compress just about any type of file.

If you want to attach images in an unzipped format so that they appear as part of the email, take care in choosing the image format. Using Paint Shop Pro you can convert your pictures into .jpg files, a format that reduces the size of the picture file, making it ideal for use in email.

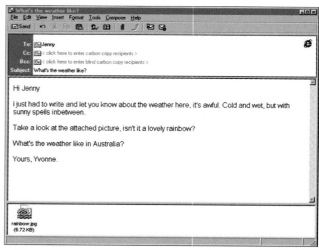

3 You'll notice that a frame has appeared under the main message body window. This contains **icons** that represent files you have attached to the mail, including their size. You can delete them by right-clicking them and selecting Delete, or simply drag the icon into the recycle bin on your Desktop.

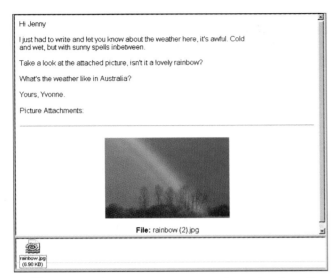

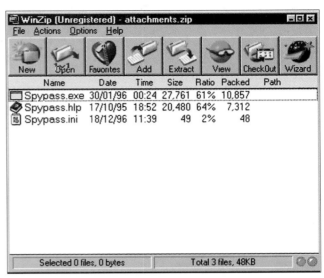

4 When the recipient gets the email, this is what they will see: the normal text message with the picture or pictures inserted below. They can **save the file** by dragging and dropping the icon as they would any other file.

6 ...and they are all added to a **zip archive** – a single file containing all the compressed files. In this case it took just a few seconds to reduce three image files in size by more than 60 per cent.

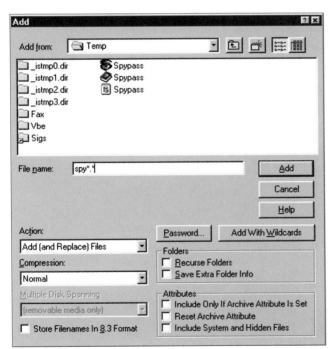

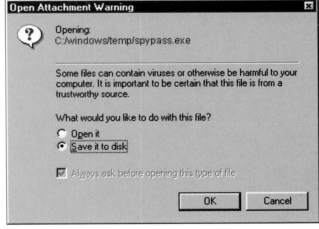

5 Making files smaller before attaching them to your email is a good idea if you have a lot to send, or they are large to start with. **WinZip** does the job easily. Just select the files you want to compress...

7 If an attached file doesn't display along with your email, it may be because it's a file that needs to be opened by another program, such as a database or spreadsheet. Don't be alarmed by this warning box. It's just telling you to be careful. Unless you are sure the file concerned is virus free, take the save option and use a **virus checker** before opening it.

Virus tip

There are a lot of hoax virus warnings that circulate, with names like Good Times, that claim email messages are infected. Don't panic. You can't catch a virus from an email message. This is a modern myth. But you can catch a virus from an attachment because these are ordinary computer files. Always virus-check unknown files before you open them.

Mailing lists

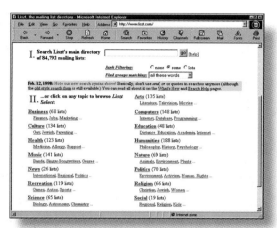

With nearly 85,000 mailing lists to choose from, finding the right one can be difficult. Use the Liszt Web site at www.liszt.com to make the job easier. Either select from broad categories, or search for a specific list by keyword.

A quick search on the word *pregnancy* uncovered 20 different mailing lists dealing with the subject. Selecting the underlined list title presents you with more information about the mailing list, including details of how to subscribe.

Mailing list tip

If you are going on holiday or will be away from your PC and email for a while, it's a good idea to unsubscribe from any mailing lists you belong to before you go. This prevents you coming home to an overflowing mailbox and a large and time-consuming email download. Simply re-subscribe when you get back.

You can get together with groups of like-minded people for an online chat about anything you like.

Mailing lists enable you to participate in email-based discussions, and there are no limits to how many people can take part. There are thousands of mailing lists operating on the Internet, covering just about any subject you can think of. They cost nothing to join, and all you do is collect your email.

Get together

Mailing lists are easy to use. Each has two separate addresses. The first is the administrative address, which you use to notify the maintainer of the list that you want to join. The second is the list address itself, which is where you send messages when you want to join in a conversation. Subscribing is easy, although there is some variation in subscription instructions from list to list. You usually won't have any trouble if you send an email with a blank subject line and the word Subscribe in the body of the message to the administrative address.

Leave the list

You will then receive email messages that are sent to the mailing list address. Every message sent to this address by any other list member will get forwarded to you, and any message you send will be forwarded to every other member. The most popular mailing lists can generate hundreds of email messages each week, and most will offer the option of getting a daily or weekly digest of the messages if you prefer.

Watch out!

Although email offers great value for money, there are a few pitfalls that can increase your bills. The first rule is never read your email online. All the time you are connected to the Internet your telephone bill will be increasing. Your email software should have an option to allow you to work offline. It will connect to your ISP, check for new email, download it to your PC and then disconnect. You can read and reply to the messages at your leisure, and send all the replies in one batch.

Internet directory

Finding someone online may seem a difficult task, but it needn't be.

The bigger the Net gets, the harder it becomes to track people down. With more than 100 million people around the world already online, and more than a million newcomers joining every month, locating the Dave Lamb you used to know is like looking for a needle in a whole field of haystacks.

There is no such thing as a printed email directory, like a telephone directory. So if you've got a person's name, and you think he or she has an email account, how do you go about tracing the person? Fortunately, this is becoming easier all the time.

Most Web search engines let you look for people as well as topics, and they make the searches as speedy and accurate as possible. If you are using one of the latest email programs, you will find it has a people search facility built in. Windows 95 and 98 let you search for people straight from the Start menu. You may not find the person you're looking for, but the task will be easier than you thought.

You will learn

- How to use the search features of your electronic address book.
- How to use the online directory services to locate email addresses of people for whom you have no mailbox details.
- How to make the most of the search options available from these directory services to ensure an efficient and accurate search.

You will need

Software A Web browser and email program, such as Microsoft Internet Explorer and Microsoft Outlook Express.
Hardware A modem or other means of connecting to the Internet.
Other An account with an Internet service provider.

How to find someone online

1 Start at the beginning, with the easiest option, the **Windows Start menu**. Simply left-click the start button to open the menu and move up to Find. If you are using a later version of Windows 95 or Windows 98, you can then select People from the sub-menu that appears. Click on this and a new window will appear, with various options for finding people.

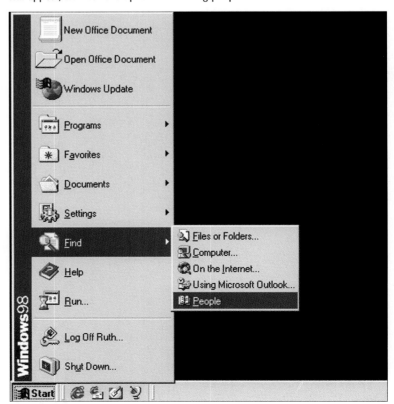

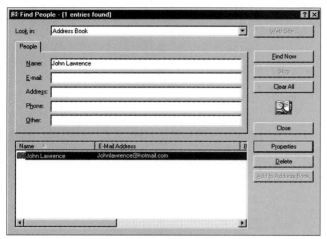

2 By default the **Find People** application will open with Look In Address Book. Entering a name in the relevant box and clicking the Find Now button will perform a search of your email address book. A right mouse click over the resulting entry in the lower window will pop up a menu that lets you compose an email to that person. However, this is only useful if you already know the email address of the person in question. If you don't, then you will need to use one of the online directory options.

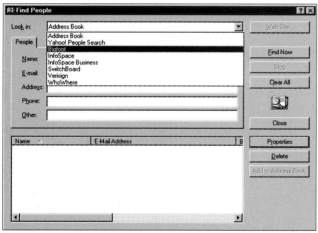

3 To do this, click on the arrow at the end of the **Look In** selection box, and a drop-down list of more choices will appear. Selecting one of these, Bigfoot, for example, will change the database of information that is searched when you ask the program to find someone. Bigfoot and the other services listed are online resources and so a connection to the Internet has to be made. Enter a name as before, make sure that your modem is switched on, then click on the Find Now button.

Jargon buster

White Pages Any online directory that contains real world information, such as street addresses and telephone numbers, rather than just email details.

LDAP Stands for Lightweight Directory Access Protocol and refers to the method used to search the databases of Internet people-finding services.

4 Your computer will now dial up your Internet service provider and connect to whichever **directory service** you have chosen to use. It takes only a few seconds for the results to appear on your screen. If the search is successful, then the relevant email details will appear in the lower window as before. If not, you will see this warning box. If this happens, just click on the OK button to clear the warning, then either revise your search criteria (perhaps use only the surname or a first initial and surname to widen the search) or choose another directory service and continue until you are successful.

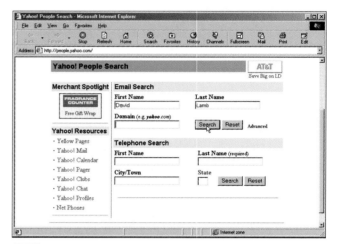

5 There are alternatives to using the Start menu method. The most popular and efficient is to use one of the many Web-based search sites. The biggest and best known for finding Web sites and services is **Yahoo!**, which can also help you find email addresses. Yahoo! bought the most popular address directory, Four11, and merged it with its own site to create the Yahoo! People Finder. To get here you must use your Web browser and type http://people.yahoo.com into the address box. Enter a name (first names and surnames have separate entry boxes) and click on the Search button.

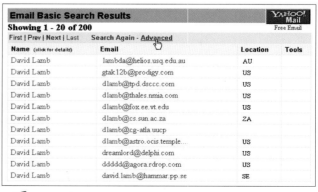

6 This search was successful – too successful, in fact, as it turned up 200 David Lambs living all over the world. However, all is not lost. Simply click on the **Advanced** link next to the Search Again option at the top of the list.

Advanced Email Search — People Search

Fill out as much or as little information as you want. All fields are optional. Enhance your search by choosing an organization name and type.

First Name: David
Last Name: Lamb
City/Town: Los Angeles
State/Province:
Country: US
Domain:
Old Email Address:
☑ SmartNames™ (Bob = Robert)

Organization Name:

Organization Type:
○ Company
○ University/College
○ High School
○ Military
○ Other
◉ All Organizations

[Search] [Reset]

7 Now you are given a form with narrower search criteria to focus the search and hone in on the right David Lamb. Let's assume you are fairly certain that the person you want lives in Los Angeles. You can enter these details and search again. If you know any other details about the person you are looking for, enter them — things such as the type of organization (university, company or military) — to narrow the search further, or the domain (if David Lamb worked at Microsoft you might enter microsoft.com as a domain) to narrow it down even further. In this example Los Angeles and US were entered because that's all that was known. Check the **SmartNames** box, which will search for Robert as well as Bob or Rob, or Dave as well as David.

Email Advanced Search Results — YAHOO! Mail

Showing 1 - 2 of 2 — Free Email
First | Prev | Next | Last   Search Again - Basic Search

Name (click for details)	Email	Location	Tools
David Lamb	rainbow70@yahoo.com	Los Angeles, US	
David Lamb	daven123@yahoo.com	Los Angeles, US	

8 The difference is amazing. It took less than 20 seconds for the Yahoo! **People Search** to get it down to just two David Lambs based in Los Angeles. Now it's just a case of emailing two people a polite and brief letter to see if either one is the David Lamb you are trying to contact.

9 With a database containing the email addresses of more than 13 million Internet users, the Yahoo! People Search still only has a fraction of the people who are using the Net. The chances are therefore pretty high that you will have to try more than one service before hitting the jackpot. Some services offer country-specific searches, such as the **Excite People Finder**, for example. Connect your Web browser to www.excite.co.uk and then select the People Finder option.

Troubleshooting

While online directory services are improving all the time, they are still not perfect. Printed telephone directories are updated only every few years, and numbers can be out of date if people move or go ex-directory.

Online directories can also contain out-of-date information. Email addresses change: if you change your Internet service provider, you get a new email address; if you decide to use one of the many free email services, you get a new email address; if you change jobs, you get a new email address. It may not be unusual for a search to return a handful of addresses that are accurate as far as the person is concerned, but dated from the point of view of the mailbox. The date of creation of the address cannot be given, nor can you find out when it was last used; most people would consider this information to be private.

Perhaps more of a problem is the fact that it can be very difficult to ensure you have the right person, especially if the name is a common one. Take US President, Bill Clinton. A search for this name will produce dozens of addresses, all for Bill Clinton. Unless you know that an official government address ends in .gov you wouldn't be able to filter out the namesakes and the deliberate fakes. It is vital, therefore, that you verify an identity by sending a polite Is this you? message before sending something personal or confidential.

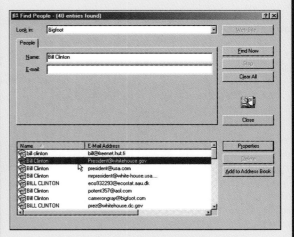

A successful search for Bill Clinton's email address turns up 40 different mailboxes. The real one is at whitehouse.gov but if you already knew that you probably wouldn't be using a directory service.

Jargon buster

Domain A domain is an Internet street address — that part of the email address that comes after the @ symbol. If you know this much of someone's address, you are 90 per cent of the way to finding the whole thing.

Lookup The act of one computer requesting information from a directory held on another computer.

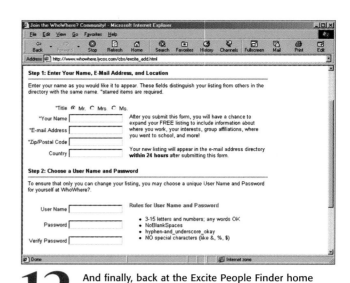

10 Excite offers a number of choices. Your first move should be to enter the name in the search box and press the **Look It Up** button. David Lamb is used once more for this example.

Search Results

David Lamb   dalam@mailcity.com
Los Angeles
us

Additional Contact Information

This Listing was Last Customized in July '98

11 Although the search this time returned a staggering 500 David Lambs, each entry has the full email address, details of the geographical location and the mailbox service provider to help narrow things down. Even better is the addition of a **More Details About** David Lamb link under each entry. Click on this and you get much more information, including an exact location (with zip- or postcode where known) and the date the entry was last updated. This gives you a much better chance of finding the right person and finding an up-to-date email address.

12 And finally, back at the Excite People Finder home page, there is the option to **Add Your Email Details** to the database, free of charge. Selecting this takes you to this data entry screen and allows you to add your details to the WhoWhere directory service used by Excite and many other services online. It's just a matter of entering your details, choosing a username and password combination so only you can change those details, and hitting Submit. Note that you can update your details whenever necessary. Then your friends should always be able to find you electronically.

Address book tip

The simplest way to keep track of the people closest to you is to ensure that you keep your email address book as up to date as the one next to the telephone. If someone gives you their email address, you find it online, or you receive email from a person you want to keep in touch with, then enter the details into your email software's address book straightaway so that you don't forget it. It's a lot less hassle searching for a name in your private email address book, no matter how big it gets, than going online to search through a database of millions.

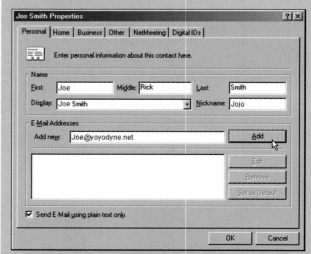

Microsoft Outlook lets you store a great deal of information in its Address Book, which is perfect for keeping track of those people important to you.

Filtering email

Set up a virtual secretary to open email and sort it into relevant folders.

Email is quick, efficient and cheap, but this is starting to cause problems. Information overload is a reality. If you receive 25 emails per day, that's 175 each week, or a staggering 9,125 a year. For many people the figures are much higher, thanks to the amount of junk email, or spam, that's sent.

Junk email distribution has become big business, attracting unscrupulous people who don't care who receives it. Even managing everyday email can be a task. With 175 emails coming in each week, it's all too easy to skip or delete an important message that has been lost among the rest.

The solution is filtering. You can set up a filter with a rule that looks for email from Aunt Marge and a command to move such messages to a folder called AuntM; or you can have a filter that looks for a phrase such as Get Rich Quick in the subject of an email and moves it to a junk folder because it will almost certainly be spam. Set up the right filters and your email will manage itself.

You will need

Software Just about any dedicated email program, such as Outlook Express, Netscape Messenger or Eudora, will let you filter mail.
Hardware A modem or other means of connecting to the Internet.
Other An account with an Internet service provider that provides you with an email address.

Organizing incoming email messages

1 Steps 1 through 14 show you how to organize your email using **Microsoft Outlook**, but the same principles apply to all email filtering. Only the procedure will change, so check your manual for details about how to apply these steps in your software. Your first step to a more organized life is to select Organize from the Tools menu or click on the Organize button on the toolbar.

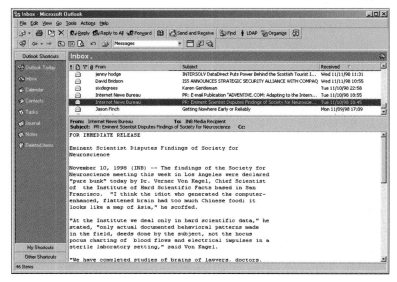

You will learn

- How to use the built-in filtering features of your email software.
- How to set up filtering rules that sort your incoming email into separate named folders.
- How to consign junk email straight to the bin.
- How to send automatic replies to let friends and family know you've received their email.

2 A new pane opens at the top of your email window, and offers four options: **Using Folders**, **Using Colors**, **Using Views** and **Junk Email**. Using Colors option lets you display messages from different people in different colours, so you can spot an email from a member of your family, for example. Using Views will change the way your email is displayed and sorted, enabling you to sort alphabetically by sender, or in date order.

3 The **Junk Email** option lets you colour or move messages that Outlook recognizes as spam or having adult content. This is a useful way to filter out unwanted or inappropriate messages, especially if the whole family uses the email account. You can even get updates of suspect email addresses to be added to the filter list automatically by selecting Click Here and downloading the updated data from the Microsoft Outlook Web site as directed.

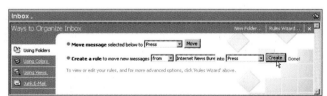

4 Now look at the **Using Folders** options, the simplest of which is highlighting a message and using Move to copy it to another folder. Use the New Folder button to create an appropriate folder. Alternatively you can create a simple rule that does this automatically every time a message is received from that sender. Choose the folder you want the messages to be moved to, and click Create. You can do cleverer things than just moving a message to a folder, and the key lies with the Rules Wizard.

5 Click on **Rules Wizard** at the top right of the organize pane, and a new window will appear. If you have just created a rule, as in the previous step, details of this will be shown. The top pane of the window shows existing rules, with a checkbox to the left of each that determines if it is activated. The bottom pane describes the action performed by that filtering rule. You want to create a new filter, so click the New button.

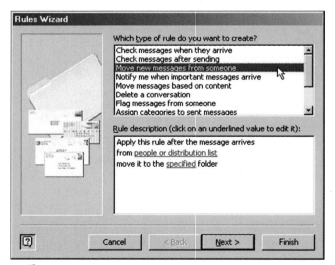

6 A new window appears with lots of options. The top box contains the most common types of filter, while the bottom box explains the action that will be taken. Start with the most useful filter of them all, one that moves messages from specified senders into specified folders. To set up this filter select **Move New Messages From Someone** and click on Next.

Address book tip

Make full use of the address book that every email program has. When you get email from someone you may want to contact again, add their details to your address book right away. Most email software makes this easy — often a right-click over the message opening up a menu that includes Add To Address Book as an option. Failing that, the same option can be found in the main program menus. Familiarize yourself with the process and it will soon become second nature.

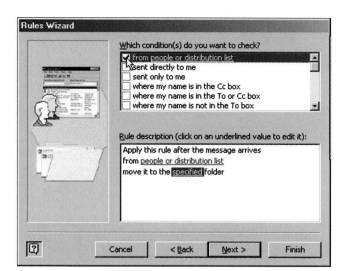

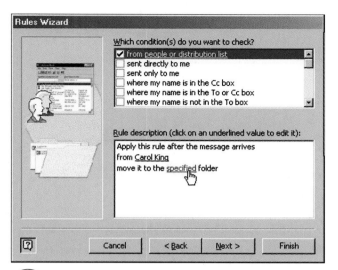

7 You are now faced with a long list of **conditions**. These are the rules governing which messages the filter will apply to, and there are plenty of them to cover all possible requirements. You can choose to move email that has a specific word in the sender's address, so that all email from one domain or mailing list is moved, or with specific words in the subject line or message text so that all messages that contain that word (maybe the name of your business or of a hobby) are moved to a folder. You can choose to move messages that are marked as important, or that have an attachment, or are over a certain size. The possibilities are enormous, but for this example choose the option at the top of the list, From People Or Distribution List.

9 You will now be taken back to the Rules Wizard window, but if you look in the **action pane** you will notice that the sender's name now appears there. Next you need to select a folder to move email from this person into, in this example the secretary of the PTA, and you do this by clicking on the word Specified which is highlighted in the same pane.

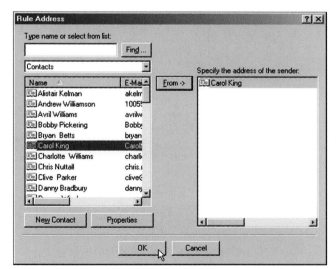

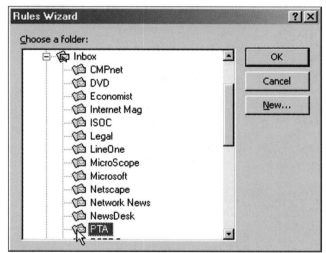

8 Click on the **From People Or Distribution List** checkbox, then move to the lower action pane and click on People Or Distribution List. Select the name from the address list that appears, which is a copy of your email address book. If the name isn't shown, you can create a new entry for your address book and select that. Once you have made your selection, click OK.

10 A **directory window** will appear that contains the folders in your email inbox. Either select a folder from here by clicking on it, or create a new folder using the New button. When you have finished, simply click OK.

Watch out!

Internet email services provide you with an email address and mailbox free of charge. The only trouble is that they are Web-based: you collect, view and reply to email using your Web browser. You can't use email software to collect the Web-based free email from services such as Hotmail, Netscape WebMail and Yahoo!, which means that you cannot filter it using your existing filters either.

Some, like Hotmail, do allow you to set up Web-based filters. You would be well advised to check if filtering options are available before you sign up with a free email service.

Jargon buster

Spam Junk email. This can be sent to millions of people for little cost.

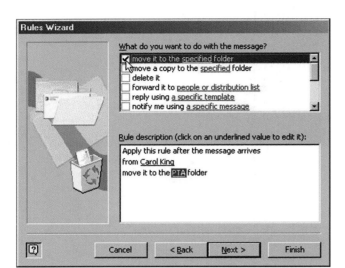

11 You will find yourself back at the Rules Wizard window, with the folder name now shown in the action pane as well as the sender's name. Click Next and the upper rules pane changes to show further options that specify what you want the new filter to do. You can move the message to the folder, or move a copy, reply to the sender using a template, be notified of the arrival of the email by way of a sound or a written message, and much more. Explore all the options and have fun at the same time as making your email work for you. Because you want to **Move It To The Specified Folder,** that's the option to select. Click Next.

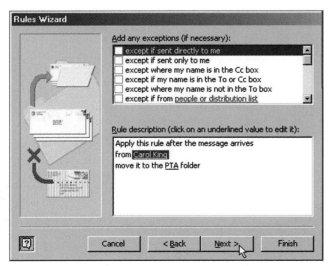

12 You now have the option of including as many **exceptions** to the rule as you want. This enables you to override the action of the filter in specified circumstances – if the email address contains a specific word (useful to separate business and personal email from the same person sent using different accounts), or if your name is in the CC box instead of the main recipient, and many other exceptions. For this example there are no exceptions, so click on Next.

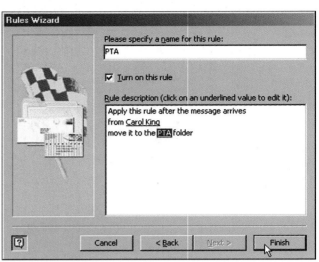

13 The final step involves giving your filter a **name** so that you can easily identify it. Since you can apply as many filters as you like, this is important. Then select the checkbox to turn the filter on, and click Finish.

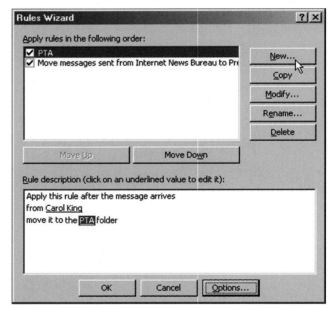

14 You will now be back at the Rules Wizard window and should see **two rules** present in the top pane. You can turn these rules on or off at the click of your mouse and edit them simply by using the highlighted sections in the lower action pane. To create your next filter, click New.

Watch out!

Junk email is a problem area. Sure, you want to filter this out, and the easiest way is by the use of certain keywords such as Get Rich Quick. But if you do this you should always make sure something important hasn't slipped through as well. The solution is simple: set up your filter so that it moves all junk email to a folder called junk rather than deleting it instantly. This way you can quickly scan what's in the folder before you trash the contents.

5

Fax, Phone & Voicemail

Use your computer to send and receive faxes and even work as your own personal assistant.

For some purposes, especially where an exact copy of printed material, or photographs or other graphics are concerned, a fax conveys more information than a phone call and can be quicker and cheaper.

Most people who want to be able to fax expect to use a stand-alone fax machine. A fax machine connects to a dedicated phone line and allows faxes to be sent and received at any time of the day or night, without restricting phone use. If your business is home-based, this convenience may be limited by space, because fax machines are quite large, especially when you take into account their paper trays.

Watch the traffic

Fortunately, if your fax traffic is not too great, you can use your PC to send and receive faxes, which it will do as a background task while you do other jobs.

Small businesses often suffer the disadvantage of not having someone always available to take messages. The solution, of course, is an answering machine, which is no larger than an ordinary phone. However, now you can use your computer as an answering machine. In fact your computer can be a much more versatile answering system than any stand-alone answering machine, able to accommodate many more messages, to sort them into categories of your own choosing and to give your callers more information than can be squeezed into an answering machine's greeting. This is voicemail.

You will need

ESSENTIAL
Software Most modems come with free software, but you can buy more fully featured packages. Windows 95 has fax software built in, but Windows 98 does not.
Hardware A modem. All modems can send and receive faxes and many can also double as hands-free telephones and answering machines.

Modem facts

False economy?

Multifunction machines may offer considerable savings over the four or five separate machines they replace in terms of price and desk space. However, think carefully about their usage. In particular, if one function breaks down, you will lose the use of all functions while a multifunction machine is being repaired.

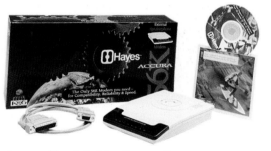

A conventional desktop format, the Hayes Accura 56K modem above performs well as a speakerphone, avoiding the sound break-up that can sometimes mar conversation.

Installing an internal or external modem turns your PC into a complete communications centre.

To send faxes from your computer, you must have a fax modem installed as well as suitable software. The people you send faxes to need a fax machine or a computer with a fax modem and suitable software, which need not be the same as yours. You can receive faxes from another computer or a fax machine.

Up to speed

Fax machines send and receive at a speed of 9,600bps (bits per second). Whatever the modem box may say about its speed, it will only communicate with a fax machine at 9,600bps, although it may communicate with another fax/modem at 14,400bps. The standard speed of current modems is 56,000bps and it is now almost impossible to buy a modem with a speed under 33,600bps, so if you do not want to use a modem to send email or otherwise use the Internet, your only criteria for purchase is that it should be capable of fax operation.

In or out?

Modems for desktop computers are available for installing internally or externally. To summarize the differences, external modems, about the size of a paperback book, use a separate power supply with cables to the computer and the phone sockets. There may be speaker and microphone sockets if the modem is a voicemail fax/modem. A row of lights on the front indicates what the modem is doing at any time. Internal modems are not as easy to install as external modems, since you have to remove the case of your PC. They don't have any status lights, so you won't know what your modem is up to, and you can't move an internal modem between two PCs.

Notebook PCs can use desktop modems, but a better option is a credit-card-size PC Card modem — sometimes called PCMCIA. These have a designated slot on a notebook PC.

Can you hear me?

One aspect of using your computer to receive fax or voicemail is that you need to keep it on all the time. While not necessarily a problem, if this worries you, choose one of the newer modems like the Pace Solo, which can receive and store messages even when disconnected from the computer.

Dedication

When you choose a fax/modem or a stand-alone machine, you'll need to decide whether to install a dedicated phone line or to share your voice line. A dedicated line is best, of course, since this keeps the existing phone line free for phone calls. But for many home users, the cost or inconvenience of an extra line makes the choice difficult. Fortunately, an automatic fax/phone switch like the Fax Friend can distinguish between incoming voice calls and fax transmissions on the same line. Plugged into your phone socket, the device will direct voice calls to your telephone and faxes to your fax machine or fax/modem, all automatically.

Multifunction devices, like the Canon MultiPASS C30, combine a colour inkjet printer with a high-speed fax, scanner and copier.

Multi-talented

Some printers come with a fax/modem built in, and some include a scanning facility too, making them multifunctional. You can also get fax machines fitted with a PC interface, turning them into multifunction devices. Both of these overcome one of the principal disadvantages of fax/modems — the inability to fax anything that has not been generated by the PC. You cannot fax a page from a book or a copy of a letter unless you scan that document into the computer first, involving another piece of hardware with perhaps a limited usage.

Hidden advantages

Fax/modems offer three advantages over stand-alone machines. In many fax machines the scanning head is buried in an inaccessible location, which means it doesn't often get cleaned. This leads to blurred and spotted outgoing faxes with telltale dark parallel lines. The owner of the fax machine doesn't realize this unless a fax recipient informs him or her, but a bad impression may have already been made. PC-generated faxes are always pristine. The second advantage is that incoming faxes are stored on your hard disk until you've read or printed them. Perhaps best of all, a fax/modem never runs out of paper.

Fax software

Microsoft Fax

To send or receive a fax using Microsoft Exchange, double-click the Inbox icon on your Desktop. If you don't have an Inbox icon on your Desktop, then Microsoft Exchange is not installed. To install Microsoft Exchange and Microsoft Fax, go to the Add/Remove Programs dialogue box in Control Panel and select the components you want. If you originally installed Windows 95 or 98 using a CD-ROM or floppy disks, you may be asked to insert the Windows installation disks. You can also open Microsoft Fax from the Start button, then Programs, Accessories, Fax.

Jargon buster

Fax on demand Fax on demand or fax back usually requires that you have installed a voicemail software program on your computer. The fax on demand mailbox is part of that system. It allows a caller to request that a fax on a particular topic be sent to him or her and for the system to respond automatically. Multiple documents are each given a number and the caller keys in that number when asked. Key 0 is usually an index to the rest.

Usually, the caller is asked for his or her fax number and the software calls that fax machine and delivers the required document. Sophisticated programs deliver the fax while the caller holds, hence at the caller's expense. The documents must be on your hard disk, of course.

Some software allows you to attach documents to a cover page, just as you would with an email. These then print out on the receiving fax machine.

Entering a subject will help you identify faxes that you have previously sent.

To send a quick fax, you can type your message on the cover page using the Quick Cover Page option.

Some fax software shows you a preview of what your fax will look like.

The software included when you buy a fax/modem is powerful enough to meet most people's needs.

Fax software works by giving you word processing capability to compose your message. You also get a Phonebook into which you can input your recipient's fax number and other details. It's sometimes possible to copy or import existing records from a different software program on your computer. You also get a fax transport program, whose operation should be invisible to you. This can incorporate options to store faxes for transmission at specified times. Finally, you get a fax viewer so you can look at incoming faxes.

Whereas Microsoft integrated its fax software with Windows 95's Exchange (also known as Windows

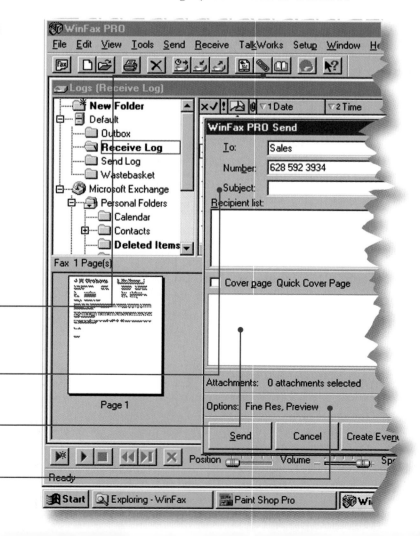

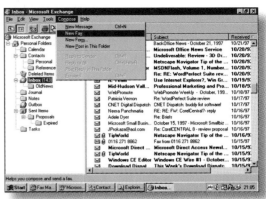

Messaging), you will have to install Microsoft's At Work fax software from a folder within the Windows 98 CD-ROM. For instructions on how to do this, see page 80. If you are using Windows 95, opening Exchange displays your file viewer in two windows. The left side lists folders, the right side lists the contents of a selected folder. Among the folders is an Inbox for incoming mail. Other folders include an Outbox, a temporary store to hold outgoing messages; Sent Items, where you'll find copies of messages you have sent; and a folder for items that you have deleted.

All fax software can be used in two ways. You can launch the program and compose your faxes directly before clicking the button to send; or you can select the fax as an alternative printer in your word processor or other application.

Microsoft Exchange, or Windows Messaging if you've upgraded, provides a universal Inbox that you can use to send and receive email. You can use the Inbox to organize, access and share all types of information, including faxes.

Software upgrades

● **WinFax Pro** From Symantec, this is probably the best-known fax software as cut-down versions are bundled with many modems. WinFax Pro is now on version 9 for Windows 95 and 98 and is packed with features. It has hundreds of cover page designs, integrates closely with Microsoft Exchange and Outlook, and can even forward received faxes to other fax machines when you're away from your PC.

● **SuperVoice Pro** Though primarily a voicemail program, Pacific Image's SuperVoice Pro also offers faxing facilities and supports video email.

● **FaxNow!** This is a deceptively simple fax-only program from Redrock. With fewer complicated features, it does the job of receiving faxes with quiet efficiency and the minimum interruption to whatever else you're doing at the time. FaxNow! stores faxes as standard .tif files, so they can be manipulated by most graphics programs.

Windows 98

Windows 98 doesn't include any fax software. The Windows 95 fax software is still available as part of the Windows 98 setup files, but installing isn't simple.

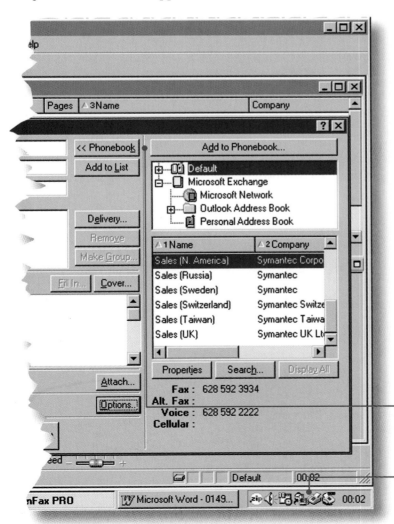

The Phonebook lets you quickly choose recipients for your faxes and you can send a fax to several people just as easily as one.

Some fax software puts icons in the system tray for fast access to certain fax functions.

Sending a fax

Jargon buster

Polling A system to allow a fax machine to retrieve documents from one or more machines while unsupervised. It can be used by shops in a chain to order stock from a central warehouse overnight.

It's easy to plug in a modem and send faxes from dedicated software or other applications.

If you have a modem and Windows 95 with its fax software, you have everything you need to send and receive faxes from your PC. There's an Installation Wizard in the Mail and Fax icon in Control Panel, or in the Inbox icon on your Desktop. Windows 98 uses the Windows 95 software but it's more complicated to install. For this or other fax software, follow the instructions. The Microsoft Fax appears as a printer in your Printers folder; to send a fax, just print to the fax, rather than to your printer.

Importing addresses

The easiest way to select fax numbers is from the address book provided by every program. Some fax software can import details from other lists you may already have. Other packages, like Microsoft Fax, are not so accommodating.

With fax software installed, you can send a fax from any application that supports a print function. Fax software sets up a print driver that delivers your document to the fax transport system before 'printing' it over the phone line.

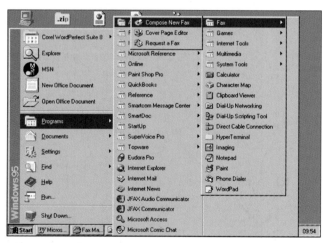

1 Microsoft Fax is in the Accessories folder under the Start button. From here you can send a fax, launch a cover page designer, poll another machine or use fax on demand. You can also start the Fax Wizard by right-clicking any file in Windows Explorer, then clicking Send To Fax Recipient.

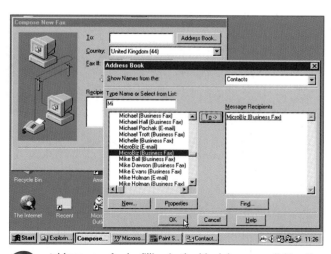

2 Address your fax by filling in the blank boxes or clicking the **Address Book** button to copy data. You can build up a list of recipients for the same fax by clicking Add To List. This is called Broadcast Faxing. Transferring recipients' data from your address book can also build up a multiple faxing list. Click OK.

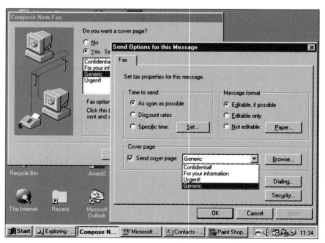

3 Next you have to decide whether to include a **cover page** and if so which one — it can be one of your own design, of course. Clicking Options brings up more decisions to be made about transmission time and format.

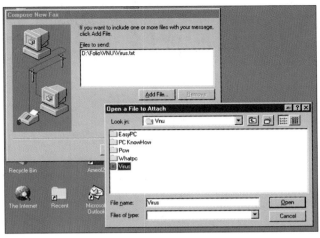

Join the line

Having prepared your document, just select Print. You will be presented with the Printer Setup window. Clicking the spinner in the printer name box will reveal alternative drivers. Choose the fax driver and click Print. A Fax Destination dialogue box will ask for the destination phone number, the time the fax is to be sent and optional cover sheet details. In some software you can transfer these from the Phonebook. Click OK, and your document will appear in the outgoing list ready for transmission at the requested time.

The fax driver will remain selected until you change it for your ordinary printer. Note also that Print in the button bar — the one with the icon — only works with the selected printer.

5 You can **attach** documents created by any application to be sent with your fax. They will be correctly formatted to print out on the receiving fax machine, provided you have the application on your hard drive. Your fax is now ready to send.

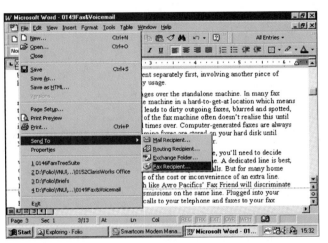

6 You don't have to start Microsoft Fax from the Inbox or Start button to send an attachment. If you have the attachment on screen, you can start Microsoft Fax from File, Send To. This calls up the **Fax Wizard** to address your fax.

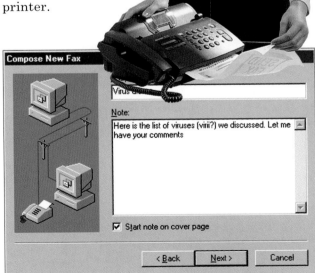

4 Giving your fax a **name** isn't mandatory, but it will make it easier to retrieve when your list of faxes sent grows. You can also opt to start your message on the cover sheet, which will usually have half a page of space available, saving the need for extra pages.

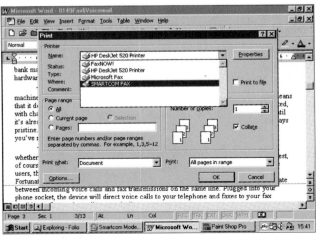

7 If you're working with an application that doesn't have Send in its File menu, use File, Print, and select your **fax driver** instead of your printer driver.

Voicemail

Voice software

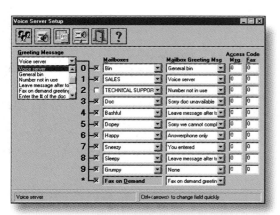

Most voice-capable modems include voicemail or integrated fax/voice software in the box. Some manufacturers supply their own exclusive program, but usually it's a cut-down version of a full commercial package.

Hayes voice modems, for instance, use their own Smartcom Message Centre LE, while Olitec has Olifaxvoice. A popular choice is SuperVoice, found with Pace and Electronic Frontier modems among others, and which can be upgraded to the more versatile SuperVoice Pro.

Voicemail navigates by asking callers to press the button corresponding to the person they wish to leave a message for. Messages can redirect callers to other people for specific topics.

Your computer can turn your home or business phone into a versatile telephone system.

Voicemail software answers your telephone for you. Working in conjunction with a modem that has voice facilities, it sits in the background waiting for the phone to ring. It will play a recorded greeting and record your callers' messages. It does this as often as needed: since it uses your hard disk it can store much more than a stand-alone answering machine using a tape. Integrated fax/voice software distinguishes between fax and voice calls, and stores them in the same mailbox for easy retrieval.

Separate boxes

A mailbox is a location on your hard disk that stores all your messages. Most voice software is sophisticated enough to allow several separate mailboxes. You can have one for each person in your home, so everyone can check their own messages. Home businesses can have mailboxes for functions such as sales inquiries, stock availability and account information. The caller is not going to know that it may be the same person reviewing them all. Some software will let callers upload data or send faxes to individual mailboxes.

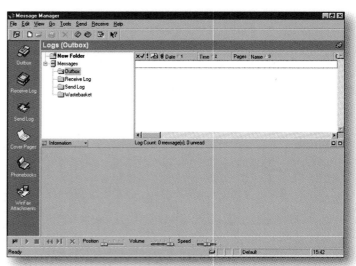

Symantec's TalkWorks is a complete messaging centre that lets you operate a sophisticated voice messaging, call tracking and fax managing service, all from your computer.

Dedicated to the task

Most voice software lets you set up a dedicated fax on demand system. This allows callers to receive prepared documents as faxes from a spoken menu or printed list. Useful applications for this can include events diaries or restaurant menus.

Voice software works by converting speech into voice files, of either proprietary or standard .wav format. In order to hear them clearly, you may need to boost your PC's memory and processor speed, and upgrade its com port and sound card.

Internet Voicemail

The Internet Voice Mail service from VocalTec lets you send a recorded voice message to anyone with an email account, anywhere in the world. You need an email account yourself, of course, as well as a MIME-compliant email program, and a copy of VocalTec's software. This works like your email program. Just enter a person's email address, record a message by speaking into the microphone, and send it off. You can even add text or attach files.

Your recipient doesn't need a VocalTec licence or a copy of the software, because you can include an Internet Voice Mail player in your message. VocalTec has a Web page at http://vocaltec.com with a free evaluation version of the software.

Voicemail tips

With your voicemail installed, please pause before setting it up and take pity on your callers. Everyone has called the sort of large company that subjects callers to a tour of its mailbox facilities before giving them the extension of an employee who's gone out for the day and asking you to leave a message. Make your messages brief and try to offer a catch-all option early on. This could include an opportunity for callers to skip over departmental routing instructions and just leave a message for anybody.

SuperVoice from Pacific Image has a whole host of sophisticated features, including a speaker phone, answering machine, paging, video email and faxing.

The Internet Voice Mail service is available to anyone with regular email access. Users will benefit from the increased speed of transmission.

Pager tips

You can set up some software to alert you by pager when a fax or voice message is received. In SuperVoice, for example, you just select or create a mailbox and click on Page If Message Is Received so that the box is checked. The Pager Info button, which is otherwise greyed out, then becomes available. Enter your pager number.

When a caller leaves a voice, fax or data message in your mailbox, SuperVoice will automatically notify your pager, which will alert you and display the mailbox number, plus the quantity of voice, fax and data messages.

Cover pages

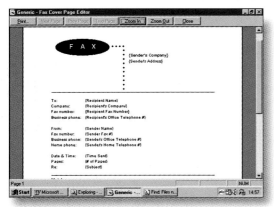

This is Microsoft's **Generic** fax cover page. There are three others: **Confidential!**, **For Your Information**, and **Urgent!**. Fax cover pages are in your Windows directory and end in *.cpe. Use them as they are, modify them, or create your own from scratch.

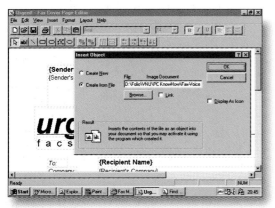

Microsoft Fax's **Cover Page Designer** also lets you insert a graphic, useful for a logo, say. On the Insert menu, click Object. You can then either use an existing object, choosing Create From File (click Browse, find the document that contains the graphic you want and then double-click it) or create a brand-new graphic by clicking Create New.

Fax tip

As a minimum your faxes should include your name and fax number plus the name of the person for whom they are intended. Microsoft's Cover Page Editor does this automatically, taking your details from the User tab in Fax Setup and the recipient's data from your Phonebook.

Fax cover pages can create a good impression and convey a lot of useful information to the recipients.

Most fax software lets you add a cover page to your faxes and most offer more than one design. If you regularly fax someone who doesn't need to be reminded who you are, omit the cover page, saving your transmission time and their fax paper. Some software, including Microsoft Fax, lets you write your message on the cover page itself, which is ideal for short messages.

If you are sending a fax to someone at a company, you will need to include information about who the fax is from and who it's for, because most faxes spill out of a machine serving a whole department. Other useful information to include is the date of the fax, the subject and the number of pages sent.

Most fax software handles all this automatically, taking your details from the information you entered when setting up the software. Recipient's details often come from the entries in your Phonebook, so it pays to keep that up to date. You can elect to fill in the cover page manually for each fax.

You might want to include a logo, which can be added as a graphic. The same goes for signatures, which can be handwritten and scanned. If you don't have a scanner, send your signature to a fax-owning friend, ask them to fax it to you and clip it out using a screen capture program (see screengrab below).

The right impression

If you're in business, remember that a fax cover page is as capable of creating an impression — favourable or otherwise — as a letterhead. Take care to ensure that it projects a professional image, preferably consistent with your letterhead and business cards.

Use the Help facility in Windows 95 and 98 to find how to paste your signature from one document to another.

Turn your PC into a fax machine

Use your PC to send faxes and you won't need to buy a fax machine.

Fax machines, a standard business tool, are also invaluable at home. Easy to use, they can deliver copies of documents immediately. Take apart a fax machine and you will find three main components: a scanner to input documents to send, a modem to transmit the data over the phone line, and a printer to print received documents.

So if you own a PC, a printer, and a modem, you've already got the key elements of a fax machine. All it takes is the addition of some software to turn your PC into a fully fledged, high-quality fax machine. Fax software treats your modem as a kind of printer; to send a fax, you print the document to your modem — most are fax-capable. You then supply destination details and the fax modem will dial out and send the fax. It doesn't matter what's at the other end of the line, a dedicated fax machine or a modem, the result will be the same: the best-looking faxes you've ever seen.

You will learn

- How to use your computer to send and receive faxes.
- How to send faxes to broadcast groups.
- How to schedule send times to take advantage of cheap rate calls.
- How to get Windows automatically to redial busy numbers without further intervention.

You will need

Software You won't need any additional software if you're running Windows 95 or Windows 98, although if you have the latter, installation is not quite so simple (see next page for instructions). To install fax software using Outlook 98 (see 1 below) you will first need to have installed Outlook 98 which is included in Microsoft's Office Suite (available either in the Standard, Professional or Small Business editions). If you do not have Office on your computer, you can use Microsoft Fax which is a standard component of Windows 95 or the At Work Fax software which is included with Windows 98 (see next page).
Hardware Apart from a PC running Windows, you'll need a telephone line and a modem.

Sending faxes from your computer

1   Before you can send a fax from your PC, you have to install fax software. How you do this will depend on whether you've got Windows 95 or 98, or Outlook 98 installed. Assuming Outlook 98 is installed, to add a fax service click Start, Settings and then click Control Panel. Double-click Add/Remove Programs, click the Install/Uninstall tab, and then click Microsoft Outlook 98. Click Add/Remove and click **Add New Components**. You then have the choice of installing extra components from the World Wide Web or from your installation CD-ROM. Choose the latter. Outlook will start Internet Explorer and connect to the Outlook 98 Components Web page. Click the Symantec WinFax Starter Edition checkbox, and then click Next. When the install is complete, quit all programs and then restart your computer.

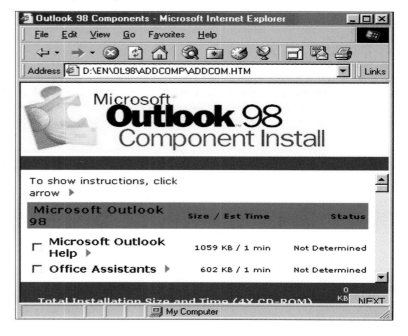

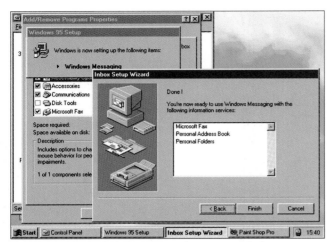

2 Adding **Microsoft Fax** to Windows 95 is simple, because it is a standard Windows 95 component. Click Start, Settings then Control Panel. Double-click on the Add/Remove Programs applet and click on the Windows Setup tab. Check the Microsoft Fax box. The wizard will ask permission to install other components, such as Windows Messaging. Click Yes and then click Apply.

Insert your Windows 95 CD-ROM when requested and the necessary files will be copied across. The Inbox Setup Wizard then launches. Click the Next button and again on the Information Services page, Microsoft Fax being the only service being installed. You're then asked to select the fax modem you wish to use, so click Next again. You're then asked if you want incoming faxes to be answered automatically or not. Click Next and enter your fax details, such as your name or the name of your business and your fax number. Click Finish when you reach the end of the Wizard.

3 Although Windows 98 doesn't come with any standard fax software, Microsoft does include the **At Work Fax** software that was originally supplied with Windows 95 on the Windows 98 CD-ROM. It's tucked away out of sight in the Tools, OldWin95, Messaging, Intl folder, and you can install this.

Before you install the At Work Fax software, you must make sure that you have a Microsoft mail client already installed on your computer. Examples of mail clients include Microsoft Exchange, Windows Messaging and Outlook 97. If you have any of these already installed, it's fine to install At Work Fax. If you haven't, then in the same folder on the Windows 98 CD-ROM, you'll also find a copy of Windows Messaging to install.

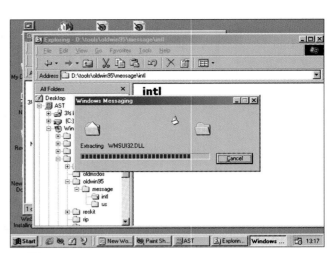

4 Either way, insert your Windows 98 CD-ROM and use Explorer to navigate down to the Tools, OldWin95, Messaging, Intl folder. Double-click on wms.exe file to install Windows Messaging. Follow the installation Wizard prompts, but where it asks you to select an Information Service, select the Manually Configure Information Services Option. For the moment install Windows Messaging with no information services. When complete, install At Work Fax by double-clicking on **awfax.exe** in the same Tools, OldWin95, Messaging, Intl folder. At the end of this installation, Windows 98 needs to be rebooted.

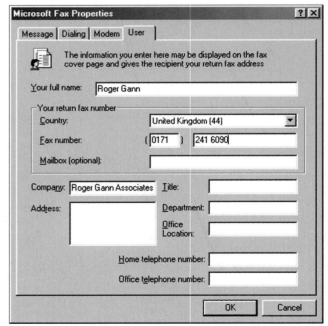

5 With Windows Messaging now installed, you'll see a new Inbox icon on your Desktop. As well as adding a fax printer, you'll also see a new Control Panel icon, **Mail** (or Mail & Fax). Double-click on this to add the Fax service. Click the Add button, select Microsoft Fax and click OK. You'll then be asked to enter your fax details. You can also specify other things, too, such as the default cover sheet, when to send and, if you're on a network, whether other users can use your modem to send faxes. By default, the modem is set not to answer incoming faxes, so if you want to receive faxes, click the Modem tab, click the Properties button and select the answering mode you want. Click OK several times to exit the Mail Control Panel applet.

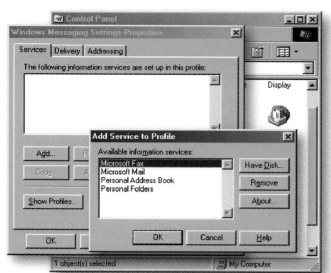

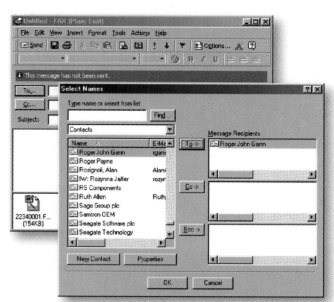

6 You also need to add two more services to Windows Messaging. Use the same Mail Control Panel applet to add a **Personal Address Book**. You can store frequently used fax numbers here. You'll also need to add the **Personal Folders** service as well. And that's it. You can now fax directly from Windows.

Faxing from within an application is very simple because Windows treats faxing as if you were printing a document. This means you can fax from any application that you can print from. For example, you can fax a page from within Microsoft's spreadsheet, Excel, or from Notepad or even Paint. Say you want to fax a letter. Open your word processor, say WordPad, and compose your letter. When you're ready to send it, select File, Print, then select the Fax Modem as your printer. Click OK.

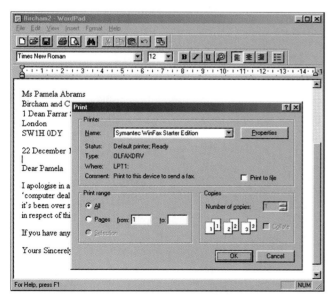

7 The **Compose New Fax Wizard** now makes an appearance. Enter the name and phone number of the recipient of your fax or pull it from your Personal Address Book by clicking on the Address Book button and then selecting it from the list and adding it to the recipient list.

Note that there can be more than one recipient. Click Next and choose a cover sheet, such as Confidential or Urgent. You can also specify other details like the send time by clicking the Options button. Click Next and then enter any additional information you want printed on the cover sheet. Click Finish to send the fax.

8 In the System tray, next to the clock on the Taskbar, you'll see a tiny **fax machine icon** which tells you the fax modem is waiting to answer incoming faxes. If you have sent a lot of faxes, a fax queue will be created, each fax being sent one after the other. Another system tray icon — a little page with whizz lines — then appears to indicate this. If you want, you can cancel a pending fax by clicking on this icon, selecting the fax and selecting File, Cancel.

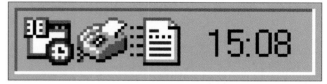

9 If the fax at the other end is busy, At Work Fax will retry a total of three times, although this number can be increased or decreased in Fax Modem properties. You can also specify the gap in minutes between retries. If it still can't send the fax, you'll get an **Undeliverable** notification.

Signature tip

You will probably want to put a signature at the end of the faxes you send. But just how do you get your signature onto an electronic document? If you have a scanner the solution is simple — you scan it in, save it as a graphics file and drop this graphic into your document where you want your signature to go.

If you don't have a scanner there is a neat way to get around the problem. Just sign your name on a piece of paper and using a conventional fax machine send it to your fax/modem. Open up the saved fax in a simple image editing program, such as PaintShop Pro or Paint. You can then crop into your signature and save that file. Now all you have to do is drop that signature graphic into any document you want to fax as if it were a piece of clip art: use the Insert, Picture, From File menu options in Word, for example.

Get Online!

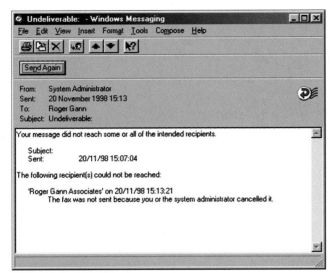

10 As well as sending directly from an application, it's also possible to compose a quick fax directly from **Windows Messaging**. Double-click on the Inbox on the Desktop and select Compose, then New Fax. This loads the Compose New Fax Wizard. Another quick way of sending faxes if you have Outlook 98 is to right-click a completed document you've already prepared, select Send To and from the destination list select Symantec WinFax Starter Edition.

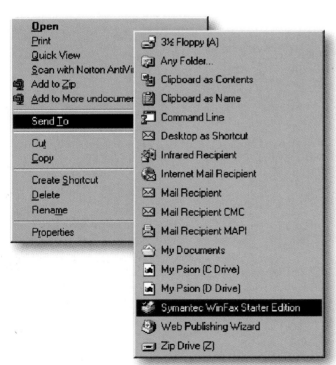

11 Receiving a fax is even simpler. Providing your PC is on and the fax modem is set to answer calls automatically, faxes will be received in the background, without you having to stop what you're doing. When a fax comes in, the fax modem answers and the incoming fax is saved as a file on your hard disk, normally in .tif format. The new fax is recorded in your email client — Exchange, Windows Messaging or Outlook — as a new message. Windows Messaging or Outlook doesn't have to be running, but if they are you'll be notified with an audio alert when a fax comes in. In this example, Windows Messaging is used.

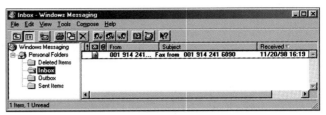

12 To view the fax, simply double-click on it. This loads a special viewer program, **Imaging for Windows**. If you have an early version of Windows, you will have a much simpler fax viewer, but you can still download Imaging for Windows from the Microsoft Web site. Not only does this program let you view received faxes but you can add comments before printing them out or even faxing them on to someone else. If it's a junk fax, it's simple enough to delete it.

13 Another handy feature is that you can **organize** received faxes to make it easier to find them again. For example, you can group all faxes from one company together. To do this, you create a separate Inbox folder for each category and then drag and drop each received fax into the appropriate folder. This helps keep your main Inbox free of clutter. To create a new folder, select the Inbox and from the File menu, select New Folder. Give it a name and click OK.

Cut the cost of calling

Talk to anyone, anywhere in the world for the price of a local telephone call.

An Internet phone allows you to talk to anyone, anywhere in the world, for the price of a local call. The first thing you need is a multimedia PC with a sound card, speakers and microphone. The second is a modem and an account with an Internet service provider. And the third is the software that lets you make the calls. Most important of all, whoever you're talking to must have the same setup as you.

Internet telephony works by setting up meeting areas on the Internet where you can talk to other people. When you install the software, you tell it your name, location, interests and email address and then, when you start the program, your details are added to the list of people who are available for a net meeting (see page 85, step 7). When you want to talk to someone, you request a conversation by double-clicking on their name in the list.

You will learn

- How to make international phone calls over the Internet for the price of a local call.
- How to set up your Internet phone profile.
- How to search through Microsoft's Internet phone directory.
- How to identify whether or not a person is ready to receive a call.
- How to accept or reject calls.
- How to use the Chat facility to write messages to those people who don't have a microphone and speakers.

You will need

Software An account with an Internet provider and Microsoft's NetMeeting 2.1 software, which can be downloaded free from the Microsoft Web site at www.microsoft.com.
Hardware PC with a sound card, speakers, microphone and modem.

How to set up an Internet phone link

1 Make sure you have a microphone in the 'mic in' socket on your sound card and that your speakers are turned on. There is a lot of software offering Internet phones. Microsoft's **NetMeeting** is used here because it's simple to set up and free. You may have a copy, but it's best to download the latest version from Microsoft. Go to www.microsoft.com and click the Downloads link and scroll through the list to find it. When you've downloaded it, double-click on its icon and follow the instructions to install it. A shortcut is added to your Start menu; find that and click on it to start the setup program. You'll see this screen.

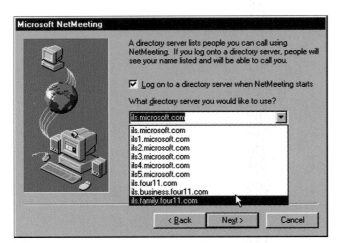

2 Click on Next and at the dialogue, click on the down arrow. You'll see a list of the **directory servers** run by Microsoft for NetMeeting users. It's hard to know which one to pick; here the family server at the bottom of the list is chosen. Make sure there's a check mark in the box above the drop-down list. When you start NetMeeting, you'll go straight to the family area.

3 Click the Next button and then fill in your **details**. Press the Tab key to move between fields. Obviously, you have to enter your name, but the other details are optional.

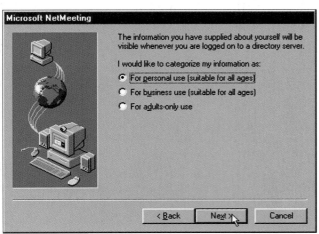

4 Click the Next button and choose a category. To talk to anyone, choose the first one: **For Personal Use (Suitable For All Ages)**.

Web phone tips

● Don't set the volume of your speakers too high. It's probably easier to use headphones than speakers, because speakers distort. Worse, you may get an echo effect which makes it hard to hear what the other person's saying.

● Similarly, if it says next to someone's entry that they're interested in adult chat and you decide to talk to them, don't expect politics or an intellectual debate. By adult they mean sexually explicit. Remember, by declining to accept incoming calls automatically, you can always reject another caller's approach, see step 8.

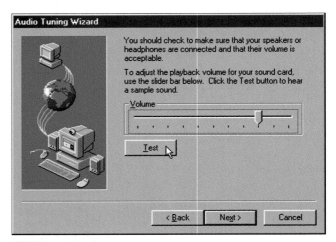

5 Click the Next button and then choose your modem speed. If you're at home and you have a new PC, choose **28,800bps or faster modem**. Click the Next button. Do the same at the next dialogue box and the Wizard will test your sound card and its settings. Click the Test button and you should hear a funny drum roll sound that goes from the left to the right speakers. If you don't, see the Troubleshooting box.

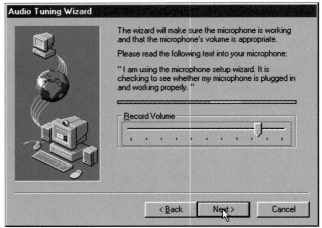

6 Click the Next button. Now you have to speak into your microphone to check the **recording level**. The Wizard will automatically check the level for you — if it's too loud the meter goes into the red — and will lower the volume if necessary. You'll see the slider move from right to left to compensate. The level should be above the green and into the yellow by about three or four blocks.

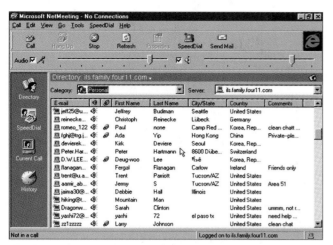

7 Click on the Next button and then at the dialogue box, click the **Finish** button. NetMeeting will load and take you to your chosen directory server on the Internet. This is what the screen looks like. In the main window you can see a list of the people currently on the server waiting to talk.

But NetMeeting tells you much more than that. If a name has a speaker icon by it, it means that person can make and receive voice calls. There's a chat facility in NetMeeting where you can type messages to people who don't have a multimedia computer (see step 12). If there's a little camera icon next to their name, it means they have a video camera attached to their PC and you can see them when you make the call. You don't need any extra equipment at your end to do this, but the faster your modem is, the smoother the pictures will be. If a name has a red sun next to it, that means the person is engaged in a call.

Which software?

Microsoft's **NetMeeting** was used for this project because it is widely available and free, but there are many other products you could use to have an inexpensive phone conversation on the World Wide Web. Searching for Internet phones at the **Lycos** directory (www.lycos.com), for example, produces over 14,000 possible sites (see below) where you would be able to find information and products to download. You should note that some of these programs won't be free, but many are available in trial versions, which typically let you talk for three minutes before they cut out. That should be more than enough time for you to try them out.

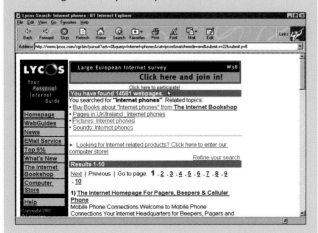

8 Before making a call, it's good to check your settings. From the Tools menu, choose Options and then go through the tabs in the dialogue box in turn by clicking on them. Check the information in each one — you'll recognize a lot of it from the stuff you typed in during the setup process — but pay particular attention to the **Calling** tab. The key option here is Automatically Accept Incoming Calls. If you click on this and put a tick in the box, when anyone else calls you, you don't get the choice of declining the conversation. Leave it blank instead.

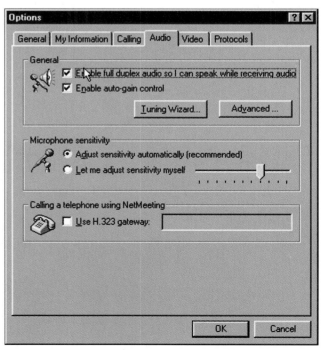

9 Click the **Audio** tab. At the top of the dialogue, there's a checkbox to enable full-duplex audio. This means you can talk and listen at the same time. If you don't have this box checked, your conversations will be like using a walkie-talkie: you speak, then wait for the person to answer before speaking again.

Web phone tip

If you're using NetMeeting, treat members who only want to talk to family and friends with respect. They'll mark their preferences clearly in the comments column.

10 If you're not still connected to the NetMeeting server, start the program again by clicking on its icon from the Start menu and find someone to have a conversation with. Double-click on their name and NetMeeting will notify them that someone wants to talk to them. If someone decides to have a chat with you, here's what you'll see on the screen. The **? ??** in this case is the actual name of the caller.

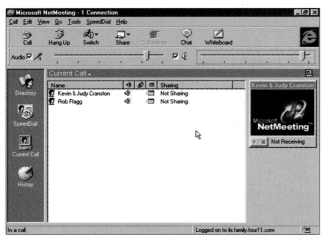

11 Here there is a **conversation** with someone. As you can see, your name (Rob Flagg) and theirs are in the centre of the screen, and if they had a video camera at their end, you'd see a picture of them in the box at the right of the screen.

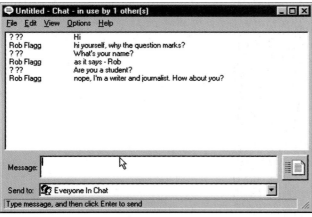

12 If two people try and have a conversation and one of them doesn't have a multimedia PC with a microphone and so on, then NetMeeting starts its **Chat** software. Instead of talking, you can type messages to each other — like this.

Troubleshooting

You may discover after having set up everything properly and made contact with another person, that you still can't talk to them while they're talking to you. The first thing to do is to check that you've set up the full-duplex option (see step 9). If that doesn't make any difference, it's for one of two reasons. It's possible that your sound card simply doesn't support full-duplex, or that you're using an old set of drivers with it. Drivers are utility programs that allow your sound card to work properly with the rest of your computer.

Check the situation by going to the Start menu and choosing Settings, then Control Panel. Double-click on the System icon and then, at the dialogue box, click on the Device Manager tab. Click on the plus sign next to Sound, Video and Game controllers and then double-click on the entry for your sound card, which is usually the second in the list. If in doubt, click on each one in turn until you find the dialogue box in the screen shot below. At the next dialogue box, click on the Settings tab and make sure there's a tick in the box next to Allow Full-Duplex Operation. After that, your Internet phone conversations should sound more like the real thing. If you don't have a dialogue box with this option in it, either contact your PC supplier to see if there are more up-to-date sound card drivers that may let you use full-duplex, or visit the Web site of the sound card manufacturer and see if there are any new drivers there that you can download.

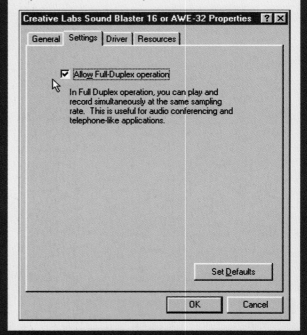

Jargon buster

Full-duplex This means your sound card is capable of recording and playing back audio simultaneously so you can have a two-way conversation. Half-duplex sound cards are less common, and only let one person speak at a time.

6

Videomail

Email doesn't have to be only words. You can send videomail just as easily.

It wasn't long ago that only the very rich or those working in the TV and film industries had access to the equipment needed to get video images into a PC, and only a small percentage of these people who had specialized training had the skill to make it work.

The equipment needed is now within reach of home users, and there are no special skills needed to get it working. Computer video has become a matter of plug and play, and all the equipment needed can be purchased in one box that will cost no more than a fast modem or a good set of speakers.

Video-conferencing over the Net is commonplace for companies around the world, and it isn't unusual to see Webcams sitting on top of monitors in most managers' offices these days. This project shows how to use these advances to send video clips by email to recipients anywhere in the world. You will discover that it's easy to keep in touch using videomail, and it's also great fun.

You will learn

- How to install a Webcam to enable real-time video capture straight on to your PC screen.
- How to install and use software to send video film across the Internet.
- How to get the best balance between quality of film and speed of transfer.

You will need

Software VDO Mail software is used here.
Hardware At least a Pentium 133MHz machine, 32Mb of RAM, a 16-bit sound card, and a fast modem. You will also need a video camera.
Other An account with an Internet service provider.

Sending videomail

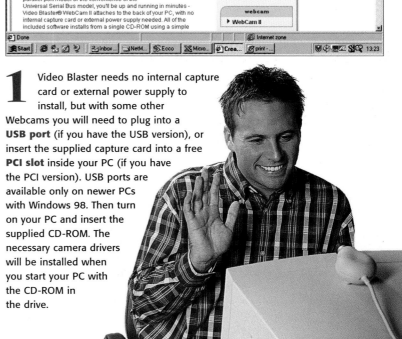

1 Video Blaster needs no internal capture card or external power supply to install, but with some other Webcams you will need to plug into a **USB port** (if you have the USB version), or insert the supplied capture card into a free **PCI slot** inside your PC (if you have the PCI version). USB ports are available only on newer PCs with Windows 98. Then turn on your PC and insert the supplied CD-ROM. The necessary camera drivers will be installed when you start your PC with the CD-ROM in the drive.

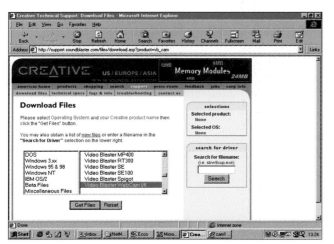

2

Select Video Blaster Webcam and follow the instructions to download the files. If necessary, click on the **Utilities icon** from the main screen and install the Direct X 5 drivers. If you are using a computer with Windows 98, you won't need to do this because they are installed as part of the operating system. Even if you are running Windows 95, there is a good chance that you have Direct X 5 installed already, especially if you play a lot of games on your PC. Direct X is a 3D driver from Microsoft that accelerates the graphics, and helps produce a better image from the Webcam as well.

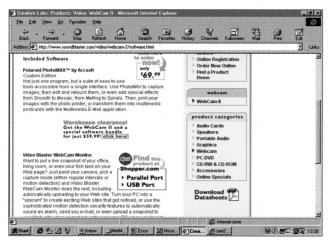

3

In Video Blaster, information on the software included will appear. Once you have restarted your PC, the necessary drivers for your Webcam and for Direct X will have been installed. Click on the **Applications icon** from the main screen. If you can, install VDO Mail instead of the free VideoLink Mail application, which isn't as easy to use or as flexible as VDO Mail. You will see a screen with some data about VDO Mail. Press the Install button to continue.

Videomail tip

VDO Mail can send a player/decoder with a videomail message. This adds about 250K to the file size and isn't necessary because the videos are sent in the standard Microsoft .avi format. Double-clicking on the video icon will automatically start Windows' Videoplayer, and the video will start playing. The best advice, therefore, is not to waste time and space sending the player/decoder.

Jargon buster

.avi Audio Video Interleave is an audio video standard designed by Microsoft and supported within the Windows operating system.

Direct X Another Microsoft standard, this one allows programmers to produce 3D and video software that will run faster and smoother than otherwise on a desktop PC.

PCI Peripheral Component Interconnect slots inside your computer are used to connect peripherals, such as a Webcam or graphics card, to your PC.

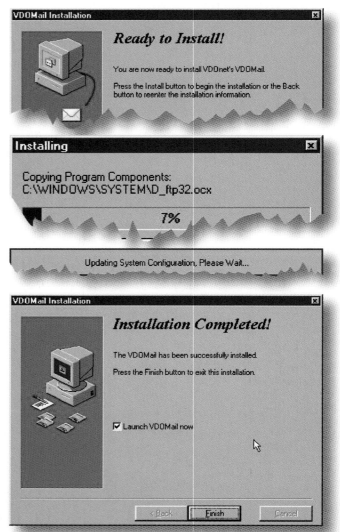

4

The **Setup Wizard** will now begin. Just press the Install button and follow the usual instructions until you reach the screen that tells you the installation is completed. Click the checkbox that says Launch VDO Mail Now and then click on the Finish button to continue. A welcome window will appear that tells you that some setting up is required before you can use VDO Mail for the first time. Make sure you have your Internet service provider account (ISP) and email details before proceeding.

5 You must enter information about your **ISP** and **email account**. Your ISP should have given you the name of your outgoing email server. If you are unsure about the server's name, call your ISP, or look in the Server Settings options of your email software. The Account Name should be the proper name for your account, not an alias, and you must enter the full domain path. Enter your full name in the Personal Information section, and your email address below. This time you can use an email alias if you have one.

7 When **VDO Mail** starts, there is a window in the middle of the screen showing whatever the Webcam is pointing at. Move the camera around and you will see video appearing in real time in this window. Use the View, Preferences menu to change the size of the screen. To get started, all you have to do is point the Webcam at whatever you want to film, press the Record button and remember to hit the spacebar when you want to stop.

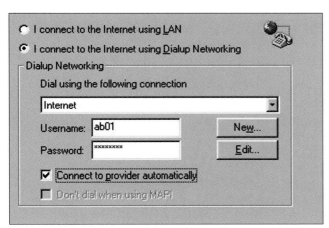

6 The next screen requires more setup information. Check the box that says you use **Dialup Networking** if you connect to the Internet using a modem. Select the connection you use from the drop-down list, enter your user name and password and check Connect To Provider Automatically to save yourself added work later on. This will result in VDO Mail automatically connecting to your ISP and sending the video by email without your having to do anything – not even opening an email program.

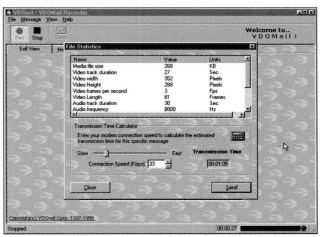

8 When you've hit the spacebar and finished filming, a **File Statistics** screen will appear. This is useful because you can see exactly how long the video is, how big the file is, and how long the file will take to upload as an email attachment. You can adjust the connection speed to match your modem. View the video before you send it, to make sure it's the masterpiece you think it is rather than a film of your hand. Click Close.

Troubleshooting

In the Preferences of VDO Mail is a useful tab marked Capture. Select this and play around with the message-quality slider. The better the quality, the bigger the file size and the longer it will take to send and download. A file size of 250Kb for 30 seconds will result in acceptable transfer times, and reasonable quality.

A warning screen may pop up telling you about skipped frames. Take heed of this. Poor quality filming could be caused by many things, not the least of which is a PC struggling to find enough resources. The faster your PC, the better job it will do of handling applications like video. Click the checkbox that will automatically adjust your recorder settings to match the recording environment, and you should get acceptable results.

If you are using a 56Kbps modem, the top speed only applies to downloads. As VDO Mail is uploading data, the top speed you get is 33.6Kbps. Make sure that you set the connection speed in the file statistics window to 33 for the best performance.

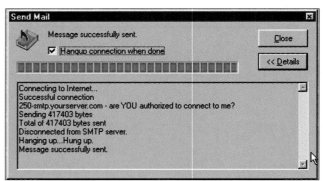

9

Click on the **Message View** tab and your video will replace the live view, and you will notice the Play/Pause control at the bottom of the video screen. Click the Play button and your video will play back. Once you are happy with the video, click on the Send icon in the toolbar.

11

A window will appear with details of the transfer. Click **Hang Up Connection When Done**. This window shows the progress of your connection and the file transfer, so that you can be sure the video has been emailed successfully.

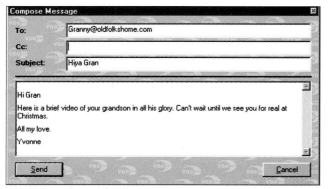

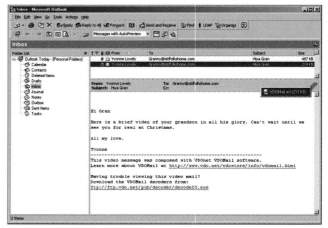

10

A **message window** will now appear, which you use just like any basic email software. Fill in the email address details for the recipient in the To: line, anyone else to whom you want to send a copy in the CC: line, and don't forget to give it a meaningful title in the Subject: line. Now write your message, making sure you tell the person that a video is attached, and when you are finished just hit Send.

12

This is what the person receiving the email will see. A message arrives as usual, but with an attachment. The message has had text added by VDO Mail, which lets recipients know a video is there and they can download a decoder if they have trouble viewing it. Double-click on the paperclip and Microsoft's **Videoplayer** will play the video, shown below.

Talking pictures

If you want to talk face to face across the World Wide Web, then you need to buy a Webcam.

Webcams are small video cameras usually placed on top of your monitor, pointing straight at you as you sit at your desk. Simply plug one into your PC and using the appropriate software (usually included with the Webcam), you can join in video-conference chats with other Webcam users over the Internet.

A snapshot of life

The swift growth in the popularity of Webcams is due to the number of people who use them to add live video feeds to their Web sites. They point their Webcams at anything and everything: office coffee machines, fish, themselves, the street outside... Whatever the subject, a Webcam puts snapshots of life from all over the world on the Internet.

This is the secret of the Webcam's success. No longer is physical distance a barrier to keeping in touch, face to face, with friends and family. With a phone connected to the Internet at a local call rate, the Internet to connect you with your friends, and a Webcam to transmit video images, you can have real-time, face-to-face conversations.

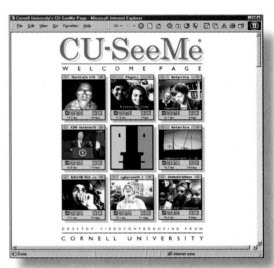

Cu-SeeMe software, often packaged with your Webcam, lets you connect directly to other Webcam users and is among the most popular methods of keeping in touch online.

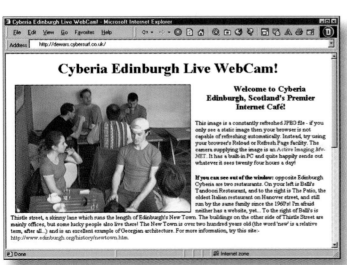

Webcams connected to Web pages can bring you live views of things happening across the world. In this case it's people who are using the Cyberia cybercafé in Edinburgh, Scotland.

Fact file

● **Video-conferencing**
Communicating with one or more people over the Internet, using live video pictures and sound as well as by typing in text.

● **Video capture card** A card that slots inside your PC and allows you to connect video devices like Webcams and Camcorders to your computer.

● **USB** The Universal Serial Bus is a port found on the back of many PCs. It allows peripherals like printers, modems or Webcams to be plugged into the back of a computer without the need for additional cards.

● **Frames Per Second** A term used to express how many pictures the Webcam can shoot in a second. The more frames per second, the clearer and less jerky the resulting video image will be.

Buying tips

● As the Webcam market has expanded, there are now more than a handful of models to choose from, so make sure you choose the one that best fits your needs and budget. First, decide whether you want a black and white or colour camera. Most new Webcams are colour anyway, and their price is less than the first black and white units used to be. However, if you only want to use it for informal Web chats, keeping in touch with your family over the Net and occasional video-conferencing, you may be able to find an older black and white unit going for not much money. Colour units offer great value, however, and the difference in perceived picture quality when it's full colour is remarkable.

● Most Webcams are designed to be mounted on top of your monitor, so they are supplied with a two metre lead at the most. If you want to place the Webcam somewhere else, check the length of the wire with the supplier and find out whether extension wires are available. It's also useful to find out how many frames per second the Webcam operates at. The higher the number, the less jerky your video images. TV programs are broadcast at 30 frames per second, and some of the latest Webcams can match that. Anything less than 15 is going to be very jerky.

Top five brands

● **Connectix QuickCam**
  www.connectix.com
● **Intel Create and Share** www.intel.com
● **Pace Colour Video Camera**
  www.pacecom.co.uk
● **VideoBlaster WebCam** www.creativelabs.com
● **Philips USB WebCam** www.pc.be.philips.com

Connecting up

Most Webcam models available today produce full colour pictures, yet they cost less than the black and white cameras of just a year or so ago. Costing no more than the average modem, a Webcam is small, often resembling a golf ball. Inside the plastic sphere is a camera lens which you can rotate to point anywhere. Look for models with a shutter to cover the lens, which can become very dusty, affecting the quality of the images captured.

Most cameras come with a video capture card that you need to install in your PC. Make sure you have a spare slot before you buy the Webcam. If you already have an internal modem, a scanner and a few other add-ons, you may have used all the available slots. In that case, you can buy Webcams that use the USB interface that many new PCs come with (check before you buy), or the parallel port that you connect your printer to. Any kind of video on your PC will need a lot of processing power, so the more powerful your PC the better. A Pentium 90 with at least 16Mb of RAM is the very minimum system configuration you should have if you want to start using a Webcam.

Software

The software you need to operate the Webcam is usually included with the Webcam package when you buy it but you can also use Microsoft's Netmeeting video-conferencing software, which is often included with the Internet Explorer Web browser. It can be downloaded directly from the Microsoft Web site at www.microsoft.com. One thing's for sure, once you've entered the world of Internet video-conferencing, you won't want to leave it, nor all the new friends you'll discover.

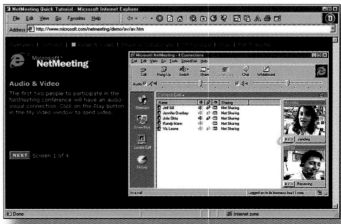

Microsoft's NetMeeting software makes video-conferencing something that you can use at home as well as at the office.

The future of communications is the Net. But what does that mean and how can you get the most out of it?

Not so long ago if you wanted to communicate with people located in many different countries, it was an expensive or slow process — often both. You could communicate by letter, but even the finest postal services around the world struggle to get your letter from one side of the world to the other in less than a couple of days. The instant answer to keeping in touch on a global basis is the telephone, but international phone charges prohibit regular or long calls. This is where the Internet has saved the day. Now you can have the best of both worlds, with electronic letters arriving overseas just seconds after you send them.

Talk on the Net

New developments in Internet telephone software have even opened up the opportunity to use the Net to talk, in real time, internationally, for the cost of a local telephone call to your Internet service provider. But to get the best out of online communications, you need to choose the right resources for the right job at the right time, and that's what is explained here. You will learn how online communication means so much more than just email, how you can have one to many conversations, join in online debates, make new friends, become part of an online community, and discover the dos and don'ts of Internet etiquette. If you've got something to say, somewhere on the Internet there is someone waiting to listen and answer back.

You will need

ESSENTIAL
Software An Internet connection software such as Internet Explorer, a Usenet Newsreader and email suite such as Outlook Express, and Internet Relay Chat (IRC) software like mIRC. If you want to make full use of private conferencing systems, offline reader software will keep the bills down.
Hardware A fast modem and a sound card, if you want to use audio chat facilities.
Other An account with an ISP (Internet service provider).

Chat tip

Remember that you are having real-time conversations, just as if you were talking face to face, and you have to be connected to the Internet the whole time for that. Bear this in mind when you get caught up in a conversation — if your connection is not a local call, your telephone bill may mount up. In these cases, chatting for hours every night will lead to a shock at the end of the first few months when the phone bill lands on the doormat.

A friendly chat

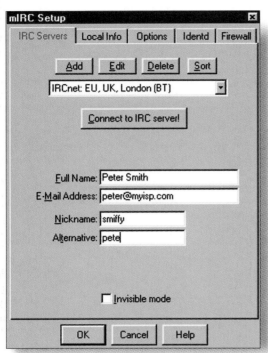

Getting started with **IRC** is as easy as loading the software (mIRC in this case) and choosing a server to connect to and a nickname to use.

You can have conversations using the written word with other Internet users all over the world.

Real-time, text-based, two-way conversations on the Internet are possible using nothing more than a connection to what is known as an IRC server, and some special software available freely from the Net. Internet Relay Chat, also known as IRC, is the resource that makes this possible.

Global chat

Although your conversations are limited to text, it's amazing how quickly you become absorbed into the flow of chat. You are not limited by geographical boundaries or by the numbers of people who can join in a conversation at any time. It is quite possible to be involved in a conversation with a dozen people from the US, UK, Europe, Russia, Australia, South Africa, the Far East, Pacific countries and Africa, all in real time. The global nature of IRC and the capacity to participate in live conversation have been the main reasons for the success of Internet Relay Chat.

Social chat

You will probably want to use IRC for social reasons — it's like being in a bar or at a party or sports function. It's not a business system, and you are far more likely to find yourself chatting with a student than a company director. Many users around the world have IRC connections through their university Internet access, and because of this, and the global nature of the Net, it's almost

Next, choose a **channel** to chat in. The software will let you filter out channels you don't want to see, such as those with adult content, and those you do, such as channels with the word Friends.

Now select a channel from the list that appears. Use the **descriptions** to help with your choice, and not the number next to each channel because this denotes the number of people connected and chatting.

unknown to connect to an IRC server and not find plenty of people ready and willing to talk, no matter what the time of day or night.

You'll need some software to handle everything — from connecting to the IRC server in the first place, to listing available channels and keeping track of your conversation. Most of this software will be shareware and among the most popular is something called mIRC.

Find a nickname

Users of IRC are known by nicknames. You choose yours as you connect but can't, for obvious reasons, use the same nickname as anybody else connected at the same time. Conversations take place in channels, each with its own group of participants and each with its own agenda for discussion.

One thing that you will notice right away is the overwhelming feeling of having to learn a new language. Because people want to have their say as quickly as possible, and with as little typing effort as possible, over the years a form of online shorthand has developed. Acronyms such as BTW for 'by the way', BRB for 'be right back' and CUL for 'see you later' do make things faster, but only after you've learned them all. Be patient. Don't expect to grasp it all at once, and you should be OK after a few sessions.

Watch out!

Internet Relay Chat (IRC) is, undoubtedly, a great way to get to know people on the Internet. It's like going into a bar and getting caught up in conversation with other customers, most of whom you've never met, and who make interesting conversation. However, watch out for a minority who, like in a bar, are there to cause trouble.

Trouble on IRC comes in a variety of guises. There are people who are interested only in sex – avoid them by simply not joining any of the many channels that have a sexual reference in the channel name. If you are pestered by someone, you can ask the channel operator to remove them from the conversation, or you can often do this yourself using the /KICK <nickname> command from your IRC software. Also avoid downloading files from IRC channels. Apart from the fact that pirated software is often distributed this way, there is an increased risk of catching a computer virus from files downloaded from IRC. Finally, unless your conversation is taking place in a secret or hidden channel, there is no privacy of conversation. Anyone else can join the channel, see who's connected and participate in the conversation.

Jargon buster

IRC Stands for Internet Relay Chat. IRC is a real-time chat system for typed online conversation on the Internet.

Usenet An Internet-based giant bulletin board, made up of more than 20,000 discussion groups.

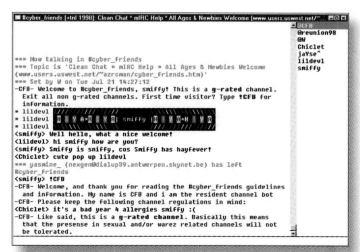

*** Now talking in #cyber_friends
*** Topic is 'Clean Chat * mIRC Help * All Ages & Newbies Welcome (www.users.uswest.net/~azrcman/cyber_friends.htm)'
*** Set by W on Tue Jul 21 14:27:12
-CFB- Welcome to #cyber_friends, smiffy! This is a g-rated channel. Exit all non g-rated channels. First time visitor? Type !CFB for information.
* lildevl //// //// ////
* lildevl H▓Y A*█I▓Y█| smiffy |H▓Y█*H▓Y▓R
* lildevl //// //// ////
<smiffy> Well hello, what a nice welcome!
<lildevl> hi smiffy how are you?
<smiffy> Smiffy is sniffy, cos Smiffy has hayfever!
<Chiclet> cute pop up lildevl
*** yasmine_ (nexgen@dialup39.antwerpen.skynet.be) has left #cyber_friends
<smiffy> !CFB
-CFB- Welcome, and thank you for reading the #cyber_friends guidelines and information. My name is CFB and i am the resident channel bot
-CFB- Please keep the following channel regulations in mind:
<Chiclet> it's a bad year 4 allergies smiffy :(
-CFB- Like said, this is a g-rated channel. Basically this means that the presense in sexual and/or warez related channels will not be tolerated.

@CFB
@reunion98
@W
Chiclet
jaYse^
lildevl
smiffy

You are now ready to chat. Most channels will give you a warm welcome as they did here, logged on as smiffy. The three windows carry the conversation on the left, participant nicknames on the right, and a small text entry box at the bottom.

Communicating using the Internet avoids anyone keeping you on hold.

Using Usenet

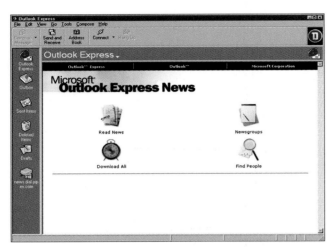

1 Start your **Newsreader** software. Microsoft Outlook Express is supplied free with the Internet Explorer Web browser. From the front screen you can select a newsgroup to join and connect to the Internet. Once you join a group, you can read messages from that group here.

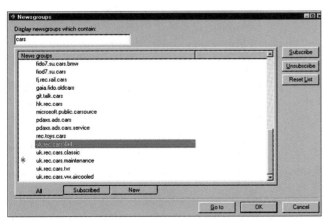

2 Once connected, select the list of **Newsgroups**. The first time you connect this may take a few minutes because the list is 20,000 newsgroups long. Once the list appears, you can enter a keyword (such as Cars) and only those newsgroups that match your criteria will be displayed, saving you a lot of time.

Jargon buster

Flaming If you annoy someone in a Usenet group, they may do the online equivalent of blowing their top — in other words an aggressive rant, known as a flame.

IRL An acronym that is often used in online conversations that stands for 'in real life', referring to your life away from the Internet.

Join online discussion groups with like-minded people who share your hobbies or interests.

While Internet Relay Chat has been compared to an online version of citizens' band radio or to a telephone that uses the written word, Usenet is more akin to a collection of bulletin boards. The analogy is a good one: unlike an email conversation, everything that you pin to the Usenet bulletin board is there for public consumption and can be read by anyone who looks at that particular board. Also unlike email, Usenet allows for threads of conversation that can include any number of participants.

Keep up with the news

With more than 20,000 separate bulletin board areas, known on Usenet as newsgroups, it's a truly massive system and one that is guaranteed to have a number of discussion forums that will be of interest to you. Everything is covered from aeroplanes to zoo-keeping, with everything you can think of in between. You select the newsgroup that interests you, and using a piece of software known as a newsreader (which will

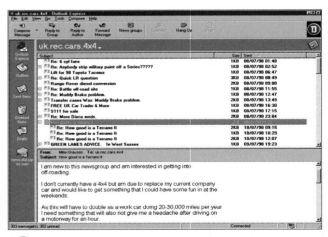

3 Select the newsgroup that interests you and **subscribe** to it. This costs nothing and just means you want to join in the discussion. At first there will be a long list of discussion names within the newsgroup; click on any that interest you and the message will be downloaded and displayed in the lower window.

Etiquette tip

Usenet has its own rules of etiquette. If you barge in and break these rules you are asking for trouble. At the very least people will ignore you, and at worst they will become aggressive. Falling foul of Usenet etiquette is easily avoided; just take the time to read the frequently asked questions file (FAQ) that can be found in most newsgroups. This will explain the rules of behaviour and outline the purpose of the newsgroup you have joined.

probably have been supplied with your Web browser by your Internet Service Provider), you can start to read and reply to messages right away. Don't confuse newsgroups with chatgroups though: Usenet newsgroups tend to be places for the former rather than the latter. You can find the answers to your gardening questions or get technical support for your computer problems. Many computer companies have official Usenet support newsgroups, including Microsoft. You can even have debates about politics and current affairs. Of course you will make friends by so doing, but it's not the same purely social medium as you find in IRC.

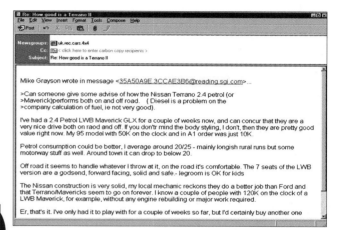

4 To join in the conversation you can either use the **Reply To Author** button to send a private email to the person you are replying to, or the **Reply To Group** button to send a message that goes into the newsgroup itself.

Jargon buster

Spamming The act of posting copies of the same message across multiple Usenet newsgroups. It is impolite, frowned upon by the majority of Usenet users, and our best advice is not to do it.

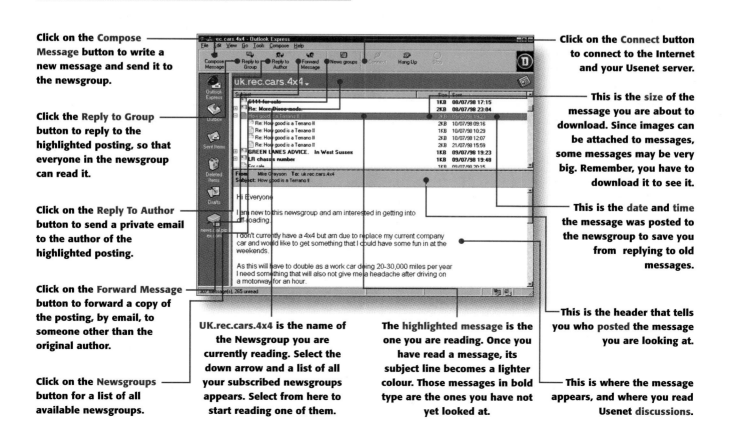

Click on the **Compose Message** button to write a new message and send it to the newsgroup.

Click the **Reply to Group** button to reply to the highlighted posting, so that everyone in the newsgroup can read it.

Click on the **Reply To Author** button to send a private email to the author of the highlighted posting.

Click on the **Forward Message** button to forward a copy of the posting, by email, to someone other than the original author.

Click on the **Newsgroups** button for a list of all available newsgroups.

UK.rec.cars.4x4 is the name of the Newsgroup you are currently reading. Select the down arrow and a list of all your subscribed newsgroups appears. Select from here to start reading one of them.

The **highlighted message** is the one you are reading. Once you have read a message, its subject line becomes a lighter colour. Those messages in bold type are the ones you have not yet looked at.

Click on the **Connect** button to connect to the Internet and your Usenet server.

This is the **size** of the message you are about to download. Since images can be attached to messages, some messages may be very big. Remember, you have to download it to see it.

This is the **date** and **time** the message was posted to the newsgroup to save you from replying to old messages.

This is the **header** that tells you who **posted** the message you are looking at.

This is where the message appears, and where you read Usenet **discussions**.

Conferencing

Conferencing systems **like CompuServe or CIX, shown here, have thousands of subject specific conferences for you to join and find like-minded people to chat with.**

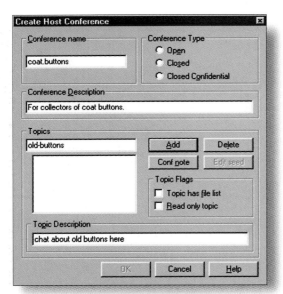

In the unlikely event of there not being a conference that covers your interests, it's easy to start a new one of your own.

Conference systems are like online clubs where you have to agree to a set of rules before you are let in.

Think of conferencing and you might think of people communicating by video on screen. While you can do real-time video-conferencing over the Net, the type of conferencing explained here is text-based and onscreen, where one or many conversations take place in small communities of people in focused discussion groups. These come in two forms, either Web-based or closed commercial systems.

Keep to the rules

Web-based conferencing systems are much like Usenet in that anyone can join in once they have been granted access. Unlike Usenet, things are more organized and you often have to agree to abide by the community rules before you are let in. These cover things like swearing and abuse of membership.

Most conferencing systems are free, but they suffer from the slowness of the Web. The majority require the participant to be online, and the Web page will need to be refreshed after each message is read or a reply is posted.

Commercial conferencing

A better option is a commercial conferencing system, such as CIX or CompuServe; there are similar systems the world over. Commercial conferencing allows for an even better quality of discussion than either Usenet or Web-based conferencing, because people are paying for the service and don't want to waste their time filtering nonsense out of the discussions.

Jargon buster

Server The network computer that you connect to on the Internet from which to retrieve information. Most familiar are the Web servers that hold the information contained on individual Web pages. However, as far as communicating online goes, these servers can include a news-server distributing Usenet newsgroups, or an IRC server hosting chat sessions.

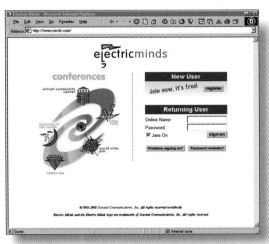

The other advantages are that there are likely to be official support conferences from PC software and hardware manufacturers, access to a high level of skills among the professional memberships, and there are no delays while using the system. Most commercial systems have developed an offline reader (OLR) which lets you connect to the system, download messages, then disconnect. This takes just a minute or two. The OLR then sorts the messages into their right place in each discussion area (or conference), and you can read and reply without the need for a live connection.

Once you have finished, the OLR will connect again, post your messages and disconnect. You save time and money, and get a database of messages that you can keep on your PC. Commercial systems cost money, but most are a good investment.

Web-based conferencing systems cost nothing to join, but may work out expensive in the long run thanks to their slowness of use and lack of proper offline reading software.

Jargon buster

OLR Stands for offline reader. An OLR is a piece of software that saves you money if you use discussion groups online. Basically, they collect all your messages which are then fed into an offline database. You read and reply, then connect again and send them back. You are online for only a few minutes instead of a few hours, which saves on your phone bills.

Watch out!

Essentially there are two types of conferencing system that you'll come across online: Web-based conferencing and proprietary commercial systems.

Although Web-based conferencing is easy to access – provided you have a Web browser and an Internet connection, you are ready to join in – and usually free, you still have to agree to abide by certain membership rules, specific to that particular group. Make sure you are prepared to do this before joining in.

Commercial conferencing systems are open to members only and again there are rules of membership that you must agree to abide by. Also membership fees apply. Usually these come in the form of a monthly subscription, so this is not a cheap option by any means.

However, because of the cost implication you tend to get more committed users on commercial conferencing systems. Whether this improves the quality of discussion depends on what you are looking for in a conversation. These systems generally have excellent archiving of discussions and bring the added advantage of professionally developed offline reading software to bring down the real cost of use, as well as making them among the easiest systems to get to grips with.

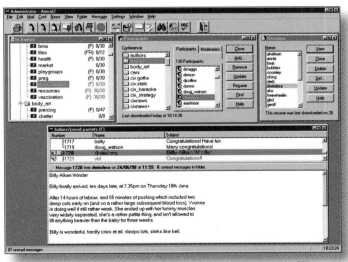

A commercial conferencing system brings ease of use and offline reading into one powerful package. You can select a conference, see details of its participants, read and reply, and even read a resumé of individuals who interest you, all from the one window.

More mailing lists

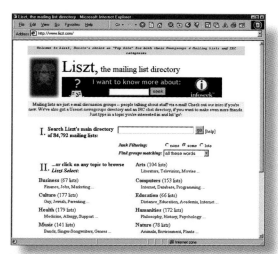

The **Liszt** mailing list directory site on the World Wide Web makes an easy job of finding the right list for you from the thousands available.

A **keyword search** for classical music produced an interesting set of mailing lists. Your next step would be to take a closer look at one.

Mailing list tip

There are thousands of mailing lists (just under 85,000 at the last count), and finding where they are based can be difficult. A site on the Web solves all that. Called Liszt at www.liszt.com, it is a search engine for mailing lists. You enter a word that describes the list you are looking for — Parenting or Sport for example — and it searches its database, gives you a selection of lists to choose from, and tells you how to join.

You can fill your email inbox with messages that really interest you by subscribing to a mailing list.

Most people are fed up with receiving dozens of emails every day from people they don't know, but that's only if the email in question is the electronic version of junk mail known as spam. Not so for the millions of people who belong to one or more mailing list; they eagerly await the arrival of yet another batch of emails from total strangers.

Join up

Mailing lists are one of the most ingenious methods of joining in online debates. Like Usenet, there are thousands of different discussion groups that you can join. But unlike Usenet or commercial conferencing systems, you don't need any special software or connections to be able to join in.

Mailing lists operate entirely through email. You subscribe to a mailing list that interests you, and your email address is added to the server that hosts that list. Then, every time anyone sends a message to the mailing list, a copy of it is forwarded to you and everyone else who is a member. If you want to

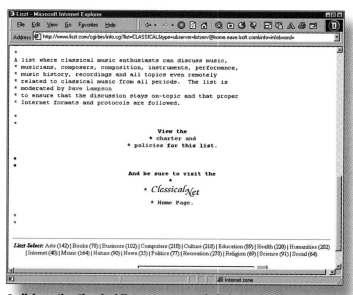

A **click on the Classical list, a recommended Liszt Select list,** reveals further information about it. This includes a brief description, some information about the list rules and policies, and even directions to a home page on the Web by the list operators.

join in the discussion, you simply reply to the email that interests you, and in the same way it gets forwarded to everyone else.

On the list

Mailing lists are easy to get involved in. You simply locate the details of a list that is of interest and send an email message to the subscription address. Just like Usenet, subscription is free. The majority of mailing lists have little human involvement with administration.

The most popular mailing list system around is called Listserv, which is totally automated. The mailing list server runs a special program that scans the email it receives for commands such as Subscribe in your email message body, and then automatically adds your name to the list requested. The Listserv system also handles forwarding messages on the list itself, which makes it a very clever piece of computing technology.

Switch it off

If the volume of email discussion becomes too much, or if you are going away for a couple of weeks on vacation and don't want a mountain of mail on your return, you can simply unsubscribe by sending a message to the same Listserv server.

Watch out!

Whatever method you are using for your online communications, whether it is Usenet, IRC, conferencing systems, mailing lists or forums, you should take some time to learn the rules of the road. Making mistakes online may not seem important, but you don't want people in a discussion group to ignore you or treat you like public enemy number one. Communication rules take the shape of an online etiquette, known as netiquette. Here are some of the most important rules of netiquette that you should consider before you start entering into a discussion group:

● Always read the FAQ file, if there is one, before you make your first posting. This rule applies to all communication formats. A frequently asked questions file does what its title says, so read it to avoid asking a question online that has been asked many times before.

● Always read to the *end* of a conversation before posting to it. Why waste everyone's time, including your own, by answering a question that has been answered already?

● Don't overquote in your postings. Communications software can make it easy to automatically paste the entire contents of the original message in your reply, which will annoy people. Only quote small passages where it aids the flow of your reply.

● Don't spam in any way, shape or form. Select the right forum in which to post your thoughts and only post them there. Nobody in a Usenet newsgroup about programming is interested in the problems your dog has with fleas; stick to the relevant conferences and make online friends, not virtual enemies.

The Usenet FAQ Archive at www.faqs.org/ faqs/ contains every Usenet FAQ file known to exist, and is the best place to go to ensure you don't make a netiquette mistake when you join a Usenet newsgroup.

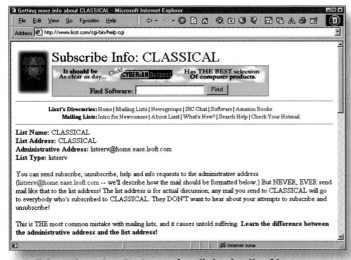

Just click on the Subscribe button for all the details of how to subscribe to the list, then sit back and wait for your email discussions to start flowing through the virtual letterbox.

Online forums

CompuServe makes it easy to find the right forum for you, offering a number of options for searching through the available discussion areas.

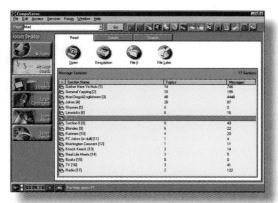

Navigating through the forum options and topics is easy thanks to the point and click interface that CompuServe provides to its members.

For a truly international debating experience, it's best to join one of the online commercial forums.

Online forums are areas of debate that differ from other communications methods in several ways. First, they are all operated commercially by ISPs. AOL and CompuServe have hundreds of forums. The forums are only open to members of those services and the cost of using them is built in to the monthly fee. The forums are all approved by the service; you can't just set up a forum of your own. Most are set up by ISPs at the request of commercial companies who get a percentage of the revenues made.

Don't get the boot

Forums usually have a well-maintained files area from where you can download files that relate to the forum content. There will be a forum operator, or moderator, on hand, and if you persistently break the rules you face being expelled from the forum and possibly from the service.

Most services have an offline reader, although these tend not to be as good as the commercial conferencing systems' software. ISPs want to keep you connected and using their service for as long as possible, and don't really want you just connecting for a few seconds to collect messages.

International flavour

The appeal of online forums is their international flavour. Unlike conferencing systems which tend to be based in whichever country they originate from, and Usenet, which is largely American and British in flavour, forums on CompuServe and AOL attract members from countries all around the world.

Writing tip

Avoid writing a hasty reply and immediately sending it. Take the time to read over your message. Once you hit the Send key, your message will be posted for the world to see. If you have acted hastily or in anger, everyone who reads it will draw their own conclusions about the type of person you are.

Exchanging notes

Find out something specific with Deja News but use Outlook Express to read and contribute to Usenet newsgroups.

There may be occasions when, rather than downloading messages for a particular newsgroup, you simply want a quick way of accessing previous messages to find out specific information on a particular topic using your Internet browser. You can do this by using the search facility at Deja News on the Web at http://www.dejanews.com. The opening page lists categories of discussions from Arts & Entertainment through to Travel and you can either click on a particular subject and read through the messages or join discussions, forums or communities devoted to these subjects. This means you can access newsgroup data on an occasional or even one-off basis but you will need to spend more time online to find what you are looking for. To gain full benefit from newsgroups, use Outlook Express, the mail software built into Internet Explorer. Follow the steps here to set up Outlook Express.

How to set up Outlook Express

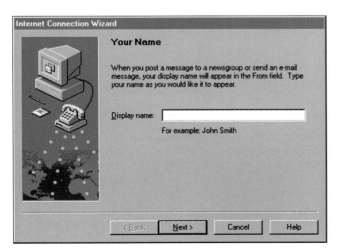

1 Load Outlook Express from the Start, Programs menu and click on the **Read News** icon. A wizard pops up to guide you through the process of setting up newsgroup access. The first thing it needs is your name; type in the name you want to appear at the bottom of any messages you send and then click on Next. Now type in your email address and click on Next again.

2 You will need the name of your Internet service provider's **news server** for the next step. Dig out the documentation that came with your Internet account and you should find the details there. Usually it will be called something like news.providername.com. Type in the name of your news server. You might have to log on to the news server with a name and password. If your Internet service provider has given you a news server account name, click the My News Server Requires Me To Log On checkbox and click on the Next button.

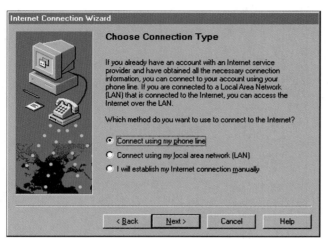

3 Type in your Internet account name and password and click on Next. Give your news account a name — News is as good as any — and click on Next again. Then tell Outlook how you connect to the Internet. For most people that's through the phone line, so click the **Connect Using My Phone Line** option.

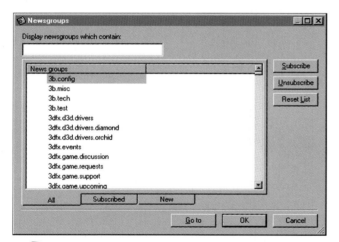

4 Outlook asks you which Dial-Up connection you want to use for newsgroup access. You'll probably want to use the news server provided by your existing ISP so select **Use An Existing Dial-Up Connection** and select your ISP from the list below. Click on Next and then on Finish to complete the setup.

Finding newsgroups

Each newsgroup has a name that should tell you the type of discussion covered. Alt.creative_cooking tells you you're in the Alternative batch of newsgroups and the topic under discussion is cooking. The main group areas are:

- **Alt (alternative)** Here you'll find any topic goes, from the sublime to the ridiculous.
- **Biz (business)** The commercial side of newsgroups.
- **Comp (computer)** Where techies discuss computing.
- **News** This area covers how newsgroups work.
- **Misc (miscellaneous)** Anything that doesn't really fit into the other categories.
- **Soc (society)** Discussions about society and culture.
- **Rec (recreation)** An area that covers any recreational topic.

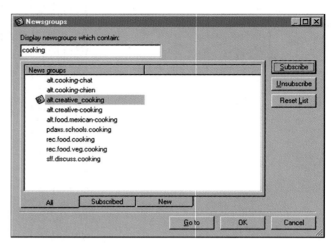

5 The next step is to pick out the newsgroups you want to follow and to subscribe to them. Outlook asks if you want to see a list of the available newsgroups; click on the Yes button. Outlook should now go online and download the list of newsgroups. Since there are thousands out there, this could take a while. Once they've all been downloaded, a list of newsgroups pops up. You can either scroll through the list until you find something that catches your interest, or you can search for a particular topic. Here you are interested in cooking, so cooking is typed in as a search phrase in the **Display Newsgroups Which Contain** box.

Say you like the look of the alt.creative_cooking newsgroup and you're going to subscribe. Simply click on that one on the list and then on the Subscribe button. You can subscribe to as many newsgroups as you like and then click on OK.

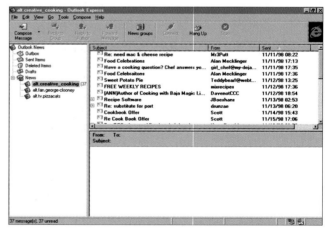

6 In the Outlook Express main window, you should now see a new folder called **News** and a list of all the newsgroups you've subscribed to. Click on any one of them to get an idea of how they work. You'll see details of messages sent in the right-hand window. To view a message click on it and it'll pop up in the bottom right window. Discussions within a group always start with one message. Follow-up messages are grouped in what's called a thread. If you see a + sign next to a message, it means there's a discussion thread there. Click on the + sign to follow the thread.

Once you're ready to contribute to a newsgroup, you can either reply to the whole newsgroup or to the author, or you can start a new discussion. To respond to messages, click on the message and then either on the Reply to Author or Reply to Group icon on the IE menu bar. Type in your response and click on Send. You'll see your message pop up in the list of messages. To start a new discussion, click on the Compose Message icon and type.

8

Legal Issues

The law is there to protect you as a computer user just as much as it is there to prevent you from going astray.

The law applies to everyone in equal measure, and that includes the computer-using public. Whether you are purchasing your first computer, upgrading to the latest specification or treating yourself to yet another essential peripheral, the law is there to protect your rights as a consumer. A computer is a retail purchase just like any other, and it is covered by laws that exist to prevent you from being misled, short-changed or cheated in any way.

Big Brother?

Legal responsibilities don't end with a successful purchase, however. As a computer user, there are plenty of ways in which the law can affect how you use your PC. Don't think of this as Big Brother interfering; this is the Internet age, and access to a phenomenal amount of information from all over the planet is just a mouse click away. What is acceptable to one culture may be unacceptable to another, and what is legal in one country may be illegal in another. Just because something is easy to obtain doesn't make it legal.

Behave yourself

While the law is there to protect you when you buy goods online, when you design and publish a home page on the World Wide Web and when things go wrong with your computer, it also exists to protect the rights of others against things that you may do, such as spreading libel on the Net or using pirated software.

Common sense

Every country has its own specific laws, and they vary from country to country. The advice given here is based upon the global commodity of common sense. If you follow these guidelines, you will be well on your way to avoiding any inadvertent legal problems.

Buying tips

● If you are buying a PC by mail order, protect yourself by making sure you get a written confirmation of both the agreed purchase price and system specifications before you part with any cash.

● When the PC arrives, sign the delivery note with 'goods not inspected' written clearly near your signature. This means you are not responsible if your computer was damaged in transit.

Copyright laws

This is the **Official Oasis Web site, as published by** the band's management company. Use of images and sound clips without permission has caused many sites run by fans to close down.

It's so easy to cut and paste images, text and sound using a PC that people often overlook copyright.

Copyright laws vary from country to country. In the UK, for example, copyright is effective for 70 years after the death of the author, after which anyone can use the material as they like. Photographs and images are treated the same as works of art, i.e. the copyright doesn't expire after a period of time. In the US, copyright is effective for 50 years after the death of the author or, for works made for hire and anonymous or pseudonymous works, for either 75 years from publication or 100 years from the time it was created, depending on which is shorter. Photographs, other images and computer programs are treated the same as text.

The best advice is that if something doesn't belong to you and you haven't asked for and received written permission to use it, then don't.

Watch it!

It's a rule that you ignore at your peril. Recently several Oasis fans set up their own Oasis fan page on the Web. They scanned in images of the band from record sleeves, out of magazines and from official merchandise. They used the Web to include some snippets of their favourite Oasis tracks, a little video footage and the lyrics of all the songs, making a great fan site — but all without copyright permission from the band's management company, the songwriters, the photographer whose images they were using and so on. It wasn't long before they got letters from the management company giving them 30 days to get the copyright permission or face legal action if the offending material wasn't removed. Similarly, Star Trek Web sites set up by fans were forced to close down by Paramount Pictures.

Protect yourself

If you have a Web home page of your own, you can take some simple steps to try to protect your own copyright. Make sure that there is a copyright statement saying who owns the rights to the work and that use elsewhere without permission is forbidden. Make sure you include this message on every page. A copyright button that links to a separate page with a legal statement on it is a neat and workable solution.

It's not as if you need to use the work of others to create your own Web page; there are plenty of CD-ROMs full of clip art images that you can use freely in your work. Just make sure when you buy the CD-ROM that it states in the manual (or sometimes in the electronic licence you agree to when installing the software) that the clip art is freely distributable or in the public domain.

There's plenty for free

The same applies to the fancy gadgets that you sometimes see on World Wide Web pages, such as visitor counters, working clocks, animated images, spinning logos and so on. If you go to an Internet search engine site, it will point you in the direction of Web sites that will either sell you a licence to use such small applications, or let you use them free of charge.

If you want a piece of code to put something like a Java clock on your Web site, don't just copy it. Use a resource like the Javascript Source page and copy it for free without breaking any copyright.

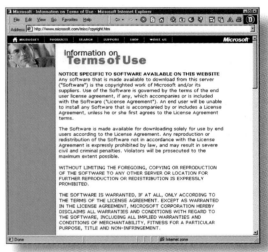

Click on the copyright link at the bottom of a page and you'll often be rewarded with the full legal notice — like here at Microsoft's online headquarters, for example.

Clip art is the popular answer to copyright-free design. Packages like Microsoft Publisher shown here have thousands of examples of clip art for you to use in your publications.

Watch out!

The Internet has become a hotbed of copyright problems, not least because it's so easy to publish your own home page. Many people don't even know they are breaking the law when they borrow an image or some code.

Remember not to copy any images, text or sound from any Web pages unless you have the express permission of the owner to do so. Don't find a Web site that you like and just cut and paste the HTML code that was used to design it. By doing so, you are stealing someone else's work and infringing their copyright.

You can instead use public domain code, which means that the item referred to — an image, sound or software — has been donated to the public by the person who created it.

Online libel

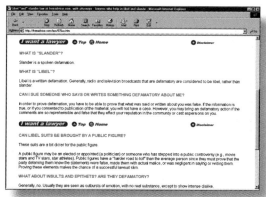

Not surprisingly, a number of **lawyers specializing** in libel are now online. Their sites also provide useful explanations of the law of libel.

England's longest-ever trial was a libel case brought by McDonald's in 1994. The **McSpotlight** site tells the McLibel story, as it became known.

Libel tips

● Don't post messages online when you lose your temper. Wait until you cool down and then reply.

● Always make sure that you are telling the truth, as far as you are aware, when posting on Usenet, especially when referring to a third party.

● If you do make a mistake, apologize quickly and sincerely, and in public in the same place the libellous statement was published. A simple apology can often diffuse the situation and prevent it from going to court.

Be careful what you say or publish online or you could find yourself being sued for libel.

The Internet can lull the user into a false sense of security. Instant communication and the ease with which you can get caught up in a conversation or a heated debate can allow you to say something you might regret later. You might really regret it later because once the heat has died down your words will remain on the Net for anyone to see, anywhere in the world. If a false and defamatory statement is seen by the person it refers to, and he thinks that it exposes him to hatred, ridicule or contempt, or that it lowers his esteem among his colleagues, loses him business or damages his reputation in any way, he can sue you for libel.

Easy to prove

The trouble is that Internet communication can seem like a spoken conversation, and slander — defamation by the spoken word — is commonplace but hard to prove. Libel, on the other hand, is easier to prove because the words have been published and can be used in evidence. What constitutes libel will vary from country to country, and, in the US, from state to state. The amount of damages awarded to the injured party also varies but can reach astronomical heights.

Watch what you say

Although Usenet seems the most obvious place for libel to occur, Web pages can also contain libellous statements. If a copy of an email containing defamatory words about someone gets into the wrong hands, it can be used as evidence, especially at work, where a systems administrator might have access to all messages sent.

9

Fun & Games

Shopping for just about anything you can think of, all over the world, has never been easier or more fun.

Shopping on the Internet is becoming ever more popular. It's easy, it's fun and it opens up the whole world to you as a shopping centre. From your Web browser you can buy a gadget you've always wanted, a book, a CD that you can't track down, or even your weekly groceries from the supermarket.

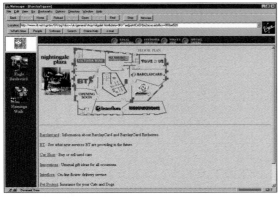

Wander around the shops from the comfort of your chair, at BarclaySquare.

BarclaySquare

Take a trip to the shopping mall at BarclaySquare. This is home to a number of shops, such as Argos, Interflora, Debenhams and Toys R Us, and you can leaf through the catalogues of some of your favourite retail outlets. While you can't buy over the Net from Toys R Us, you can get a good idea of what products are available and find out the latest prices. At the Argos store, if you're short of ideas for birthday presents, use the gift selector. Simply fill in the age and sex of the person you're buying for and you get a helpful list of suggestions. You can view products and prices online and you can even place an order.

Jargon buster

Browsers These are software programs such as Netscape Navigator or Microsoft Internet Explorer that allow you to view pages from the World Wide Web. They let you enter Web site addresses to control which home pages you want to visit, and then move backward and forward between pages on different sites.

At the Car Shop, you can buy and sell cars online, or get a free valuation. Also in BarclaySquare, you'll find travel shops, insurance companies and Barclays Bank.

Internet Bookshop

Even the best-stocked bookshop can fall short of a bookworm's ideals. Perhaps a title is not in stock, or the shop doesn't cater for special interests. This is where the Net comes into its own, with miles of virtual shelves to browse and easy facilities for searching and ordering.

Two of the biggest bookshops on the Web are the Internet Bookshop and Amazon.com. There are millions of titles and it's easy to search for books by title, author or subject. You can look at book charts, read about authors and benefit from special offers.

Watch out!

In most cases, you will need to set up an account with the shop you want to buy from. This is usually just a matter of entering a few details, such as your name and address. A company may want you to pay by credit card and may assure you that it offers a completely secure way of receiving your details over the Internet. However, the Internet is not absolutely safe for such sensitive information, and most reputable companies will be happy to take details over the phone or by mail. In any case, you should be absolutely sure of the company's reliability before parting with your credit card number.

Shops in the US are easily accessible when you use the Internet.

Compact Disc Connection

CD Connection is the ideal place to look for obscure music CDs. The site is full of facilities for searching and browsing, so it could turn up both elusive old titles and obsolete CDs. Ordering is easy, too.

Supermarkets

Most of the big supermarkets have a presence on the World Wide Web. You'll certainly be able to find Tesco, Asda and Sainsbury's, for instance. These sites have information about the latest products and incentive card schemes. They also let you order gifts such as chocolates, wine and flowers. You'll need to supply credit card details, but your purchases will usually be delivered within 24 hours.

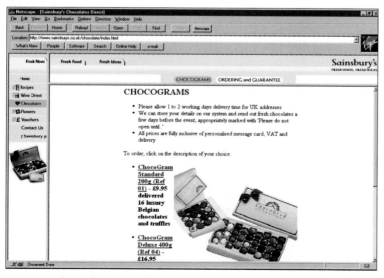

You can order a Chocogram from Sainsbury's Direct services.

Jargon buster

Search engine When you don't know the address of a Web site you would like to visit, or simply want to find out about a particular subject on the Internet, you can use a search engine in much the same way as you would use a telephone directory. Simply type in the name of a topic such as 'dogs' or 'wine' and search engines like Alta Vista or Magellan will give you a long list of related sites. But watch out: if you type in a common word, prepare to be amazed by the amount of information that appears.

At the Tesco site, you can go round the virtual shelves, clicking on the items that you need. You can even select fresh fruit and vegetables, specifying the required weight.

Home Hunter

You can search for a new house on the World Wide Web. The facility is still in its infancy, but some of the more enlightened estate agents have realized the convenience for clients of posting house details on the Internet. Some agents, such as Home Hunter, cover the whole of the UK, so you can quickly get a feel for house prices and availability anywhere in the country. You can easily browse around to find the house of your dreams and you can even sell your own house online.

Where to go

WEB SITES

- **BarclaySquare**
  www.barclaysquare.co.uk
- **Internet Bookshop**
  www.bookshop.co.uk
- **Amazon.com**
  www.amazon.com
- **CD Connection**
  www.cdconnection.com
- **Sainsbury's**
  www.sainsburys.co.uk
- **Tesco**
  www.tesco.co.uk
- **Asda**
  www.asda.co.uk
- **Home Hunter**
  www.homehunter.co.uk

All sites were active at the time of going to press.

Laughs online

Take a break from all your hard work and have a laugh, courtesy of the Internet.

Everybody likes a good laugh. When you've got the whole world participating in the joke, it can only get better. Of course, not everyone shares the same sense of humour or tolerance for endless puns or knock-knock jokes, and you'll certainly have to weave your way through some near-the-knuckle stuff, but for those who look, the Net is a great source of fun, as you're about to discover.

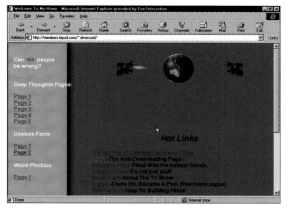

The Deep Thoughts pages (to be found at http://members.tripod.com/~silvercord/) provide examples of the offbeat humour to be found on the Net.

Deep Thoughts

This is one of the collections of aphorisms and one-liners you'll come across if you search. Masquerading as philosophy, the host pokes fun at almost everything, but mostly at his own bizarre view of the world — think Eddie Izzard or Robin Williams. Sample joke: *If you ever fall off the Sears Tower, just go real limp, because maybe you'll look like a dummy and people will try to catch you because, hey, free dummy.*

Be persistent and you'll be rewarded with some gems.

Jokes.com

More than just a joke site, this is a searchable database of jokes, stories, one-liners and other funny stuff. Entries are rated and it is possible to search for specific content. For example, you can look for gags that are one-liners, have a general content and have scored equal to or higher than five. You can sign up for the joke-a-day email ($1 US a month), email a joke to a friend, or check out morphed celebrity photos. There are also some excellent real-life lists, such as the 50 great newspaper headlines feature. Sample: *Typhoon Rips Through Cemetery; Hundreds Dead.*

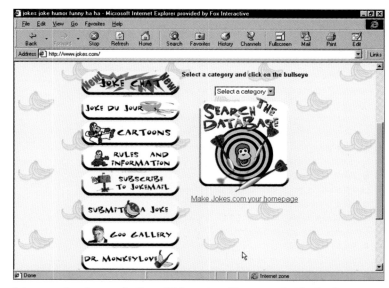

Jokes.com is a huge selection of jokes stored in a searchable database.

Kids online

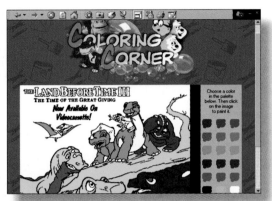
Coloring Corner is part of the Kid's Playroom site.

Submissions to the Refrigerator are created with real crayons or paints on real paper.

The Net is a giant playground for kids. Used wisely it can be safe and educational as well as entertaining.

There's plenty for kids to do online: they can find information for a project, play games, watch cartoons, explore all kinds of entertainment sites and keep in touch with the activities of their heroes and idols. Thousands of Web pages are devoted to pop groups, sports and personalities from all walks of life.

Play and learn
Some sites are specifically designed for children, such as Kid's Playroom, which is a site run by Universal Studios. It features games, puzzles, songs, video clips and a colouring corner where children can create pictures online or print them out in black and white and colour them in later.

The Refrigerator runs a rolling competition for young artists. The best picture sent in each week is displayed on the front page of the site for seven days and then takes its place in the Hall of Fame.

Visit Disney's site for games, entertainment and advertising. Check out Cartoon World! where there are pictures, videos and sound clips of every cartoon you can think of. Children can print out masks of favourite characters and colour them in.

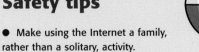

Safety tips

● Make using the Internet a family, rather than a solitary, activity.
● Choose an appropriate ISP. Some of them offer unregulated access to newsgroups while others remove the potentially offensive ones.
● Never give out home or school addresses and telephone numbers on public Internet sites.
● Give your children pseudonyms for use with their email accounts.
● Allow children to use Internet Chat and take part in newsgroups only under supervision.
● Find penpals or email pals for your children through reputable sites like E-Pals. Don't use Soc.penpals or similar newsgroups.
● Make your children aware that not everything on the Internet is true and that people they meet on the Internet might misrepresent their true motives, age or sex.

Cartoon World is a one-stop source for everything related to cartoons, animations and animated movies.

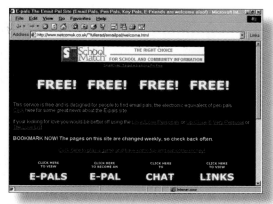
E-Pals is a safe place to find electronic penpals.

Games addicts will find lots of shareware and demonstration products on the Web. Parents who are concerned about the suitability of games for young children should visit the Non-Violent Games site, where each title is vetted for violence and unsuitable content before being made available.

The Natural History Museum in London runs a terrific site where children can tour the museum by examining the highlights of each gallery. There are special treats too, such as being able to download virtual reality fossils which can be enlarged, rotated and examined. You'll find links to a host of other sites and plenty of suggestions on using the Net effectively at Yahooligans. This is a US-based resource centre for children and their parents.

Hazards for the unwary

You can prevent access to unsuitable Web sites by using features built into your Web browser. In Internet Explorer 4 click on the View menu, select Internet Options, then click the Content tab and the Enable button to start the Content Advisor. (In version 5, select Internet Options from the Tools menu.) Slider controls allow you to set tolerance levels for language, nudity, sex and violence.

Other browsers have similar controls but their effectiveness depends on the ratings systems loaded into the browser. Internet Explorer 4 and 5 default to RSAC (Recreational Software Advisory Council) ratings, but you may subscribe to other ratings.

Disney.com is commercial, but kids love it.

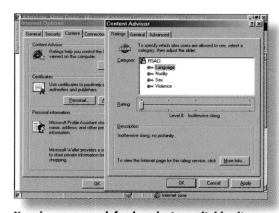
Your browser can defend against unsuitable sites.

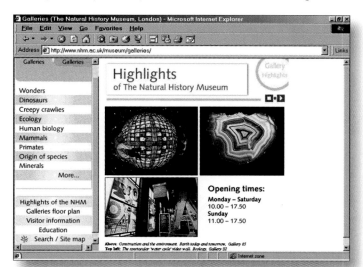
The Natural History Museum has one of the top UK Web sites, and other museums around the world are equally fascinating.

Web sites
- **Cartoon World!** www.cet.com/~rascal
- **Disney** www.disney.com
- **E-Pals** www.netcomuk.co.uk/~fullerad/emailpal
- **Kid's Playroom** www.mca.com
- **Natural History Museum** www.nhm.ac.uk
- **Non-violent games area** www.kolumbus.fi/roberto/area
- **The Refrigerator** www.artcontest.com
- **Yahooligans** www.yahooligans.com

Online games

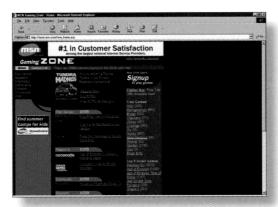

MSN's Gaming Zone includes a number of games you can play against real opponents.

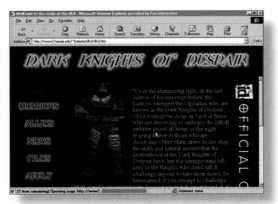

Quake is one of the most popular games that you can play over the Internet, with tournaments and distinctive teams called clans who take their gaming very seriously indeed.

You can play Microsoft's Age Of Empires against other people over the World Wide Web. Here you are about to join in a game that is already in progress.

The real gaming revolution is the ability to play against real opponents over the Internet.

To play games over the Internet you need a game with a multiplayer option, a modem and an account with an Internet provider. Then it's just a case of hooking up to an Internet games arena. You'll discover that each arena has its own rules, its own software you have to download, its own interface, pricing policy, and so on. Start with something like Microsoft's Gaming Zone at www.zone.com where you can play titles like Age Of Empires for free.

Real opponents

The attraction of online gaming is that instead of playing against the computer, you are pitting your wits against a real opponent. Sometimes you're up against several opponents, which makes games more unpredictable and more enjoyable.

There's a wide selection of games that you can play online, although the most common are either strategy games or first person shoot 'em ups. Quake and its variations are by far the most popular shoot 'em ups and have given rise to an entire subculture called Quake clans, which run online tournaments, modify the game's code to produce distinctive clothing, skins and weapons, and generally take themselves very seriously. You needn't go that far, and if you can overcome the occasional technical hassles that are part and parcel of doing anything online, there's great fun to be had.

Around the world in 80 minutes

Use your Web browser and word processor to create a globe-trotting quiz.

Although this project has fun and games as its aims, it is also highly educational. You'll design a multiple choice quiz based on Web sites representing different locations around the world — a sort of Internet treasure hunt. Participants later have to visit the sites and bring back their answers and evidence of the visit for checking against an answer sheet.

You can tailor the quiz for individuals, teams or a class. It can even offer a new way to run the monthly pub quiz. Subjects range from general knowledge to the narrowest of specialities, and you can make the questions as hard or as easy as you want. Although we've chosen a globe-trotting theme, you might prefer sport, movies, music, politics, hobbies, TV programs — or even PC programs.

You will learn

- How to design a quiz.
- How to use Microsoft Internet Explorer for basic surfing.
- How to make simple Web searches using Yahoo!
- How to make more precise searches with Yahoo! and Alta Vista.
- How to take screenshots without special software.
- How to format multiple choice questions with Microsoft Word.

You will need

Software Any Web browser, such as Microsoft Internet Explorer 4 or 5, or Netscape Navigator 4.5, and a word processor program such as Microsoft Word.
Hardware A 486-based computer or better, running Windows 95 or 98 or Windows 3.x, a modem and a printer.

Make a round-the-world quiz

1 It's likely that you'll take the first steps on this project when you're stuck in traffic or taking a shower — anywhere other than in front of your PC. Inspiration for quiz questions can come at any time. Assume you've chosen your theme and have a few ideas in your head. Open Microsoft Word, start a new document and give it a name. Make notes of any questions that have already occurred to you plus other subject areas or locations that you think may be useful. Include any auxiliary questions that arise logically, perhaps for bonus points. At this **draft stage**, content is the important issue; format and presentation come later.

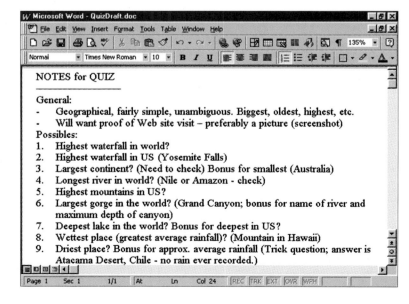

NOTES for QUIZ
─────────────
General:
- Geographical, fairly simple, unambiguous. Biggest, oldest, highest, etc.
- Will want proof of Web site visit – preferably a picture (screenshot)
Possibles:
1. Highest waterfall in world?
2. Highest waterfall in US (Yosemite Falls)
3. Largest continent? (Need to check) Bonus for smallest (Australia)
4. Longest river in world? (Nile or Amazon - check)
5. Highest mountains in US?
6. Largest gorge in the world? (Grand Canyon; bonus for name of river and maximum depth of canyon)
7. Deepest lake in the world? Bonus for deepest in US?
8. Wettest place (greatest average rainfall)? (Mountain in Hawaii)
9. Driest place? Bonus for approx. average rainfall (Trick question; answer is Atacama Desert, Chile - no rain ever recorded.)

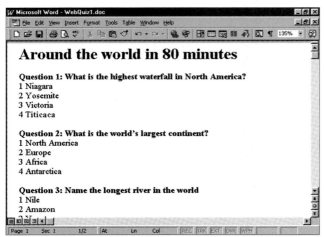

2 Start turning your notes into a presentable format. Give the document a new name, then neaten up the information. At the stage shown here, a header in a large bold font has been added. More important is your allocation of **multiple choice answers**. This can be hard work, because you need to research and enter three incorrect but reasonable alternatives. But it's worth it, because it makes everything clear and unambiguous. If your choices are carefully made to trigger discussion on certain subjects, it can also add to the fun.

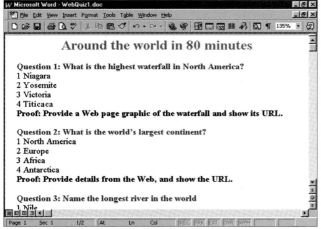

3 To make sure participants get answers from the Web, not an encyclopedia, you need **proof of surfing**. This could be a note of the site's URL (Web address), and you could also ask for a screenshot. So add appropriate ideas at this stage. You'll be able to amend them when you go online, but you may be incurring phone charges then, so advance planning is worthwhile. Remember, there may be many valid Web pages providing the correct answer. You can keep things simple by specifying one, but that would reduce the fun. Anyway, given the dynamic nature of the Web, that specific page might suddenly vanish without trace.

Internet tip

● **Keyboard** As a break from using the mouse, most surfing in Internet Explorer can be done with keystrokes. For example, you can use Tab and Shift+Tab to select hyperlinks, and go to the address by pressing Enter.

Jargon buster

● **ActiveX** A Microsoft software technology standard that lets Web authors use a set of controls that add animation, scrolling banners, live sound and more.

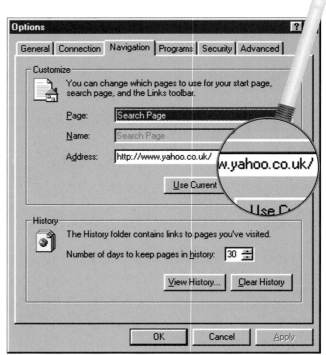

4 Now connect to the Internet. Once you're online, if it's not loaded automatically, start Microsoft Internet Explorer. If you haven't already set your search page, do that next. Click View, Options, and select the Navigation tab. In the dialogue box, select Search Page from the Page list, and enter the **Yahoo!** address as shown here. Then click OK. Now, whenever you click the Search button you'll go to the Yahoo! home page. Try it now.

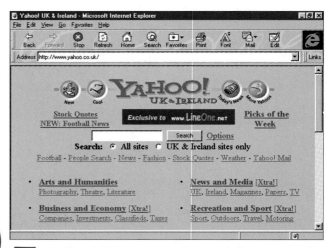

5 You'll probably want to experiment with the many **search engines** and **directories** available. There's no foolproof way of finding targets quickly. Yahoo! is simple. You enter keywords and click the Search button. If Yahoo! finds matching pages in its own directory it will display them. Otherwise it will automatically use Alta Vista, and show you the hits from that.

Internet tip

● **Previous sites** While surfing in Internet
Explorer, to return to a page you recently visited click
Back, or use the keyboard shortcut Alt+Left Arrow. Alternatively,
up to five of the most recently visited links will be listed when
you click the Go menu, and clicking one of them will take you
directly back to it.

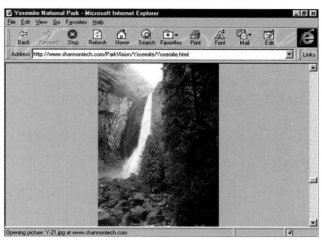

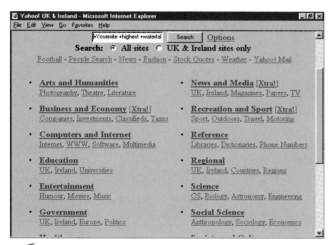

6 In order to see more of the page content, you can switch
off the tool and status bars from the **View menu**. Now
consider the first question, about the highest waterfall.
The best keywords to enter depend on circumstances, including
whether you already know the answer, as you do here. But if you
just enter Yosemite Falls you'll be overwhelmed with some 80,000
results, most of which will be largely irrelevant. Most will contain
either 'highest' or 'waterfall', rather than the phrase 'highest
waterfall'. If you precede a keyword with +, all hits will contain all
words. Try +Yosemite+highest+waterfall.

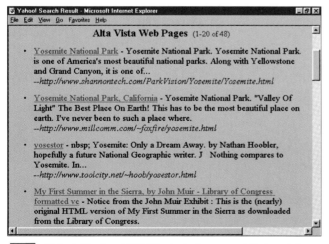

7 This yields about 300 hits, including several that contain
the details you are looking for. However, in order to
discover how much more **focused** you can make this sort
of Internet search, try improving it by doing a new search with
yosemite+'highest+waterfall'. This produces about 50 much more
relevant hits, a few of which can be seen here. Click on the first of
these to go to that site.

8 You now need to record appropriate notes about this site
in a Word document that will become your master answer
sheet. **Record** this site's address by selecting its URL and
copying it to the clipboard using the Edit menu or Ctrl+C.

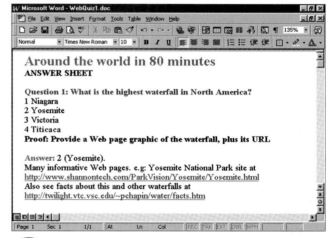

9 Go back to Word (which should still be open), and paste
the Web address into your document using the Edit menu
or **Ctrl+V**. Note how Word 98 recognizes a World Wide
Web address and formats it specially with a blue, underlined
typeface — although you normally have to press Enter to activate
that. Alternate between this document and your Web browser to
transfer further relevant World Wide Web addresses and other
information in the same way. In practice, you would surf to other
sites now that you're online, covering this waterfall question and
the other quiz topics.

Troubleshooting

● **Lost site** If you've recently surfed a Web page,
you'd expect to find it by clicking Back. Sometimes this
doesn't work. The reason is that clicking Back only tracks
unbroken series of links. If you occasionally go back and
branch off in a different direction, you break the series. To
get around this, open a new Internet Explorer window
whenever you're about to divert from your path. Each
window will preserve the links you've visited.

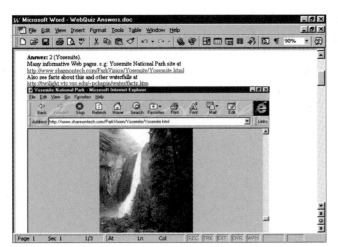

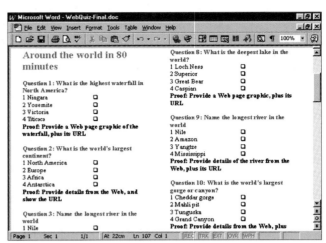

10 You can transfer screenshots of sites to your answer sheet. With the site full screen in your browser, copy it to the clipboard by pressing the **PrintScreen** key at the top right of your keyboard. Then paste it into Word as before. When you have enough data, terminate your Internet connection.

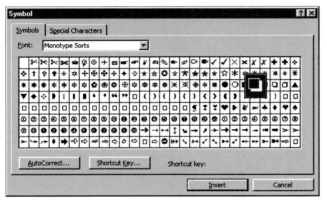

11 It's convenient to have small **check boxes** alongside each multiple choice answer. Place the cursor in the position where you want the first of them, select the Insert menu and choose Symbol. From the Font drop-down list choose Monotype Sorts and select your preference. We've chosen the fifth from the right in the third row. Click Insert and then Close. Then just copy and paste it successively to the other lines.

12 To convert your answer sheet back into a question sheet for participants to use, delete the answers and other notes and give it a new name. For a final professional touch, you can present it in column form by highlighting the text to be converted into columns and using **Format** and **Columns…** from the main menu. After printing, you're ready for fun and games. Have a great trip!

What's the difference?

● Here **Microsoft Internet Explorer 3.02** was used. While the navigation and other details will vary, you should have no difficulty using an alternative such as **Netscape Navigator**. If you use **Internet Explorer 4 or 5**, you'll also have the benefit of some additional World Wide Web searching facilities.

● To present the questions in a professional format, **Microsoft Word** is used. Alternatively, if you don't need extensive formatting, colour, columns, and so on, they could be printed from a text editor such as **Notepad**.

● A more sophisticated way to present the quiz questions would be to include specially prepared graphics in your Word document, based on the target Web sites. You could use these graphics to give obvious or subtle clues. To create them, you might use software such as **PaintShop Pro**. The graphics could either be for display on the participant's PC or printed out with a colour inkjet printer.

● Here a screen resolution of **640 x 480dpi** was used and **256 colours** to accommodate all users. However, most of today's PCs allow larger sizes, such as **800 x 600**, and with many more colours, so use these if possible for improved appearance.

Internet tips

● **Censorship** If you're doing this project with children at home or at school, you might want to control the level of sexual content and violence that they encounter. Internet Explorer lets you do this to some extent.
Go to View, Options, click the Advanced tab and then click Enable Ratings. After setting a supervisor password, you can set various restrictions. However, the effectiveness of this depends on page owners or authors giving their sites a rating in the first place, so normal supervision is still the best all-round approach.

● **History** If you want to revisit a page that is further back in your current surfing session, from the Go menu click Open History Folder, and make your choice from that listing.

Troubleshooting

● **Searching** Sometimes you'll find that the search field awaiting a new search does not accurately display the search you've just made, especially when using phrases in quotes. Just ignore this bug and enter your new search from scratch.

10

Road to Riches

Find a good idea and follow it up properly and you could become the next online millionaire.

There is no obvious road to riches but a few people have made a lot of money from the Internet. Take the two students who started with a PC or two in their college room and ended up, a few years later, running the Yahoo! directory pages; or how about the guy who had the brainwave to set up an online bookshop; he called it Amazon, convinced the public it was a great idea and is now a billionaire on paper.

Internet millionaires

These are the real success stories, the ones that make front-page news. Even so, there are thousands more out there, online and making money. The beauty of the Internet is, of course, that there's absolutely nothing to stop you from joining them. All you need is the right idea with the right approach to realizing it, and more than a modicum of determination, and you could be the next Internet millionaire making the headlines.

But don't get carried away with the notion that this is an easy ride. For everyone who has made money online there are hundreds who haven't. There is no such thing as a guaranteed moneymaker. So don't part with your cash unless you can afford to lose it. We can't promise that you will get rich from the advice given here, but you will stand a better chance if you understand the options and the pitfalls.

Route to riches

There is no obvious route to riches. You need to have an idea that fills a gap in the market and exploit it professionally. This section tries to point out the areas that anyone can turn into a moderate money-spinning venture, given a lot of hard work and all the lucky breaks you can get along the way.

You will need

ESSENTIAL

Software To browse the Internet you need an Internet browser. If you use Windows 95 or 98, you'll already have Microsoft Internet Explorer, which is represented by a globe icon on the Desktop. If you don't have a browser, your Internet service provider should supply one, such as Netscape Navigator, when you open an account. A browser displays pages retrieved from the Internet and presents them in a form you can understand, combining text, graphics and sound.

Hardware A modem.

Other An account with an Internet service provider. For a small monthly fee, an account with an ISP gives you unlimited access to the Internet, and you just pay the cost of a local telephone call while you're connected.

Advertising

Electronic Advertising

The Quickest Way To Get Sponsored

eAds pays a nickel per click!

If your Web site is a popular one, with plenty of visitors, then a banner advertising agency offering to pay you every time someone clicks a banner ad on your site could be a money spinner.

Jargon buster

Banner ad The advertising medium of choice on the Web. The small and discreet banners you see advertising goods and services. Usually these are interactive: a mouse click takes you to the advertiser's own site.

Join the advertising revolution on the World Wide Web and reach out to a huge potential audience.

The magic money-spinning word for many Internet entrepreneurs has been advertising, and there's nothing to suggest that it won't continue to be so for some time to come. As the Internet continues to grow, with more people getting connected, the potential audience that can see advertisements gets bigger, as does the number of customers who might end up buying the products or services advertised.

Online revolution

In the world of TV and magazine advertising, the potential audience is known well in advance and different rates are applied. Online it's different. Unless you are a multi-million visitors per day Web site — like Netscape's Netcenter, Microsoft or Yahoo! — it's unlikely you will ever be able to command fees that will make you rich. This doesn't mean that you can't join in on a smaller scale.

The first option is to aim for targeted sponsorship. If you run a Web site about your local high street, ask the local shops if they would like to advertise. If your site deals with your hobby, ask the shops you deal with if they want to advertise. You won't make a fortune, but you can charge enough to cover your costs. As your site grows, you can extend your advertising opportunities to bigger firms and charge them proportionately larger fees.

Banner exchange

One way to attract advertisers is to show them that you are already successful enough to have people renting space on your pages. The simplest way to do this is to join a banner exchange. There are lots of these services, the best known being Link Exchange at www.linkexchange.com. You simply register with the service — it's usually free — and the benefit you get is twofold. You can add an advertisement for your site to the database of banners — the larger exchanges have tens of thousands of sites registered — thus exposing your Web pages to a wide audience. The main benefit is that every time someone visits your site a different banner ad will be displayed at the top of the page. Some of the ads will be for large and well-known companies, which may make visitors think that you've pulled off some very good deals indeed. In fact, it's the banner exchange that makes the most money because it charges the companies for advertising space on thousands of Web sites. Nevertheless, your site will look good and may attract more advertising as a direct result.

E-Ads

If that doesn't appeal to you, there are companies such as e-Ads at www.eads.com that will pay you to take their advertising banners. They charge advertisers for the opportunity to advertise on thousands of sites in the same way as the banner exchanges do, and by registering you get those ads appearing on your pages. The difference is that they share the profits with you. The downside is that you only get paid for people who visit the advertiser's site by clicking on the banner. The amounts are not huge — something like 5 US cents for each person who clicks through — but if your site is busy you can still make money at it, without any hard work.

Some forward-thinking companies, like Amazon at www.amazon.com, let you enter an associate plan where you put a Buy Your Books at Amazon link on your site. For every customer from your pages who buys a book, you get a commission ranging from 5 to 15 per cent. This is a clever idea. You help sell Amazon to your visitors and Amazon cuts you in on the proceeds, so everyone wins out. Even the customer benefits from Amazon's 40 per cent discounts on books.

Advertising tip

To make any real money in the online advertising game, you will first need to find a way to attract visitors to your site. After all, nobody will see those ads if nobody ever visits your pages. So if you have a Web page featuring pictures of your pet cat you will not become a new media advertising millionaire. The three essential steps to success are: first, design a site that will appeal to a wide audience; second, get your site registered with as many search engines as you can; third, once you've caught people's attention, keep them coming back for more.

Become an Amazon Associate and earn up to 15 per cent commission on any sales that come through customers from your site. You can choose the logo, buttons or banners you want to display.

Banner exchange schemes such as the Link Exchange can help advertise your site to millions while at the same time attracting big name advertising to your pages.

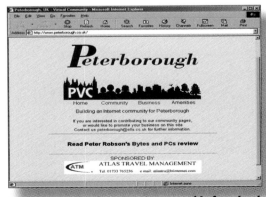

Local community sites attract sponsorship from local businesses. Targeted advertising makes sense for small sites and it's easier to convince advertisers they will see a return on their investment.

Winning moves

Casino Links is just one of many online casino sites. This one points you towards online casinos and tries to help you get the best from them. It's a good starting point for the would-be Web gambler.

Online lotteries, such as this one from Virginia, USA, offer jackpots in the millions.

Watch out!

The Internet is an unregulated place to do business. Although the laws of whichever country the site is based in will apply, that won't help you if you are in another country, with different laws, a thousand miles away. Before you part with any cash or your credit card details, especially when it comes to online lotteries and casinos, try to get some solid, trustworthy references from other people who have used the sites. Find out how long the business has been in operation. A couple of years usually qualifies as well-established.

You can make an online fortune or lose one just as easily at gambling and competition sites on the Net.

Everyone dreams of winning the lottery or the football pools, or backing the winner of the Derby, or even of waltzing out of the casino with a briefcase packed full of bank notes. The World Wide Web has more than its fair share of competitions, lotteries and even gambling casinos based on exotic Caribbean islands.

Internet casinos

Where do you start looking for these opportunities to win your fortune rather than earn it? Any search engine will turn up more than enough sites if you enter an appropriate keyword. Typing Internet Casino into the Yahoo! search box returns 20 such sites in far fewer seconds, and with Lottery there are more than 350 sites to browse.

To get straight into the action, however, the Casino Links site at www.casinolinks.com is a good starting point. It offers links to Internet casinos and online lotteries, as well as a hints and tips section to help you get the best possible experience and avoid frustration and being ripped off.

Cashing in

You may well find that you need to download special software to play the casino games at some sites. This is very similar to playing a computer game of cards or roulette but with one important difference: it's costing you money every spin.

Generally these sites work by taking credit card details and letting you buy casino credits. You bet with these credits and if you win you are paid in credits. When you have finished you can cash in your credits, although how you turn that into hard cash varies according to the casino. Some online casinos might make a transfer of funds to a designated account. Others will pay out some form of electronic money that can be used to purchase goods and services online — a bit like amusement arcade tokens. Some casinos will pay out credits for use in that casino only — it seems like they are the only ones on to a winner there!

Why not try your hand at an **Internet competition** or two? Most are free to enter; all they want is for you to visit the Web site and take a look around. Prizes on offer include cars and holidays, and the odds of winning are better than the lottery.

Some lotteries let you help good causes while trying to win a small fortune. **Plus Lotto** supports the International Red Cross.

Jargon buster

Click thru rate The number of times a banner ad gets clicked by visitors to your site. The click thru rate is normally used to measure how successful the ads on your own pages are, and can also be used to calculate what you get paid if the agreement is on a per visit basis.

It's worth checking the rules and regulations of each casino very carefully before you start playing.

Lotteries

Most countries, or states in the US, run their own online lotteries, offering big dollar prizes and jackpots running into millions. Some online lotteries support good causes; perhaps the most famous of these is the Plus Lotto at www.pluslottery.com, which raises money for the International Red Cross. It has a jackpot of $50 million, and 2,000 prizes of $1 million each.

If gambling doesn't appeal to you, you might still win some cash by entering one of the thousands of competitions operated over the Internet at any given time. The Volition site at www.volition.com/prize.html lists dozens of competitions in different categories with prizes including holidays and travel, computers, home electronics, music, art and, of course, cash.

E-commerce

Welcome to the...
**The British
Canine Shopping Centre**
The Supermarket in Cyberspace for dogs and their owners in the UK.

Shopping Areas
Food
Insurance
Products
Gift Ideas
Health & Grooming
Education/ Training

About The Shopping Centre
Links
Miscellaneous Info
Pup of the month
Contact the Shopping Centre Manager
Keep up to date

Service Areas
News
Events
Breeders
Holidays
Property For Sale
Socialising

If you need proof of the need for a unique selling point, look no further than the British Canine Shopping Centre, which caters for all your dog's needs in cyberspace.

Jargon buster

● **Secure server** A safe method of exchanging credit card details between customers and a shop The credit card information is encrypted or scrambled so that if someone were to intercept it on route, it would be scrambled. Most ISPs that offer shopping facilities to their customers will have secure servers available for their use.

● **E-commerce** The business of selling goods or services across the Internet rather than in the real world. It is the fastest growing Internet resource, and is already a multi-billion dollar market.

Service tip

The key to electronic commerce is efficiency and interactivity combined. Because both email and the World Wide Web are fairly immediate media, your customers will expect and demand fast service. That includes fast handling of orders and inquiries, emailing out notifications of the order arriving and the goods being shipped, as well as quickly turning the orders around. Just as a customer would leave a shop if the assistant ignored them, so they will leave your online shop unless they feel that they are being served. Remember, you are not the only person selling online.

Put your small business on the Internet and people from all over the world can shop with you.

Big money is being made by small businesses on the Net. The Web is a global medium, which means shopping online has no geographical boundaries. So a small-town pottery selling novelty teapots has found business is booming, with orders pouring in from all over the world, thanks to its Web shop front. A specialist confectioner, making luxury chocolates that it sells mail order from another small-town address, has seen the profits piling up since it entered the global export market on the Web. If you have something to sell, the Web is the place to sell it, and you don't need a massive investment to get started.

Get shopping

All you do need to get started is a Web page to set up shop on. At the simplest end of the selling curve, you can get by with a one-page site that just advertises what you have to sell, how much it costs and the details of how people can buy it. You can include contact details for email, phone and fax, as

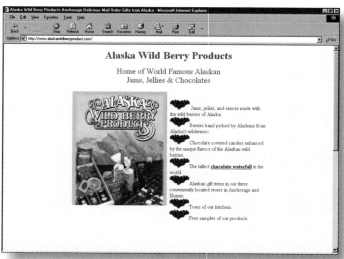

Here's an Alaskan company selling traditional fare to a worldwide market over the Web. It's proof that you can go global and export around the world, with a little online help.

well as postal address and a statement of what payment methods you accept. A more advanced site would have multiple pages, with more details of your products in the form of an online brochure, and perhaps the ability to take credit card payments by email, phone or fax if you already have merchant facilities with a credit card company.

Who would have thought the Japanese would go crazy over pumpkin seeds? But the presence of a Japanese version of this site would seem to suggest they have. Another triumph for the Internet, and more business for this company.

State of the art

The most advanced step on the e-commerce ladder is an electronic shop front, complete with interactive product lines, shopping basket facilities and secure server Internet credit card transactions.

How you go about selling online depends largely on what you have to sell. There seems little point in going to the expense of a fully-fledged electronic shop front if you are only selling knitted teddy bears as a sideline. If you have a full-time business and hope to make a living from it, the better the shop front, the more inclined customers will be to part with their cash. The good news is that whichever option suits you best, it's not that difficult to implement.

Shopping cart facilities make ordering a pleasure for customers, who can see exactly what they are buying and how much it will cost.

Templates to go

Most HTML editing software packages come with pre-structured templates for running an online business. Just follow the guidelines, making your own creative changes where necessary, for a site that will not only look business-like but will work properly as well.

At the other end of the scale, you can buy off-the-shelf shop fronts that include the all-important secure shopping basket facilities that you see at places like Amazon and Music Boulevard. This lets you concentrate on the important things, such as producing enough goods to meet the increased demands from that global market of 100 million Internet users.

E-zines

Make use of the Internet to check out the details of taxation on any income you generate from online activities. Trading in cyberspace doesn't exempt you from paying tax, as you'll soon discover.

Watch out!

Always bear in mind that just because your store is located somewhere in cyberspace, it doesn't mean that the laws of the land will not apply to you and the business that you do. This means that what you are selling must be legal in the country where your Web pages are situated. You should also check that the goods are legal in other countries, remembering that what might be acceptable on one side of the world is often not so on the other. Legal disclaimers should be displayed if there is any doubt in this matter.

Next, the law of the land applies to the way you do business and you can be prosecuted for committing fraud, or selling goods using misleading descriptions, or selling faulty or dangerous goods. The Internet is not an excuse for shoddy practice, nor an easy place to sell stolen goods. In fact, the truth is just the reverse: the Internet is full of people who know more about the law than you do, and who are quite willing and able to ensure it is adhered to. Someone, some day soon, will find you out.

Finally, make sure that you keep fully detailed accounts of all your online transactions. While there may not currently be an Internet tax on goods sold online, the profit that you make is still a taxable income. If you don't declare it as such, you could find yourself on the wrong end of a tax inspector and a large demand for unpaid taxes.

Setting up an online publishing company is much easier than launching a printed magazine.

Publications like fanzines and newsletters, well produced and presented in an exciting and readable way, have always had good potential. This applies even more to Web-based magazines, known as e-zines, and there is money to be made once your readership builds up.

Have you got what it takes?

The great thing about an e-zine is that it doesn't take much money to get started. You don't need to budget for printing a large number of copies, for example. One copy will reach a million readers. You don't need expensive equipment to get into print either — a basic setup of an Internet access account, some free Web space, a PC with a Web page editor and a scanner to get some pictures on to the page are all that are needed. Well, not quite all. You also need the creative talent, the writing skill and a unique selling point to make it a success.

E-zines can be simple in design, like this one devoted to words and the way they can be used to create poetic sculpture. In this case, the message is the medium, and complex design would get in the way.

Interesting to all

There's no point publishing a magazine about your pet dog because nobody will read it. You need to find something enough people care about to want to keep coming back; you need to be passionate about the subject yourself; and you need a unique selling point that makes your e-zine different from the rest.

Then you need to spend a lot of time keeping it on top form. That means updating it weekly, finding other people to contribute, and never giving up. If you can build up a massive readership, you have the power to negotiate with advertisers. You can also think about setting a subscription charge for the magazine, and maybe even getting a publishing company to print and distribute it.

Business tip

Be careful not to abuse the opportunities the Internet offers. Don't go into Usenet Newsgroup discussions with a sales pitch, don't try to advertise your wares in inappropriate places, and never resort to spamming. Ignoring these simple rules will ensure that your online business will be a resounding failure.

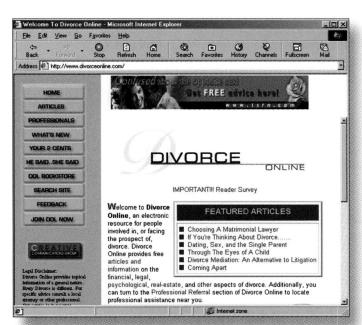

This e-zine shows how a unique selling point can come in the shape of combining comprehensive but specialized content with eye-catching and professional design. Note the advertising banner at the top of the page.

Internet tips

● There's no guarantee you will make money online. However, you won't make a penny unless you try. What's more, you won't make enough to make it worthwhile unless you exploit all the opportunities the Net presents. You need to adapt to the way things are done online.

● Don't treat the Net as you would a business in the high street or a printed publication. It's a different medium and unless you respect this and play by its rules you'll get nowhere. Make the most of the interactivity it allows and keep in touch with your customers and with Internet developments.

● Don't abuse the system. Nobody likes a spammer and nobody will buy anything from one. Use email to keep in touch with customers by all means, but give them the choice to go on a mailing list or not.

● Do your market research before setting up. The Net is the perfect research medium; all the relevant information about your business, your customers and your competitors is out there.

● Remember that exporting goods and services around the world means customers getting in touch at all hours. Make it clear that you will reply to all enquiries within 24 hours, not within the hour unless you don't ever intend to sleep.

● Use the unique linking ability of the Web to join forces with other businesses. Scratching backs is good business. So provide links to similar services from your page on the condition that they do the same; form online alliances and double your market penetration power.

● Above all else, don't think that the Internet is an easy route to riches. Unless you win the lottery, making money is hard work online and off.

CAUCE
Coalition Against Unsolicited Commercial Email

Take back your mailbox

Read the facts about spamming at the Coalition Against Unsolicited Commercial Email site at www.cauce.org. Avoid spamming, no matter how strong the temptation may be to get the news of your business venture out to millions.

Jargon buster

Spamming Sending the same message or advert by email or Usenet Newsgroup message, to thousands of people whether they are interested in what you are selling or not. It is despised by the Internet public.

Online consultants

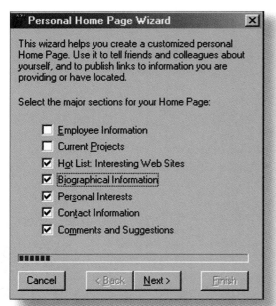

Even the novice designer can produce acceptable pages using something like FrontPage Express, part of the Microsoft Internet Explorer package.

Portfolio tip

If you expect anyone to take you seriously as a Web designer, you need a portfolio of sites. These don't have to be for real companies; they can be an assortment of page styles that apply to different businesses.

Put your computing and Internet skills to good use as an online design or technical consultant.

There's money to be made online just by knowing how to create simple Web sites, or how to help people with their computing and Internet related problems. Big design agencies charge small fortunes to get large corporations online, but they are missing out on the vast numbers of small businesses and individuals who would love to have a Web page, but have no idea how to go about it. They can't afford big agency prices, but would be delighted to find a knowledgeable individual who could put together a site at a reasonable cost.

Go for it

Designing Web sites is likely to appeal to you if you enjoy working with HTML design packages and already have your own Web site. You will probably enjoy creating sites and the experience and challenges it produces and be appreciative of the money it brings in. While big agencies talk about large budgets, you should be thinking small to start with. Spread the word in your community that there's someone who can produce decent Web pages for a small amount and the work will mount up.

The same goes for being an Internet consultant. A surprising number of ordinary people would gratefully pay you a fee to spend an hour helping them set up their modem and Internet account, or troubleshoot a problem with slow downloading speeds. Place an ad on your Web pages, help people in the Usenet Newsgroups to establish your credentials and get a name for knowing your stuff.

Good relationships

You could combine the two talents, offering to design Web pages for local businesses and then helping them to get online. If you can get the right relationships established, it opens doors to all sorts of money-making opportunities. Those same businesses that know and trust you may be interested in exploring banner advertising, with you designing and implementing the banners, or maybe placing the ads on your Web site.

Explore investments on the Internet

Buying stock can be a risky business, but the Net swings things in your favour.

If you want to get into trading stocks and shares, you may think a bank or stockbroker is the direction in which you should be heading. It is possible to use the services of an online share dealer, but different regulations in different countries make buying and selling over the Internet difficult. For the personal investor, it can be more expensive than using a local bank.

Use your usual investment services for trading, but use the Internet to provide the background knowledge that will ensure you aren't taken for a ride. Using the Internet, you can play before you pay and see exactly what's involved in joining the world of the shareholder. You can build your own portfolio of fantasy stocks in real companies, and track their progress over the course of a month, watching how they perform.

You will learn

- How to set up a personalized online investment portfolio, using a set of fantasy shares so that you can get a feel for the markets before you part with any cash.
- How to track your investments over a period of time and monitor their individual performances on the stock market, using nothing more than your Web browser and an Internet connection.
- How to maintain a printed record of these performances, building an archive of share price movements to help you become an expert investor.

You will need

Software A Web browser such as Microsoft Internet Explorer.
Hardware A modem and a printer.
Other An account with an Internet Service Provider.

Building up an online portfolio

1 To get your online portfolio started you first need to connect to an online investment service by pointing your Web browser in the right direction. The **Interactive Investor** site is based in the UK but tracks markets in New York, Paris, Frankfurt and Hong Kong as well as London. Type www.iii.co.uk in your browser address bar. The first thing you need to do upon arrival is register as a user. This process is free and brings the power of online investment tracking directly to your Desktop. Select Register on the left of the screen to continue.

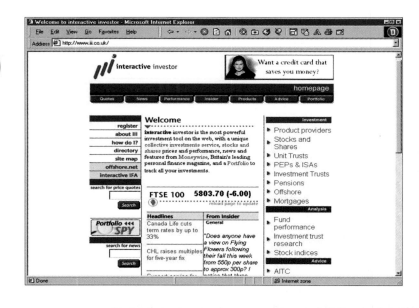

2 The next screen you see will explain that registration is free, and asks that you select one of three joining methods. As a private investor you should select the button nearest the left of the screen, clearly marked **Private Investor**. The other routes are for financial advisors and brokers only.

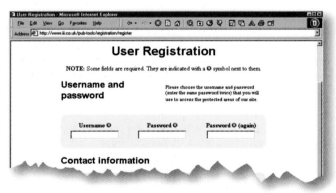

3 Now you can complete the online **registration form**. Only the entries marked with a white R against a blue circle are required for the process. You don't have to give any of the other information unless you want to. Remember to choose a user name and password that you won't easily forget. At the bottom of the form there are two checkboxes: uncheck the first unless you want to receive an email newsletter about financial services and trends. Before you check the second box, make sure you read the terms and conditions and agree with them. By checking this box you are signing a contract that says you have done this. Once you are happy with the information you have given, click on the Register With Interactive Investor box at the bottom of the screen.

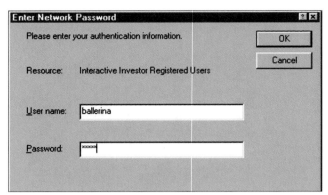

4 Before you can proceed you will be asked to complete a **user survey**. But this only takes a few seconds and you can safely choose to check the No Comment option for most questions. Once you've done this, click on the Submit Questionnaire box to continue. A pop-up box will appear on your screen asking for a network password. Don't panic. All this is asking for is the user name and password that you chose during the registration process earlier. So make sure you enter these exactly as chosen, and then press OK to continue.

5 Now you have entered the registered users section of Interactive Investor, and can choose where you want to go first. In order to track investments or to check out a company's performance before you invest, select the **Portfolio link** or click on the portfolio button that appears at the top of every screen. To get things started you will need to enter the details of the stock you are interested in. This is made easy by the built-in portfolio Search facility. Enter the name of the company (or the stock ticker if you have it) and select the type of investment or market from the drop-down list. Now hit the Search button to move on to the next – and extremely impressive – step towards building your own personal portfolio.

Jargon buster

Equity The shares offered for sale to the public by a company.

Offer The price at which a broker is prepared to sell shares.

Safety tip

You will want to keep a printed record of your portfolio in case of a hard disk disaster, and as an archive of your investment performance. Luckily, it's easy to do this. Simply go to your online portfolio, and once it has fully loaded and is displayed in your browser window, just click on the printer icon on your Web browser toolbar. You can do the same thing with share performance graphs as well, and compile them all into a hard-copy folder for future reference.

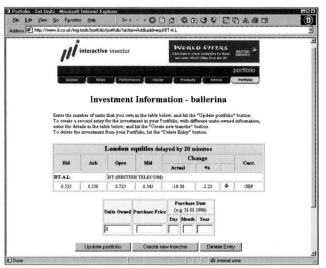

7 When you press the Add button you will see this screen. Here you can see that the British Telecom stock has been added, and you can also update your Portfolio by entering a number of shares that you have purchased and at what price. This enables you either to track a fantasy set of shares at real prices, or to keep a close eye on the performance of real shares that you have inested in. Once you have entered the purchase price and quantity simply press the **Update button** to refresh your portfolio. The Create New Tranche option allows you to set up another spearate portfolio of shares in the same company should you want to follow different investment plans. The Delete button removes an item from your portfolio. Continue adding stocks in this way until you have completed your portfolio to your satisfaction.

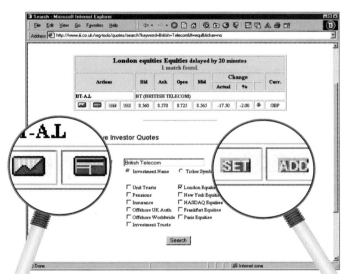

6 This search on British Telecom gives all the essential information on screen, including the stock prices and whether the price is rising or falling. All the prices are delayed by 20 minutes, so this isn't a real-time ticker. It's as close as you need for tracking a portfolio of shares. The four icons at the bottom left of the **information window** provide a degree of interactivity that is unique to the Internet. Click on the first blue icon at the left of information window – it looks like a small mountain range – for a company profile, provided one is available. Click on the second blue icon, which looks like a letter T inset, to request an email alert when the price of the stock reaches a certain value. Click on the Set icon for news items related to the company concerned. Click on the Add icon to add this stock to your personal portfolio. Remember that you are not buying the shares, just tracking them to see how they are performing. You can buy the shares for real through normal stockbroker or bank channels. Select the highlighted stock name, in this case BT (British Telecom) to get a graph showing how the shares have performed for a set period of time.

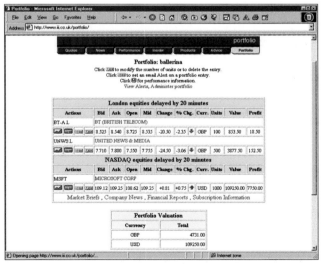

8 A completed portfolio looks something like this. As you can see, there are two entries on the London Stock Exchange and one in the United States. The Add button has been replaced with a **Mod button** that enables you to modify share quantities or delete entries with ease. Details of how many shares you own, together with their value, are now shown, and an extra column presents the amount of profit or loss that your investment has returned within the last 20 minutes. The Portfolio Valuation box at the bottom of the screen shows an instant snapshot of your investment value for each market that you are playing, here the UK and US exchanges are shown.

London equities delayed by 20 minutes										
Actions	Bid	Ask	Open	Mid	Change	% Chg.	Curr.	Units	Value	Profit
BT-A.L	BT (BRITISH TELECOM)									
	8.530	8.545	8.725	8.540	-20.00	-2.29 ⬇	GBP	100	854.00	19.00
UNWS.L	UNITED NEWS & MEDIA									
	7.710	7.750	7.550	7.730	-27.00	-3.38 ⬇	GBP	500	3865.00	140.00
NASDAQ equities delayed by 20 minutes										
Actions	Bid	Ask	Open	Mid	Change	% Chg.	Curr.	Units	Value	Profit
MSFT	MICROSOFT CORP									
	109.00	108.75	n/a	108.44	+0.00	+0.00 ●	USD	1000	108437.50	6937.50

Market Briefs , Company News , Financial Reports , Subscription Information

9 Click on **United News & Media** to get stock performance graphs.

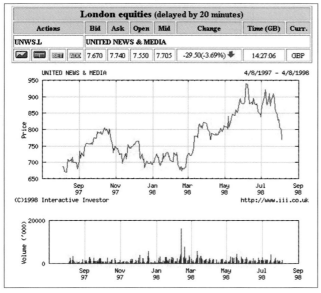

10 Choose a Timeframe of results to chart of between three months and five years. Click Compare to compare the results against the FTSE 100 stocks if you wish. You can add other stocks to track in the same graph using Other Symbols, although this can be confusing at first. Choose between a simple line graph for clarity or a more complex high/low comparison graph from Graph Type. Finally, click on the **Plot button** to display the resulting performance graphs.

11 By selecting any of the stock name links highlighted in blue, you can **graph the performance** of that stock over a given time, enabling you to spot upward or downward trends and decide whether the shares are a good investment or not. Use the configuration options to determine the time scale of the graphs; anything from three months right through to five years can be shown. Once you are ready, just hit the Plot button and a performance graph is displayed showing exactly how well, or badly, the shares have performed during that period.

Jargon buster

Bid The price a broker will pay for shares, always less than the price he will sell at.

Yield The annual profit that your shares return.

Troubleshooting

A Web-based investment resource that offers a personalized portfolio service will need to know who you are when you connect to the service in order to be able to provide you with your, and nobody else's, information. In order for this to work efficiently, there are some things that you need to be aware of.

First, you will be asked to register with the service. The registration process will be straightforward, but make sure you complete it carefully. Mistype your chosen username ('charliw' instead of 'charlie' is easily done with a slip of the finger) or password and you won't be able to get back in and access your portfolio.

Some services will require you to enter your username and password every time you visit your portfolio to ensure that it's really you who is requesting it. Others may move a small file downloaded on to your hard disk, called a cookie, that contains your user details. When you connect to the service, their computer looks for the cookie relating to that Web page and if it finds it, it will automatically let you in. This saves you from having to remember your username and password, and from some time-wasting typing, while ensuring only you can gain access. However, if you have turned off the cookie function in your Web browser it won't work. Using Internet Explorer, go to the View Internet Options menu and select the Advanced tab. Scroll down the list of options and make sure that Always Accept Cookies has been checked and you won't have any problems with the site letting you in.

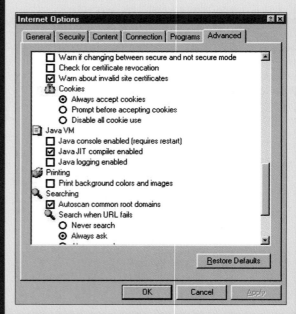

Investment trading

You too can make money – or lose it – trading stocks and shares on the World Wide Web.

A few years ago, the world of stocks and shares was a mystery to most of us. Most people's experience of investments was limited to a savings account with a bank, post office or building society. That changed with the steady privatisation of large companies and an increasing range of new ways to invest money. But the idea of looking after their own shares was anathema to many people, and they usually went to a broker, bank or share shop.

In the past few years, that's changed. You no longer need to rely on someone in an office with a Reuters terminal to track the progress of your shares, or to trade them on your behalf. Thanks to the Internet, you can check the value of your shares almost immediately, and send an instruction to buy or sell.

It's not necessarily easier to manage your stocks and shares online. Using the Internet to look after them can be just as bewildering as understanding how markets work. Here are some of the best sites for information, advice and tips to help you deal with your investments.

Financial Times

The pink paper is one of the first places to look if you want information about the markets, or to find out what a company's been up to. The online version is equally loaded with information. You need to register before you can access this site, then type in a user name and password each time you want to pass the front page. Registration is free but helps the *FT* to keep track of who looks at what.

Once you're in, there's general and financial news as well as share prices, which are updated every 20 minutes. You can construct a portfolio by telling the site what shares and investments you have, then ask for a snapshot of their individual current value, or of your total investment, with a couple of mouse clicks. It's one of the best free financial sites on the Net.

Moneyweb

If the thought of market spreads, bulls and bears makes you break out in a cold sweat, perhaps a better first stop is Moneyweb. The site is highly rated and is considered to be one of the best in the UK for personal investors. It's packed with explanatory articles about every aspect of finance, including what type of tax you will have to pay on different investments, and how to tell a genuine investment from a dodgy one. Even if you know the basics, Moneyweb is worth a visit to refresh your memory, or to find out where to get independent advice in your area.

You will need to register before you can read the *Financial Times* online.

The Moneyweb site is a great first stop for financial newcomers.

Interactive Investor

This is a good site if you want to keep up to date with market swings. As with the *Financial Times*, you can construct a portfolio on the Web site and see how the value changes each time you connect. The service is free, but you'll need to register, which involves filling in two screens' worth of information about your investments. You can arrange to receive a regular newsletter with investment tips.

If you want to track the performance of specific shares, the site can produce a graph. You can choose to see the share price over five years, for example, plotted against the FTSE-100 index. This will give

you a good idea of how well it compares with the rest of the market — a great way to separate hype from hard figures.

Electronic Share Information

One thing common to many of the share price services on the Internet is that the figures are all delayed by around 20 minutes, which is fine if you just want a rough idea of the value of your building society shares. But if you're thinking of selling a large number of shares, or you want to make a major investment in a volatile market, a 20 minute delay can make a big difference to the figures.

That's where sites such as Electronic Share Information come into their own. As well as a free service with delayed prices, there are different levels of paid subscriptions available that offer you more information and facilities, including company credit reports.

For £5 per month, you can trade your shares online, although you'll still be

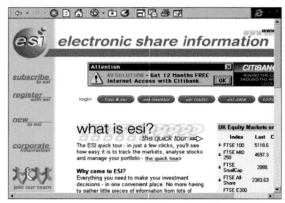

Electronic Share Information is the place to go if you just can's wait for the latest prices.

restricted to a 20 minute delay on many prices. If you're serious about making money on the markets, take a look at the Trader service. For £20 per month, this will give you the same live information that people in the City of London have, as well as many other facilities.

Those who don't want to trade will also appreciate the site because it's packed with plenty of other useful investment facts and information.

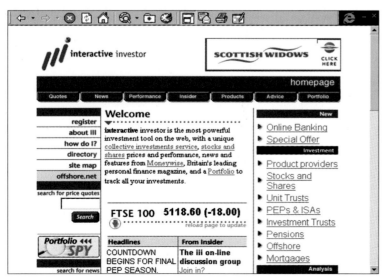

Keep up to date with the latest market trends at Interactive Investor's site.

CNN Financial Network

If you would like to invest further afield than the UK and Europe, the CNN Financial Network could be for you. There are hot stories, market reports and special reports focusing on key sectors of

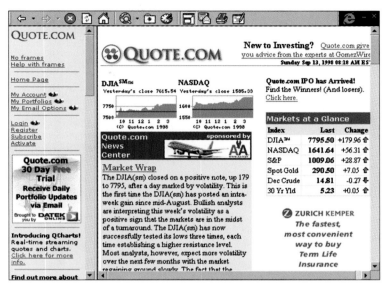

Quote.com provides a useful service for serious online investors.

For market reports from all over the world, pay a visit to the CNN Financial Network.

the economy. You can customize the news you'll see on screen so you don't have to wade through masses of irrelevant stories to reach the ones that will affect your investments. And if you don't want to read everything, you can see video reports from the TV network as well.

Quote.com

For the serious investor, Quote.com gives up-to-date pricing information throughout the day. It's designed for the US and Canadian markets rather than European ones. The basic service costs $9.95 a month, for which you will receive delayed pricing information. For up-to-date prices, you'll have to pay a hefty $99.95 each month; that will give you access to the major financial news services such as Dow Jones, Reuters and the Associated Press, and reports can be emailed direct to you at the end of each day's trading. If you do not subscribe, there is still plenty of information, and you can check US share prices free if you don't mind the delay.

Trustnet

For many people, dealing with the ins and outs of different stocks and shares is just too much trouble. The best solution is to invest in a trust, where a trust manager looks after the daily work of deciding what stocks and shares to sell or buy. As with the shares themselves, trusts can go up and down in value, and that's where Trustnet comes in. It's designed to help you monitor the performance of trusts. You can call up a chart showing you the best performing trusts, then click to see the details of a particular fund, some of which may be complicated.

Infotrade

Looking at figures online is confusing, and you'll be clocking up the phone bill. Infotrade helps you to avoid that by

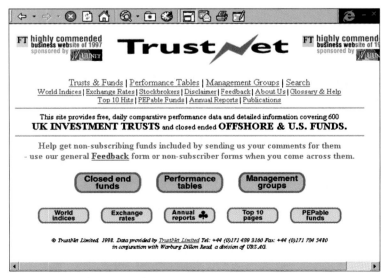

Monitor the performance of trusts online at the Trustnet site.

Find out what's involved in buying shares at the London Stock Exchange.

Video player tip

If you want to see video reports from financial news sites such as CNN Financial News, you'll need to download a video player program. The most widely used is the RealPlayer from Real Networks. You can find it at www.real.com.

giving information you can download to your own PC. You can, for instance, download the latest closing prices each day, then use a personal finance program like Quicken to view them at your leisure.

If you want to subscribe, Infotrade also operates as an Internet service provider, providing additional features such as live share prices and online trading.

London Stock Exchange

When you're looking for information about the markets, why not go straight to the horse's mouth? The London Stock Exchange Web site is worth a look, whether you're a seasoned investor or a newcomer to the market.

For new investors, or those thinking of taking the plunge, it contains useful explanations of what's involved in buying and selling, what the tax implications are, and how to find someone who can help.

There are also detailed articles on how the Budget will affect people with stocks and shares, and a useful glossary which will help you make you way round many of the other sites on the Internet.

FIND

FIND stands for Financial Information Net Directory. This site aims to give a guide to all the financial information on the Net for people in the UK.

Everything's classified by categories, with a short description of the sites in each area, and you can do a search,

although it isn't very sophisticated. Searching for Ethical, for example, will list the sections of the site in which the word appears, rather than give direct links to sites about ethical financial products.

New York Stock Exchange

Its banner proclaims: 'The world puts its stock in us.' For people not familiar with stocks, it provides a useful one-stop introduction to the world of trading, including a glossary of terms, and details the regulations you need to know to work in the markets.

Tokyo Stock Exchange

This is the first stop for anyone wanting to check out the Asian markets. It is in English as well as Japanese, slickly designed and easy to navigate.

Where to go

WEB SITES
- **CNN Financial Network**
  www.cnnfn.com
- **Electronic Share Information**
  www.esi.co.uk
- **Financial Times**
  www.ft.com
- **Find**
  www.find.co.uk
- **Infotrade**
  www.infotrade.co.uk
- **Interactive Investor**
  www.iii.co.uk
- **London Stock Exchange**
  www.londonstockex.co.uk
- **Moneyweb**
  www.moneyweb.co.uk
- **New York Stock Exchange**
  www.nyse.com
- **Quote.com**
  www.quote.com
- **Tokyo Stock Exchange**
  www.tse.or.jp
- **Trustnet**
  www.trustnet.co.uk

All sites were active at the time of going to press.

11

Designing a Web site

Get on the Web to advertise your business, promote your hobby or introduce yourself to the world.

An increasing number of people are discovering that they can have their own presence on the Web. There are people who operate small businesses on the Web, selling things like children's clothes, confectionery, handicrafts, collectibles and more, and large corporations that use the Web as a shop front selling anything and everything from flowers to cars to houses.

Join the club

There are others for whom the Web is a great way of attracting members to their club, circulating newsletters and spreading the word about their particular hobby. There are poets and artists who use the Web as an outlet for their creative talent, a gallery that's only too happy to display their work in front of a global audience. And there are plenty of people who just want to be a part of the World Wide Web because it's there and it's available — with Web sites that declare the beauty of their home town, what's different about their families, even the cuteness of their pets.

Become a master

Whether you are interested in the Web from the perspective of your business, your hobby or simply for fun, there is an opportunity waiting for you. To exploit that opportunity, you first have to become a Webmaster — a grand title, but one that merely refers to anyone who takes a do-it-yourself approach to Web pages. As a Webmaster you will be responsible for the planning, design, maintenance and marketing of your Web pages. The success or failure of your site will rest entirely on your shoulders, so it's important to get things right.

You will need

ESSENTIAL
Software A Web browser such as Internet Explorer or Netscape Navigator, Web design software, such as FrontPage, and a graphics manipulation program, such as Image Composer.
Hardware A fast (at least 33.6K but preferably 56K) modem, an inexpensive scanner or budget digital camera. High-resolution images are not essential on the Web, so high-cost imaging equipment is not essential.
Other An account with an Internet Service Provider (ISP) that provides free Web space such as AOL or CompuServe.

What makes a good

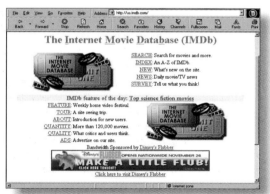

The Internet Movie Database at **www.imdb.com** is an example of a site that combines content everyone wants with a simple, uncluttered design. Take note of how everything the user could want from this site is easily accessible from the home page. First impressions count on the Web, and this is one site that makes sure that the first impression is a good one.

Before you start put, some thought into what you want your Web site to say and how you want it to look.

A good Web site requires a lot of thought before you start producing pages. You wouldn't attempt to write a novel without some idea of the plot, the beginning, middle and end, the characters involved and whether it's a romance, thriller or comedy. In the same way you shouldn't jump right into Web design without plenty of pre-production planning.

Get skilled

You must decide what you want your Web site to accomplish, and set your goals accordingly. But there is more to a good Web site than just thorough planning. A whole range of skills in areas such as graphic design, audio editing, writing ability, HTML programming, marketing and management are called for. Don't worry if that list sounds daunting; these are all skills that you can master using the right combination of hardware and software, and by following the basic principles covered in this book.

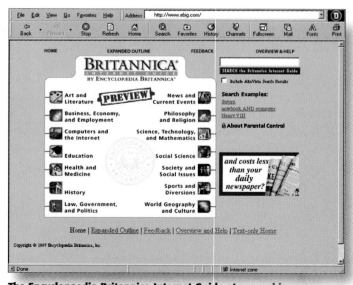

The Encyclopaedia Britannica Internet Guide at **www.ebig.com** proves the importance of planning. Like all good Web pages it is simple, yet packs the information needed on to the screen. A visitor can easily get to the information he or she wants, and the inclusion of a simple search facility on the home page is a nice touch.

Web site?

Content is king

The best sites show an understanding that content is essential. However clever the design, however flashy the technology implemented, if the content isn't good then the Web site won't be either. So before you start to look at what software you'll be using to create your site, you need to focus on what you are going to put on the pages.

Organize your thoughts

A good word processing program, such as Microsoft Word, will help you to organize your thoughts and ensure that you get such basics as correct spelling. Try to avoid long rambling pages of text. Remember the medium in which you are writing: Web pages have little in common with book pages. Break your editorial content up into blocks of text, write concisely and clearly, and always bear in mind your target audience as stated in your list of goals.

To get an idea of how to write for the Web, take a look at some sites. The pages shown here are all examples of good design. Choose pages that relate to the site you want to create: if you are producing a site about your hobby, visit other hobby sites.

Vespa Fascination at www.leonardo.nl/showcase/vespafac is a great example of how your hobby or obsession can make a good subject for a Web site. If you are passionate about a subject, your Web page should reflect this. It's obvious the Vespa fan has spent hours working on the site. Sheer enthusiasm and love shine through.

Web tip

Setting goals Use your word processing program to compile a list of achievable goals. If you want to sell handicrafts, for example, your goals may include producing an interactive catalogue of goods to reach a wide audience and enable customers to buy online. When you can confidently explain what your Web pages will do, you are ready to move on.

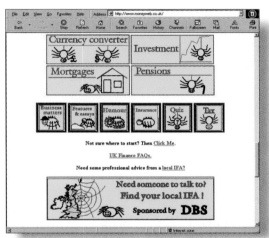

MoneyWeb at www.moneyweb.co.uk illustrates two good home page design essentials: letting the visitor know what the site is about, and using simple rather than complex images. The childlike simplicity of this design is very effective; it attracts your attention and informs at the same time.

Jargon buster

Web browser This is the program that you use to navigate and view pages on the World Wide Web, for example Internet Explorer or Netscape Navigator.

Home page This is the name applied to the first page on a Web site, the first thing that visitors to a site will see. It is often also used as an alternative term for a personal Web site — so people may refer to the entire site as your home page.

Frames These are windows that can be displayed within a single Web page at the same time. For example, you may have an index frame at the top of the page that stays in view while you browse other parts of the same site in a separate frame that takes up the rest of the page.

.gif This stands for Graphics Interchange Format. These files are among the most common images found on the World Wide Web, thanks to their small size and high quality.

Web Page software

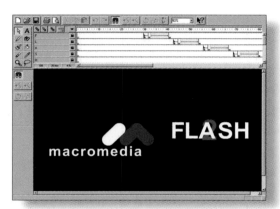

Macromedia Flash enables Web designers to produce complex animations and sounds for use on their pages. The interface is easy to understand and the final results never fail to impress.

There are plenty of programs available that make designing Web sites simple, even for complete beginners.

Microsoft FrontPage makes it easy to create Web sites using templates for pages, such as a search facility, a frequently asked questions page, feedback forms and more. It will also hide the HTML codes from view, unless you want to see them, of course. FrontPage offers all the design options you need, including drop-down menus and toolbar buttons.

Image Composer lets you manipulate pictures before you incorporate them into your pages, making complicated design techniques, such as this Neon Glow effect, just a matter of clicking the mouse.

The Preview view does exactly what you would imagine and lets you see the Web page as it would look to a Web browser.

Select the HTML view when you want to see exactly what code is being used to create your Web page. This can be very useful to help you learn more about HTML programming itself.

In Microsoft FrontPage you use the Normal view for general creation and editing. This hides the HTML code from view and lets you proceed with the job of designing the page without clutter or confusion.

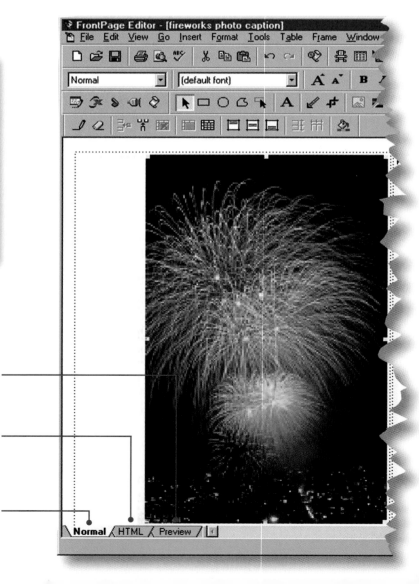

Animation

You can use image manipulators, like Microsoft's Image Composer, to crop areas of a picture for your Web site, lower the resolution (and therefore the size) and add special effects. Gif Animator lets you turn a small set of pictures into an animation that will play when someone loads the Web page. Alchemy Mindworks Gif Construction Set from www.mindworkshop.com is another gif animation program well worth checking out.

Animations can be created using an application such as Macromedia Flash. As well as adding sound to animations, Flash can create banners, navigation buttons and introductions. The program comes with more than 200Mb of clip art and typefaces.

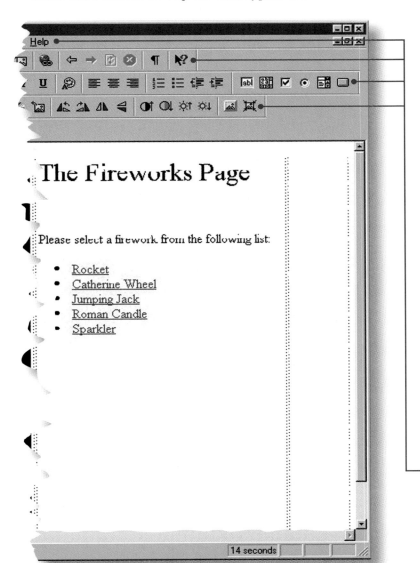

Which software?

● **Free software** The simplest Web page creation programs cost nothing, with free versions available from the Web itself, as is the case with HTML Assistant which you can find at www.brooknorth.com. Other Web creation programs are included in applications such as Internet Assistant for Word which is part of Microsoft Word 97. But free Web design software is limited and certainly won't bring the best out of you. You would do much better to buy a wysiwyg ('what you see is what you get') program. They don't cost a lot and they help you easily create great Web sites.

● **Microsoft FrontPage** This program is the best for ease of use, with its slick drag and drop interface and ready-made templates to produce great-looking pages quickly.

● **Macromedia Dreamweaver** This program is a powerful wysiwyg Web page designer that allows you to incorporate dazzling Shockwave animations and effects into your Web pages and manage your site remotely.

● **PageMill, Go Live CyberStudio, HotMetal Pro** are other Web design software packages, which may lack some of the more advanced features of those above.

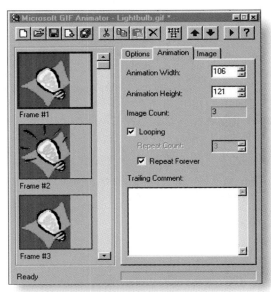

Gif Animator makes animating logos extremely simple. Results aren't as complex as MacroMedia Flash, but they can be produced very quickly.

These four toolbars contain the keys to just about everything you need to create a Web page. If you want to insert an image, create a hyperlink, add a heading or change the background colour, it can all be done here. Designing a Web page is as simple as creating a word processor document, thanks to powerful tools in Web editors like FrontPage.

Designing a page

Creating a World Wide Web page is no more difficult than writing a letter in a word processor.

To illustrate how easy it is to create a simple Web page once you have your images and text, here is The Fireworks Page which was produced in just 15 minutes.

Sit down and think about the site you want to create. Ask yourself what it's about, who it's aimed at, and how it will be presented. The site here is about fireworks, aimed at anyone with an interest in how they work. The page contains pictures of different fireworks with descriptions of the principles behind their operation. The information is presented simply, with a picture on one side of the page and text on the other.

Plan your pages

Think about your home page. This is the first part of your site that a visitor sees and it needs to be attractive without taking too long to load. Then plan what each of the following pages will contain. Figure out how you will get images and text for your pages. Remember, you cannot use other people's copyrighted work. Only then are you ready to run your Web page design software. In this example Microsoft FrontPage was used.

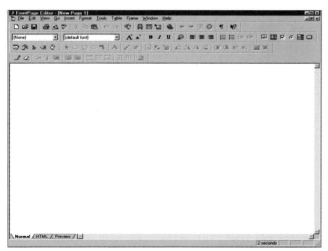

1 You start with a blank screen like this in Microsoft's FrontPage Express, but in less than 15 minutes you can create your first basic Web page. To start the ball rolling, select **New** from the File menu.

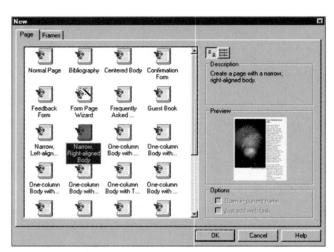

2 There are a number of pre-defined templates to choose from and, just like in a desktop publishing program, they help take the hard work out of Web design. Here choose the **Narrow, Right Aligned Body** option.

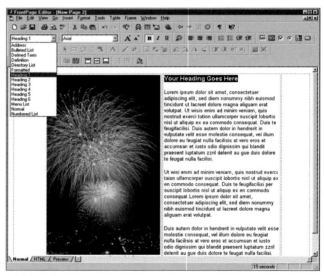

3 Highlight the **Your Heading Goes Here** text and type in a name for your Web page. Using the drop-down formatting box you can choose to make this Heading 1, which is the best format for a page heading.

Jargon buster

Plug-ins Programs that are installed on your computer and used by your Web browser to view specific content on a Web page. An example of a plug-in would be a program to allow video to be displayed on a Web page.

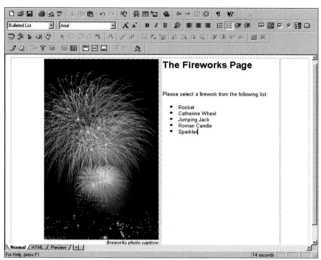

4 Delete the remaining stand-in text, then create a bulleted list of fireworks to be featured on the site. Just select the **bulleted list icon** from the second toolbar and hit the Enter key between each item entered.

6 And that's it! You've created a very simple home page with a bulleted list of hyperlinks, and all that's needed now is to create the pages to which the list **links**.

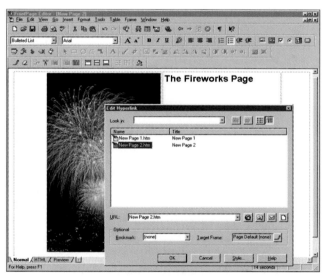

5 Make each entry in the list interactive by highlighting and selecting **Hyperlink** from the Edit menu. Clicking on the page icon creates a new page and links the selection to it.

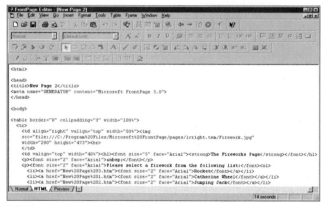

7 If you select the **HTML tab** at the bottom of the screen, you can see the complex code that lies behind the page created, which you don't have to worry about.

8 Here's the page as seen through the eyes of a **Web browser**. While it may not be a masterpiece, remember that it took just 15 minutes to produce.

The right image

Jargon buster

Hit One person visiting your Web page is equal to one hit. You can install a counter on your site to determine the number of hits it gets to gauge its popularity.

Editing an image

1 Load the picture that you want to change in Image Composer, and then select the **Cutout** option from the tools menu. Select the shape that you want to use – in this example it's a circle – and drag the outline around the image until you are happy with the positioning. Then press the Cut Out button.

2 In a matter of seconds you have turned a standard **photo** into something a little more interesting for your Web page.

Create your own Web graphics to make your site stand out above the millions of sites on the Net.

There are plenty of sites on the Web that have collections of images, buttons and logos that you can use in your own pages. But if your site uses the same images as hundreds of other sites, it will be dull. So create your own images using image editing software, such as Microsoft Image Composer or Paint Shop Pro.

Pixel perfection

Make sure you are using the right image format for the Web. Browsers recognize .gif and .jpg graphics. Use .gifs for logos, cartoons and images that have blocks of solid colour, and .jpgs for photos. To ensure images load quickly, reduce their size by cropping excess areas or reducing the number of colours. Experiment to get the best balance between size and quality.

You can scan in a photo or draw an image, then change its shape, produce an animated logo to add a bit of a sparkle to your site, and make your pictures smaller and faster.

3 It doesn't matter if the picture you have is too big. You can easily use the **Arrange** toolbox to resize the image. Reducing the image by more than half is just a matter of resizing the boundary lines around it with the mouse – and reversing it takes just one more click.

Creating an animation

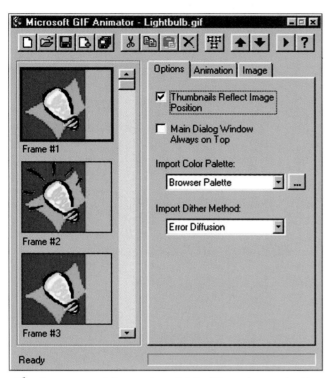

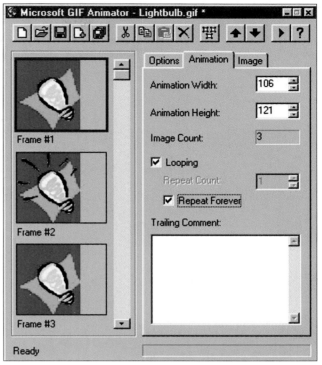

1 Create a set of three or four slightly different images, in this case a simple flashing light bulb — and load into Image Composers Gif Animator program.

2 Select the **Repeat Forever** option in the animation settings and your light bulb will flash continuously when anyone visits its Web page location.

Jargon buster

HyperLink Components of a Web page that take readers from one piece of information to another, often to another page or Web site, at the click of the mouse. HyperLinks are generally images or highlighted text.

Thumbnail A postage stamp sized version of a larger image. Often used on the Web to speed up access time on pages which are image intensive. If visitors want to see the full picture, they just click on the thumbnail image.

3 Use the **Preview** option to play your animation and see it as it will appear on your Web site. That's all there is to it.

Buying tip

Try before you buy Although FrontPage, Image Composer and Gif Animator are used here, there are many similar packages available. Trial versions of most Web design programs can be found on the Web. Make sure that the software meets your needs and your skill levels before you part with your cash. You have nothing to lose but the time it takes to download the demos.

Site management

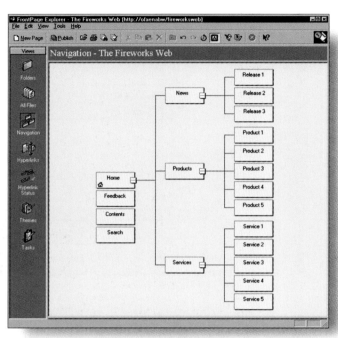

FrontPage can help manage your site. Here you see a graphical representation of a Web site. The icons on the left allow access to broken hyperlink reports among other things.

Make sure you check your Web site regularly to update information and replace any missing links.

If you want your Web site to be a success, you'll need a practical management strategy. It's neither as demanding nor as boring as it sounds if you follow this five-point plan.

Web management rules

● Connect to your site at least once a day to check that it's still accessible. If you can't get a connection, contact your Web space provider to find out why.

● If your site contains links to other sites, try out the links regularly to check that they work. Web sites frequently disappear or move to new homes.

● Make sure that the information in your site is up to date. If it isn't, change it as soon as you can. An out-of-date site is worse than no site at all.

● Encourage people to visit your site by getting it indexed by Web search engines like Yahoo! (www.yahoo.com) and Lycos (www.lycos.com).

● FrontPage includes an explorer interface that gives you an overview of your site in a simple graph format. It also has a publishing wizard that all but automates the task of uploading new pages to your site.

Web site maintenance tips

● To make updating easier, use a style guide and templates in your Web site design. Not only will you have a consistent look and feel, you won't have to start from scratch when adding something new.

● If your Web site has a large number of links, consider paying a link validation service to 'spider' or check your site monthly and email you back a list of dead links.

● If you move your Web site, change its URL or remove key pages from it, leave a visible trail to redirect users. Referral pages can be set up on your server or host with a redirecting link. If you change your URL, do a search on Alta Vista to find out who links to your site (enter link:URL in the field), then email everyone to notify them that your URL has changed.

● Always encourage feedback on your Web site, either with a link to the Webmaster or your own email address, or a feedback form. Also consider using Web log statistics software to track hits and movement on your Web site. Take all feedback seriously, and correct all errors as soon as possible.

Design tip

Remember that the Web is full of millions of pages, and most people who browse will quickly move from one to another unless their attention is held. First impressions are vital, so make sure the first page that visitors to your site will see is a good one. The home page should be clear, concise and above all else should make it clear what your pages are about.

Create a family Web site

Keep in touch with family all over the world with a Web bulletin board.

As life gets busier, it becomes harder to keep in touch with your family, particularly if they're spread all over the country or the world. It means lots of letters, duplicating photos and making expensive phone calls.

Why not let them come to you by creating a virtual bulletin board on the Net? In this way, you can put all your news in one place and contact everyone with a single email message when something happens in your family. Of course, your relatives need to be connected to the Internet, but PCs are no longer rare in homes.

The Web lets you deliver family news in an interesting, dynamic way because you can use words, photos and even sounds, so relatives can see the family on an outing or on holiday.

You will need

Software A World Wide Web page design program, such as Microsoft FrontPage 98.
Hardware Some way of copying family photographs on to your PC, such as a digital camera or a scanner.

You will learn

- How to design a family bulletin board for the Web.
- How to insert images like photographs, graphics and animated pictures.
- How to create hyperlinks to other pages on your Web site.
- How to put your email address on the page so people can contact you.
- How to turn a photograph into an image-map so that clicking on various parts of the photo takes visitors to different parts of your site.
- How to add a recorded message to your site.
- How to change the background texture and colour of your Web site.

Create a multimedia Web bulletin board

1 Start FrontPage by double-clicking on its icon. From the first dialogue box, choose the **Create a New FrontPage Web** and then click on the Blank FrontPage Web radio button. Choose OK. The program asks you to choose a location for your Web site. Either accept the default that's there, or create one that makes sense to you (for example, D:\family). Then, in the dialogue underneath, give your Web site a name and click on OK. If FrontPage can't find the location you've specified, it will ask you if you want to create it. Click on Yes. When you've done that, you'll see this screen.

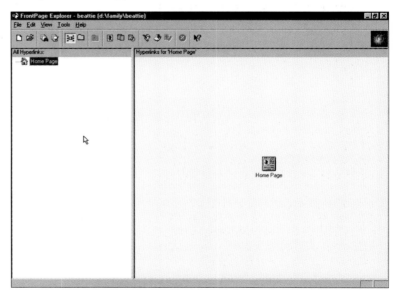

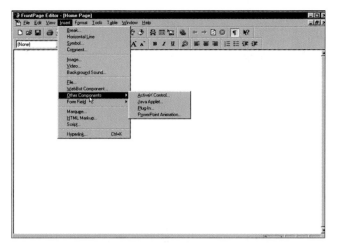

2 Double-click on the Home Page icon in the middle of the right-hand part of the screen and the **FrontPage editor** appears. It looks a lot like a conventional word processor and works in a similar way. Check out the menus though, and you'll see a number of different options and choices.

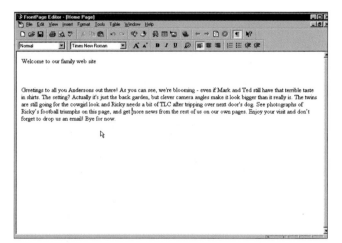

3 The first thing you need is a title and an **introduction**. You can either type directly on this editing screen or use a word processor and then copy and paste into FrontPage. Get some text on there so it looks a bit like this. Just make sure there's at least a one-line space between the title and the rest of the text.

Troubleshooting

To view your Web pages properly, you have to look at them through your Web browser. For it to work smoothly, follow this sequence.
● Design your Web page using FrontPage.
● Save your work.
● Click on Preview to see how it looks in your browser.
● If you want to change anything, switch back to FrontPage by holding down the Alt key and pressing Tab.
● Make any changes you need to and save them.
● Switch back to the browser with Alt and Tab again.
● Click on the Refresh button.
● You'll now see all of your changes in your Web browser.

4 To liven things up a little, hold down the Control key and press A to **select the text**. Go up to the button bar and click on the Centre Text button, which is sixth from the right. Click anywhere on the screen to deselect the text and then move the mouse pointer up to the G in Greetings and select that paragraph by highlighting it.

Increase the text size by clicking once on the largest A on the button bar. Click anywhere on the screen to deselect the text and then highlight the title. Click on the A again, four times so the heading is almost the same width as the paragraph. Finally, with the heading still highlighted, click on the colour palette icon on the button bar, choose a bright red colour and then click on OK to close. Click anywhere on the page. It should now look like this.

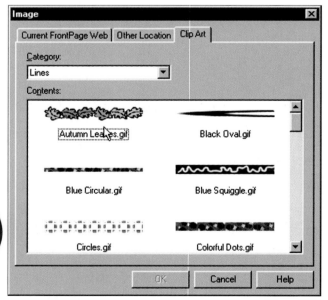

5 Divide the title from the main text by using some **clip art** that comes with FrontPage 98. Move the cursor until it's blinking on the line between the title and the text and then go to the Insert menu and choose Image. There are three tabs along the top of the dialogue box. Choose Clip Art. From the drop-down list under the Category heading, choose Lines. Pick one by clicking on it and choosing OK.

Save Image to FrontPage Web

Save this image to the current FrontPage web?

Save as URL: Autumn_Leaves92B1.gif

Yes | Yes to All | No | Cancel | Help

6 Go to the File menu and choose Save. When this dialogue appears, click on the **Yes To All** button to save your graphic along with your text.

7 To add a **photograph**, make sure the cursor is on the line between the line of leaves and the text. If it isn't, move to the end of the leaf line and press Return. Then, just as you did in step 5, go to the Insert menu and choose Image. When the dialogue box appears, select the Other location tab and click on the Browse button. Then using the standard Windows commands, find the folder where you've stored your family photos, pick the one you want and click on the Open button to insert it on the page.

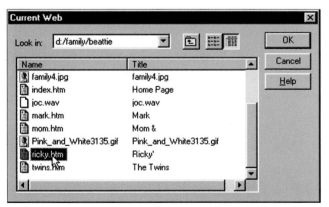

8 To create a second Web page go to the icon on the right of the button bar that looks like a sheet of paper. Click on it. Give it a title (here it is Ricky's Page) and format it. Enter some text, then save the page, giving it a title. From the Window menu, choose Home Page to return to your first page, move the cursor to the phrase 'this page' and drag over it to select the text. With the text highlighted, go to the Insert menu and choose **Hyperlink**. Click on the Current FrontPage Web tab, then the Browse button and select your second page from the list. Click on OK and then OK again. The blue underlined text indicates that the words 'Ricky's Page' have become a hyperlink.

9 Next, create other pages as you did in step 8 for other members of the family. You can turn the text into hyperlinks as before, or follow step 10 for a different approach. Here, you're previewing the Web site in Internet Explorer. To do this, from the FrontPage editor, click on the **magnifying glass/world icon** next to the printer.

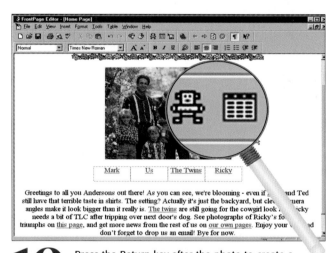

10 Press the Return key after the photo to create a blank line. Then, go to the **table button** right of the little robot, click and hold with the left mouse button, then drag down one and across four to make a table that's one row deep by four columns across. Then let go of the mouse button. Move down to the table and type in one family member's name in the first cell, another in the second and so on. After that, go back and highlight each entry in turn, centring the text and increasing the size one notch. Then, go through and hyperlink the four names in the table to their pages as you did in step 8.

Internet tips

● Plan your Web site on paper; it's especially useful for working out how the hyperlinks fit together.

● People don't like to read from computer screens very much, so keep the words per page to a minimum.

● Talk to your Internet service provider about the best way to publish your site on the Net.

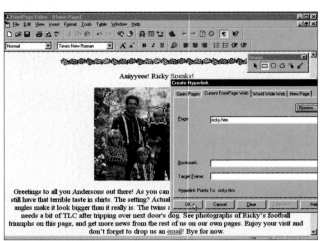

11 Now add some sound to the first page. Use Windows **Sound Recorder** to record a few sentences and save the result into the same directory as your Web site (here called D:\family). Go to the right-hand side of the leaf line and hit the Return key. In the new space type something like 'Ricky Speaks'. Double-click on the Speaks to highlight it and from the Insert menu choose Hyperlink, and at the next dialogue, click on the Current FrontPage Web tab. Click on the Browse button and scan down until you find your sound file. Double-click to select it, and click on OK to close. Save the whole file and preview it in your browser. Make sure your speakers are turned on and click on the sound link.

13 Although what is produced here will be the basis for a family Web site, there are a few extras you may enjoy. Click on the photograph. A little floating menu appears. Click on the **rectangle button** and the cursor turns into a pencil. Position it at the top left of a family member's head and, holding down the left button as you do so, drag down and right until you have a tight square round the head. Let go of the mouse button and a dialogue appears.

Make sure the Current FrontPage Web tab is selected at the top and click on the Browse button. From the drop-down list, select the person's page by double-clicking on it. Click on OK to close. Click outside the photo and the square disappears. Save and preview in your browser again. When the cursor moves over the chosen head, it turns into a hand. Clicking on the head will take a visitor to that person's page. Repeat for other family members.

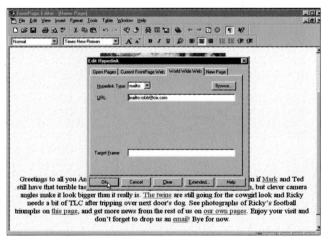

12 Change the background to something a bit more Web-like by going to the Format menu and choosing Background. Make sure the background image box is checked and click on Browse. At the next box, click on the Clip Art tab and choose **Backgrounds** from the drop-down list. Double-click on one you like and then click on OK to apply it to the page. Finally, add an email address so all your relatives can stay in touch. Go to the end of the text and highlight the word Email. Click on the Insert menu and choose Hyperlink. At the next dialogue, click on the World Wide Web tab and from the Hyperlink Type list, choose Mailto:. In the box below, after the Mailto: type in your email address. It'll look something like mailto:andersons@homenet.com. Click OK to close. Save the page and preview it in your browser as you did in step 9.

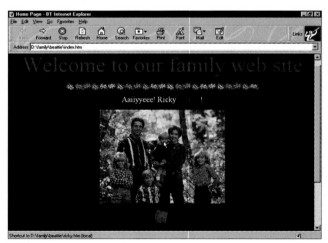

14 Finally, try this. Move the cursor in front of the first letter of the main copy (here the G in Greetings) and press Return. Move the cursor up into the space you've just created. Go to the Insert menu and choose Image. Click on the Clip Art tab and make sure **Animations** is selected from the drop-down list. Scroll down and select House.gif by double-clicking on it. A blob appears in the screen. Select Background from the Format menu. Make sure Background Image doesn't have a check next to it and choose black from the Background drop-down list and white from the Text drop-down list. Click on OK. Save the page, preview it, and you'll see how much it's changed.

12

Improving Performance

Configure Windows and your modem to take full advantage of the World Wide Web.

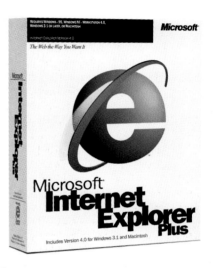

The Internet has an increasingly important role to play in enabling you to get the maximum benefit and enjoyment from your computer. If you don't have Internet access, you won't just be prevented from seeing all the information on the World Wide Web. You'll also miss out on lots of software that can be downloaded, including updates to Windows that will help your computer run better.

Connecting to the Internet requires you to configure your modem to act as a network adapter and to set up the protocols to enable your computer to communicate on the worldwide network that is the Internet. That sounds hard, and it can be. However, Windows does as much as it can to make getting on to the Internet a painless process. Here you can see how to get connected to the Internet.

Linking to the Internet

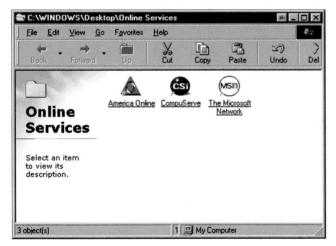

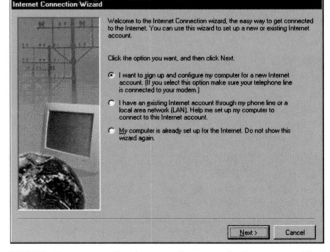

 One way to get on to the Internet is to choose one of the online services, which you will find in the **Online Services** folder on your Desktop. Services like AOL, CompuServe and The Microsoft Network provide access to the Internet and add new services of their own. They are designed to be easy to set up and use. To achieve this, they use their own software instead of the standard Internet software supplied with Windows, so much of what is described here won't apply.

Online services often charge a flat fee for unlimited access or an hourly rate. Internet access providers usually charge a flat rate per month for unlimited access. Online services can be easier to set up and use, and provide better help for the beginner. But Windows makes using a standard access provider pretty easy, too, and includes all the software you need. It's your decision.

 To get on to the Internet using a standard access provider, choose **Connection Wizard** from the Internet Explorer item on the Programs menu. Make sure that the top item I Want To Sign Up And Configure A New Internet Account is checked and click Next. The Wizard will use your modem to dial the Microsoft Internet Referral Service and obtain a list of access providers that serve your area.

Choose a provider and follow the instructions displayed by the Wizard. You will need to give your credit card details in order to open your new account. Once the account has been opened, the Wizard will set up your computer with the correct settings to allow you to connect to the Internet using the access provider you selected.

Jargon buster

Domain name service server A computer that looks up Net addresses like microsoft.com and converts them to numerical IP addresses.

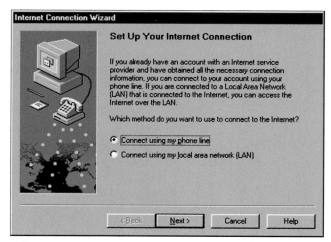

1 If you already have an account with an access provider you can use the Internet Connection Wizard to set up your computer to use it.

Start the wizard and select the second option, **I Have An Existing Account**. Click Next. The next page will ask you to confirm that your account is with a service provider, and not with an online service like The Microsoft Network or AOL. Click Next again, and select the option to Connect Using My Phone Line.

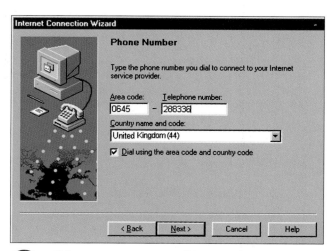

2 Click Next once more. You will be asked whether you want to create a new **dial-up connection** or use an existing one. You can use the latter option to change the settings of an existing connection. If you are setting up a new account choose the first option.

Click Next again. You will be asked to enter the phone number you will use to connect to your access provider. You should have been given this information with the details of your account. Enter the area code and number. Check the country name is correct, and ensure that Dial Using The Area Code And Country Code is checked unless it is a local number in the same area as your own phone.

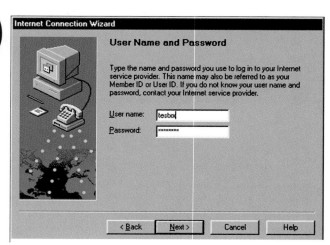

3 Click Next again. On the next page you will have to enter your **user name and password**. Again, you should have been given this information when you received the details of your Internet access account. Type your password carefully: it is shown as asterisks so no one can see it, which of course means that you can't see if you make any mistakes when entering it.

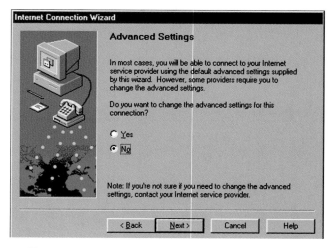

4 Click on Next again. The wizard will now ask you whether you want to configure or change the advanced settings. With most Internet access providers you shouldn't have to. However, if the instructions with your new Internet account require you to set up **IP addresses** (sets of four numbers separated by dots) or to use a script to log in to the system, you will need to change these settings.

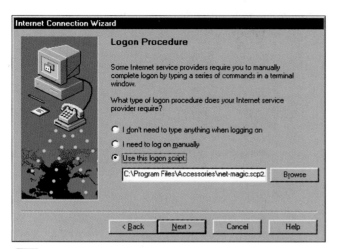

5 If you change the advanced settings you will have four extra wizard pages to complete. On the first one you must specify the connection type. **PPP** (Point to Point Protocol) is almost universally used, so select it unless you are specifically told to do otherwise.

On the following page you must specify the procedure for logging on. Your account information should tell you this. If you don't need to type anything, choose the first option. If you need to log on manually, choose the second option. Usually, though, manual log ons can be automated using a script. If this is the case, your access provider should provide you with a script. Copy the script into a folder (or type it in and save it using Notepad), then locate the script file using the Browse button after selecting the third option.

7 In the remaining steps the Internet Connection Wizard will set up your email and news reader software so that you can send and receive electronic mail and participate in electronic bulletin boards called newsgroups. These steps configure the Microsoft **Outlook Express** software that comes with Windows. If you don't want to send and receive mail or news just now, or if you would prefer to use different software, you can answer No here (and to the corresponding question for news) and skip these steps.

6 The following two advanced settings pages allow you to enter the IP address you will have when you use the Internet, and the addresses of two domain name service (DNS) servers. Most access providers allocate these automatically when you log on, in which case you won't need to enter anything here. If you have been given addresses to use, however, you should select the **Always Use The Following** option and type the addresses carefully into the appropriate boxes.

After you have done this, you will arrive at the page that anyone who didn't choose to change the advanced settings has already reached. All you need to do now is enter a name for the connection. The name of the access provider will do.

8 If you choose to set up an Internet **mail account**, click Next and specify whether you want to create a new mail account or change an existing one. It can be valid to have more than one mail account. Some access providers let you have more than one mailbox, so different members of your family can have their own email address. Click Next again, and enter your name or the nickname you would like to be known by when corresponding using email.

9 Click on Next again, type your **email address** into the box provided. Usually this address will be specified in the documentation that you received with your new account. The address you enter will appear in the header of every message that you send to say who the message is from, and it is the address that the recipient's mail software will use when replying to you. It is important to get it right, otherwise any replies will not find their way to your mailbox.

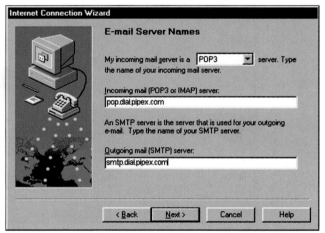

10 On the next page you must enter the details of your **mail server**. Again, the information you enter here should have been supplied to you by your access provider. The incoming mail server is nearly always a POP3 server, but its name will be specific to your access provider. It will often be something like mail.provider.com (and the outgoing mail server may have exactly the same name), but your access provider may be different. Check the names if you aren't sure.

Jargon buster

Network protocol This is akin to a language that allows computers to communicate over a network. If a computer uses the wrong protocol, other computers won't be able to understand it. Your computer must also be set up so that it knows who it is (its Internet address) as well as the name and password to use to get connected to your Internet access provider.

11 Next enter the **account name and password** you use to access the incoming mail server. The account name is often the same as the first part of your email address.

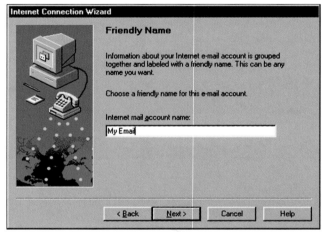

12 Give the account a **name**. If several members of your family have email accounts, identify each one by a different name.

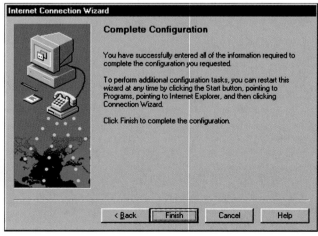

13 Setting up a **news account** is similar to setting up mail. Enter the name of the news server and you will be asked about setting up an Internet Directory Service. After that you will come to the final page of the Internet Connection Wizard. Click Finish to complete the configuration.

Net doctor

Windows Troubleshooters can help you out if things go wrong with your Internet connection.

Using the Net may seem as easy as clicking on links in your Web browser or buttons in your email program. But a lot of work goes on behind the scenes to bring Web pages, email, downloads and other things from servers on the Internet to your PC.

Windows simplifies the process of connecting to the Internet as much as possible, and your Internet software hides the nuts and bolts of how the connection is achieved. If everything works, there's no need to try to understand what is happening. But if your Net connection doesn't work, some knowledge about how your connection is set up can go a long way towards helping you identify and solve the problem.

Trouble-free surfing

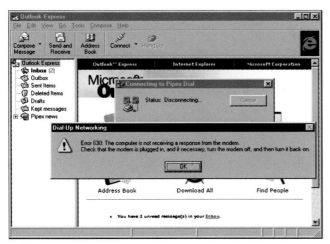

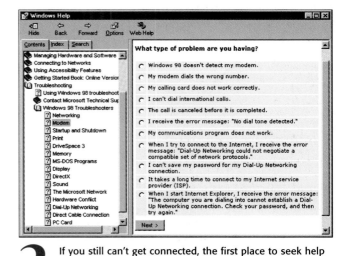

1 Before your computer can connect up to the Internet, three things have to be properly installed, set up and working. First, your **modem** has to be connected to your computer (or installed inside it, if it is an internal model), and it needs to be recognized by Windows using the appropriate modem driver. Second, the **TCP/IP** communications protocol must be installed and correctly configured for your Internet service provider (or for each ISP, if you have more than one service provider). Third, the **dial-up networking software** (DUN) must be properly configured to dial in to your ISP and establish communication between your computer and the Internet.

If your Internet connection stops working, the reason might be a simple one: your modem or the dial-up networking software needs to be reset. Shut down the PC and turn off the modem, wait a few minutes and try again; or the problem might be a temporary fault at your ISP. Wait a couple of hours and try again before you decide that the problem is at your end.

2 If you still can't get connected, the first place to seek help is Windows Troubleshooters. Problems with your modem and DUN are dealt with by the **Modem Troubleshooter**. Click Start, Help and open the Troubleshooting chapter of the help system. The Modem Troubleshooter can help with faults, such as your modem not being detected, problems with dialling and failure to establish a connection after your modem has dialled your ISP. To use it, click the radio button next to the description of your problem, and click the Next button at the bottom of the page. Try the remedy suggested by the Troubleshooter. Click another radio button to tell it what the result was, click Next and so on.

Modem tip

If you experience problems connecting to the Internet, a modem log (shown in step 6) will often show what is going wrong.

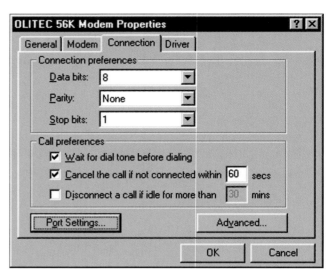

3 If the Modem Troubleshooter fails to solve your problem, you will need to dig deeper. If you still think that your modem might be the cause of the trouble, check its entry in **Device Manager**. To get to Device Manager right-click My Computer, left-click Properties and then the Device Manager tab. Expand the Modem entry to show the modem device. If it is marked with a little exclamation mark, there is a problem with it, such as a hardware conflict. Click Properties to get more information about the fault. If there is a conflict, try the Hardware Conflict Troubleshooter to see if that can resolve the problem.

If Device Manager doesn't show your modem's specific make and model but shows it as a Standard Modem, although the modem may be working, you will probably not be getting the best performance from it. You will need to install a driver provided by the modem manufacturer. Consult the manual that came with the modem for instructions on how to do this.

4 Poor performance can be caused by using the wrong **port settings**. You can check the settings from the Connection tab of the Modem Properties. The preferences should be Data Bits 8, Parity None and Stop Bits 1. The modem should always wait for a dial tone before dialling. ISPs usually answer the phone after a couple of rings so you can save time by selecting Cancel The Call If Not Connected Within and specifying a shorter interval. Click Port Settings to open the Advanced Port Settings dialogue. PCs made in the last few years have a 16550 compatible UART chip, so the box at the top left of the dialogue should be checked. If it isn't, your PC may have an old-type UART. In that case leave the check box alone, but consider upgrading your serial port.

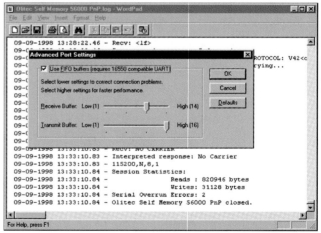

5 A 16550 UART chip can store 16 characters of data in each direction in a buffer. This improves performance by avoiding the need for the PC to fetch each character one at a time. The sliders in **Advanced Port Settings** determine how full each buffer can get before the PC must move the data out of the buffer. Set them too low and performance will suffer because the buffers will never be fully used. Set them too high and characters may be lost because the PC may not manage to empty the buffer in time to make room for the next. If this happens, it is called an overrun error.

Overrun errors harm performance because the lost data has to be re-sent. You can find out if they are occurring by getting Windows to log each connection and inspecting the result. If errors occur, move the Receive Buffer slider to the left a notch. The Transmit Buffer slider can be left at maximum, but reduce the setting if you have problems uploading files. It isn't a good idea to move the Receive slider to maximum because errors may occur, but you can try it.

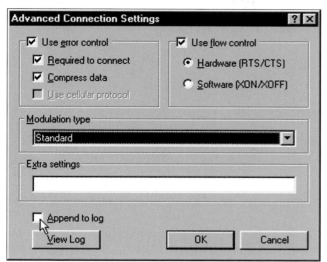

6 Click the **Advanced... button** on the Modem Properties dialogue to bring up the Advanced Connection Settings dialogue. You tell Windows to create a modem log by checking the Append To Log box. To view the log in WordPad, click View Log. The session statistics, including the error report, will be at the end of the log. If everything is working well, you can turn logging off again. At the top of the Advanced Connection Settings dialogue, Use Error Control and Compress Data should always be checked. Check Required To Connect, too. This makes Windows drop a line rather than attempt to use a connection with no error correction. Modulation type should be Standard. Use Flow Control must be selected, and the type of flow control must be Hardware. If you can't get a connection to work unless you disable hardware flow control, there is probably a fault in your modem cable.

8 You'll need to open the **Dial-Up Networking** folder in My Computer to check the dial-up networking and TCP/IP protocol settings. Select the icon for your ISP, right-click it and select Properties. The General page specifies the phone number to dial for this ISP. Use Area Code And Dialling Properties tells Windows to take account of the settings made using Control Panel's Telephone icon. The Telephone settings include important information for Windows, such as how to disable the Call Waiting signal which can crash your Internet sessions.

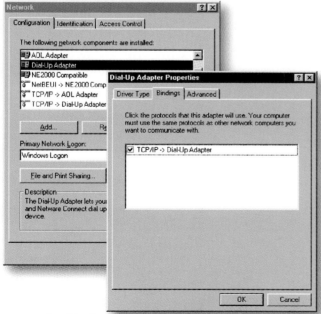

7 If nothing happens after your modem connects to your ISP, the fault might be with the **communication protocols**. Open Network in Control Panel. If your PC isn't part of a network, the only items you need to have in the components list on the Configuration page are a Dial-Up Adapter and TCP/IP. If you connect to the Internet using AOL, you will see an AOL Adapter instead. Select the Dial-Up Adapter and click Properties. The only protocol that should be associated with this adapter is TCP/IP. If others are listed, their check boxes should not be checked.

9 On the **Server Types** page, ensure Type of Dial-Up Server is PPP: Internet, Windows NT Server, Windows 95 or 98. If it isn't, you won't get connected. None of the Advanced options on this page are needed. Enable Software Compression is not required and will not speed up your connections because data is compressed by your modem. The option usually does no harm, but if you experience problems getting a connection, try disabling it.

You will often find Log On To Network is selected. This causes a delay in establishing a Net connection while your PC looks for a Windows network at the other end of the line. Additional delays can be caused by having allowed protocols other than TCP/IP. If you use Dial-Up Networking to connect to a Windows network, you will need Log On To Network and other network protocols, but for Net access the only box that needs to be checked on this page is TCP/IP.

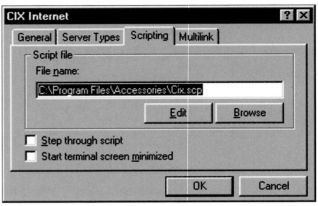

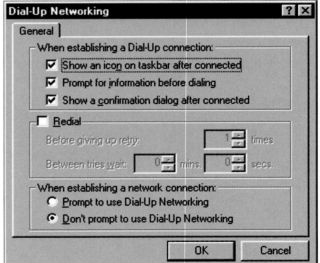

11 Some ISPs require your PC to log in to their network after dialling the number by typing your user name and password. Because this would be tiresome for you to do every time you connect, Windows will do it for you. What to type and what prompts to watch for are controlled by a script. However, many ISPs now use a different method of logging on that doesn't need a script, which is simpler. If your ISP does require a scripted log in, click the **Scripting tab** and check that the name of the script file appears in the File name box. If you click Edit, you will be able to view and change the script in Notepad. You shouldn't need to write or modify the script yourself; your ISP should provide one.

The Step Through Script box should not be checked. Start Terminal Screen Minimized is usually checked. If it isn't, when you dial the Internet a small window will pop up showing the prompts from your ISP's server and the replies that Windows types back.

10 Click the **TCP/IP Settings button** on the Server Types property page to check the protocol settings for your Internet connection. The settings to use in this dialogue box are dependent upon your particular Internet service provider. However, most ISPs nowadays assign you an IP address — a different group of four three-digit numbers that uniquely identifies your computer on the Internet — each time you log on instead of allocating a fixed one. This simplifies setting up, because you don't have to type in an address. If you have been given an IP address, however, you should click Specify An IP Address and type the numbers into the boxes below. The same applies to the Name Server addresses in the group below.

IP header compression can make things work a little quicker, but if your ISP doesn't support it, you won't get connected at all. If you can't get connected, try deselecting this option. Use Default Gateway must be checked.

Jargon buster

UART Stands for Universal Asynchronous Receiver/Transmitter. It's a chip that receives data from the modem whenever it arrives and stores it ready for access by your computer's processor. It does the same thing for data going from the computer to the modem.

TCP/IP Stands for Transmission Control Protocol/Internet Protocol. This is the network protocol used to send information over the Internet.

12 Some Dial-Up Networking settings are accessed from the Dial-Up Networking folder. Click **Connections** on the menu bar, then Settings. A dialogue appears. The first panel determines what happens when you make a connection. Show An Icon On Taskbar causes an icon showing two connected PCs to appear in the Taskbar's system tray. The screens flash to show data transfers. You can shut the connection by right-clicking this icon and choosing Disconnect. Prompt For Information Before Dialling controls whether Windows should display the Connect To dialogue so you can enter your user name and password before dialling. If you don't choose this option, Windows will go ahead and do it using previously stored values. At the bottom, Prompt To Use Dial-Up Networking will make Windows ask if you want to connect to the Internet each time you start an Internet application.

Speed it up

Browsing the Web can be painfully slow, but you can speed up your connection.

The World Wide Web is a superb resource, but sometimes it can take an age for the information you want to load on to your screen.

One reason for this is that the Internet has become so popular. Everyone wants to use it and at certain times of the day the Net slows to a crawl because so many people are online at the same time. Try not to use the Internet between 9am and 10am US time or 7pm and 8pm US time. AOL reports that in America evenings are the busiest time.

It's worth upgrading your modem to 56Kbps, to ensure you have as fast a connection from your PC as possible. Contact the modem manufacturer — search the Web, as they probably have a Web site — to see if they can upgrade your existing 28.8K or 33.6K modem to 56K technology. Failing that, if you can afford to buy a new modem the 30 per cent increase in downloading performance between a 33.6K and 56K model is worth it.

The really clever methods of speeding up the Internet don't cost a fortune. They just rely on a little

inside knowledge coupled with the right use of the best software. Here you can learn how to get more out of the Internet and in a lot less time.

You will need

Software A Web browser such as Microsoft Internet Explorer and various Internet utilities like interMute and DUN Monitor, that can be downloaded directly from the Internet.
Hardware A modem, ideally 56Kbps speed.

Speeding up your connection

1 No amount of clever software or insiders' tricks will speed up your Web browsing if your modem isn't set up properly. Open your Windows Control Panel from the settings menu (select the Start button from the bottom left corner of your Windows Desktop), and click on the **Modems** icon.

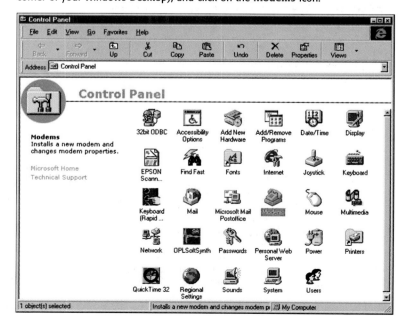

You will learn

- How the Internet delivers information to your computer.
- How to monitor the speed of your connection.
- How to tweak your hardware to ensure your PC and modem are performing at their best.
- How to filter out the things that slow down browsing, like advertising, Java applets, animations, background images and music.

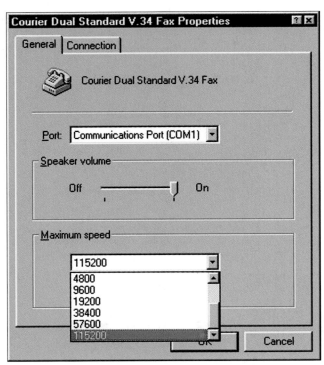

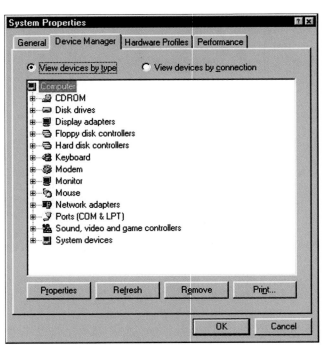

2 Select your modem and click on the **Properties** button. This will open a further window with an entry box that shows the maximum speed you have enabled your modem to connect at. Set this at 115,200 for the maximum speed. Note that you can also turn off the modem speaker volume from here, but leave it on because you will learn to recognize the sound of a proper connection and can redial quickly if the noises sound wrong.

4 You have now sorted out your modem setup. The next step is to do the same with your computer. From the Control Panel select the System icon. This will pop up a window that shows information about the version of Windows that you are running and who it is registered to. Along the top of this window are some tabs. Select the one marked **Device Manager** and make sure that the View Devices By Type box is selected.

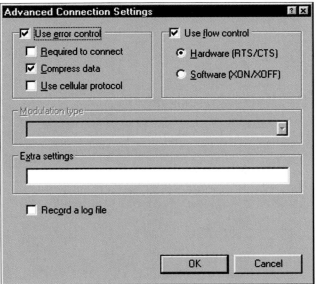

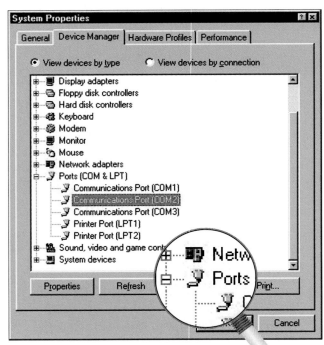

3 Select the **Connection** tab at the top of the window and select the Advanced button at the bottom right of the window that appears. You need to make sure that both the Error Control Compress Data option and Use Flow Control Hardware (RTS/CTS) option have a check mark against them. This will ensure that your modem connection runs as smoothly and as quickly as possible. Click on the OK buttons until you are left with the modem properties window only, and then click on Cancel. You should now be back in the Control Panel.

5 Look down the list until you find the entry that says **Ports** (COM and LPT), and click on the little plus sign to the left of it. This will expand the listing to show all the communications ports available on your computer. Double-click on the one that your modem is connected to – if you can't remember, you can always check by going back to the modems selection in Control Panel.

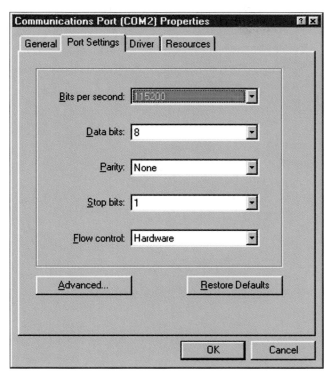

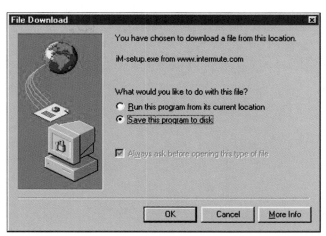

8 Follow the instructions to download the software, choosing to save the file to disk when the option window pops up asking what you want to do with the file. Once it has downloaded, exit your Web browser and disconnect from the Internet. Click on the Start button from your Windows toolbar and choose Run. Select the file **iM-setup.exe** and click on OK. If you can't see the file in this window, use the browse button to go to the Temp directory where you downloaded it to and select it there.

6 From this window select the tab marked **Port Settings** and select the speed to match your modem configuration – 115,200 bits per second. Although there are faster speeds available here, you don't want to select these because you are trying to get an exact match between your modem connection speed and the speed at which the communications port operates. Before closing this window, select the Advanced button and make sure that both sliders are at their maximum settings with the knob towards the far right of the window, and that the Use FIFO Buffers box is checked.

9 The installation process will ask you where you want to install the software. You can safely accept all the defaults offered. Within just a few seconds you will have a copy of interMute up and running on your PC. Now when you start your computer, a small icon will appear in the system tray in the bottom right-hand corner of your screen. Click on this icon with the left mouse button and select **Open Control Panel**. You can now configure interMute to speed up your browsing.

7 Now that your modem and computer are configured to work at their optimum speed, you need to get the World Wide Web itself working faster for you. This can be done with the help of a piece of software called **interMute**. You can download this from the Internet, by going to www.intermute.com and selecting the Download Now link. The software takes about five minutes to download and you can use it for a free 14-day trial. Once you have used it for two weeks, you probably won't want to go back to the slow Web browsing you knew before, and will happily pay the small price to register.

Jargon buster

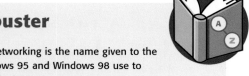

DUN Dial Up Networking is the name given to the utility that Windows 95 and Windows 98 use to connect you to the Internet.

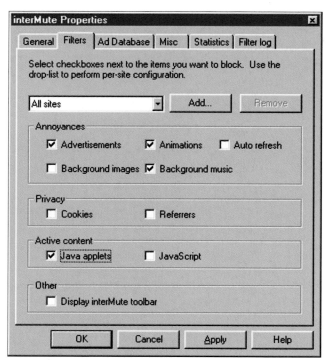

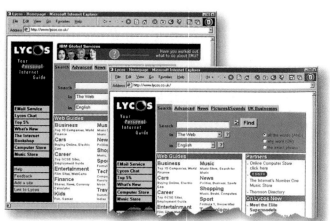

12 Spot the difference? interMute has **filtered out** the ad, and you would never know it was there to start with. The Web page loads quicker because you haven't had to download the ad in the first place. On sites with lots of ads, your browsing time can be dramatically shortened.

10 Select the **Filters** tab and you will see a host of options that you can configure. In the Annoyances section at the top are the things that tend to slow down your Web browsing, so place a checkmark against the following: advertisements, animations and background music. This will speed up Web browsing by filtering out the banner ads before you see them, displaying only the first frame of an animation instead of the whole thing, and not downloading big background music files that you haven't asked for. Checking the Java Applets box further down the screen will prevent Web pages from downloading these small applications, such as clocks and Web counters, that can also slow down your surfing.

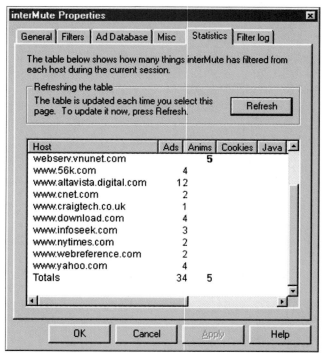

13 If further proof is needed of the time you are saving, click on interMute's **Statistics** tab and see how many ads have been removed.

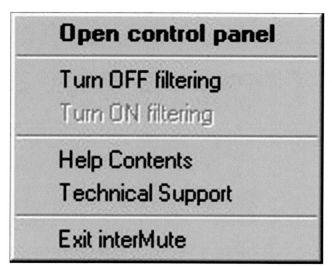

11 You can play around with the settings to see which works best for you. If you find that a Web site doesn't function properly because you have disabled Java applets, you can always turn off the interMute filtering. Click the right mouse button over the interMute icon in the system tray and then select **Turn Off Filtering** from the pop-up menu that appears.

Cache tip

Use the local cache feature of your Web browser to store Web page images in a directory on your hard disk. In Internet Explorer you will find the settings in the View/Internet options menu. Locate the Temporary Internet Files entry in the first window displayed, and click on Settings. Use the slider to select how much space on your hard disk the cache will use. The bigger the cache the more images can be stored and the faster your browsing will be, but don't overdo it.

Surfing the Net offline

Use Microsoft Internet Explorer 4 or 5 to surf the Web offline and save time and money.

Working offline means you don't have to keep connecting to the Net to download the same information again and again. You can maximize the amount of time spent looking at Web data and minimize the amount of money you spend on your phone bill. If you are using Microsoft Internet Explorer 4 or 5, you have everything you need to save time and money.

The simplest way to browse offline is to use the cache, a directory on your hard disk that stores images and text from pages you visit. Once you've visited a page the browser stores the data in the cache, and if you revisit the same page it first looks in your cache to see if any of the required data is stored there before trying to download it from the Web. You can browse complete pages from your cache without connecting to the Web.

Another method of offline browsing is subscription. You tell a Web site what pages you want and when you want them. Internet Explorer connects during off-peak hours and downloads the files. The page can be viewed later from your Desktop without having to reconnect to the Web.

You will need

Software Microsoft Internet Explorer version 4 or 5.
Hardware A modem or other means of connecting to the Internet.
Other An account with an Internet service provider.

Browsing offline with Internet Explorer

1 The first step to accessing the offline capabilities of Internet Explorer 4 or 5 is to start the program and select the **Work Offline** option from the File menu. Once selected, this will stay as your browser default until you select the option to disable it.

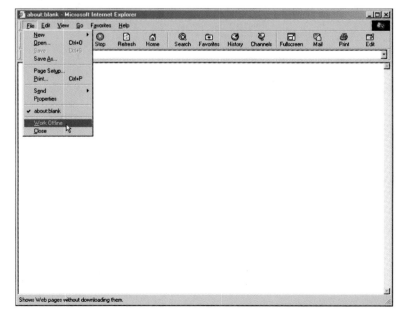

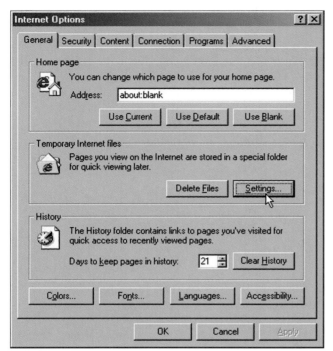

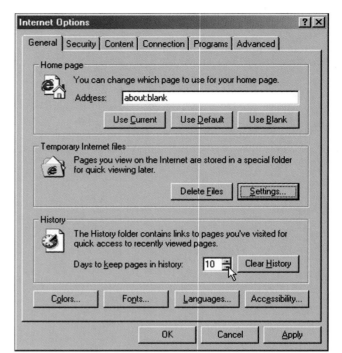

2 Go to the View menu (or the Tools menu if you are using version 5) and select **Internet Options**. A window will pop up that enables you to configure the way that Internet Explorer works, including the all-important settings for working offline. The first settings to look at are the ones marked Temporary Internet Files, so click on the Settings button.

4 Set the number of days of browsing you would like the **History** feature to store. This will determine how many days of Web browsing are available to you to view offline. Choose a low number if you visit lots of pages every day, and a higher number if your browsing activity is more limited. When you have entered the appropriate number, click on the Apply button and then the OK button.

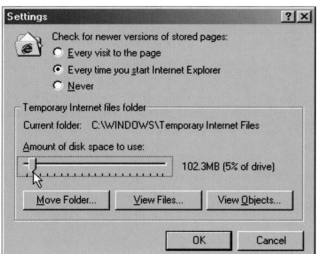

3 Use the **slider** to set the size of the Internet Explorer cache folder. The bigger it is, the more of your hard disk will be allocated to storing Web pages for offline viewing. If you are low on hard disk space, set a low figure; if you have plenty of space then 5 or even 10 per cent will provide ample storage for even the busiest of browsers. Click on OK when you have finished.

5 Now you can continue to browse the Web normally. It will take a few moments before the offline working process takes effect. This is because you have to build up the content information stored in the cache and the details of your browsing activity in the History file before you can browse offline. When you enter a Web address that doesn't have the necessary information in your cache, you will be advised that the page content can't be displayed and asked if you want to connect to the Internet to find it. Select the **Connect** button to connect to the Web as normal.

Jargon Buster

Cache A directory on your hard disk that stores temporary information such as images and html files to speed up your everyday browsing. It can also be used as a simple way to view Web pages stored offline.

OLR Stands for Offline Reader, and applies to any application that enables you to perform the majority of your online tasks without being connected to the Internet the whole time. Using one, like the Internet Explorer 4 or 5 offline capabilities, can reward you with considerable savings on your telephone bill.

You will learn

- How to browse Web sites offline, without having to stay connected to your ISP.
- How to connect to the Internet while you are asleep, download the latest information to view offline.

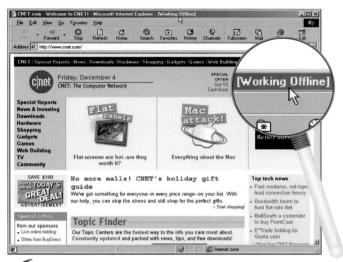

6 The next time you enter the same address when not connected to the Web, Internet Explorer will load the page from the files that have been stored in your cache without having to go online. Notice the title bar at the top of the browser window says **[Working Offline]** next to the name of the site you are connected to. If you select a link from the page that you haven't visited before, you will get the same option of connecting to reach it. Soon you will build up a set of pages that interest you, and you will be able to move between linked pages offline. Do bear in mind, though, that it can be very tiresome having to keep reconnecting and disconnecting in order to acquire a set of cached pages to read offline.

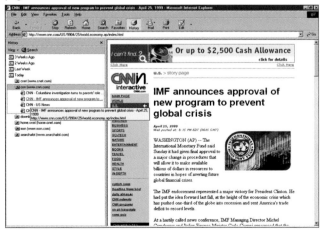

7 You don't have to type in an address to work offline; you can also use the **History** feature. Click the History button in the Internet Explorer toolbar and a frame will open on the left-hand side of your browser. Click on any day to get a list of all the sites you visited on that day. Click on a site and all the pages that you visited at that site will be listed. Select any of these and they will appear in the main browser window on the right, without you having to go online. The History feature makes Web browsing offline enjoyable and efficient, as well as being an excellent way to revisit sites that you forgot to bookmark at the time.

8 To get even more from your offline Web browser, you can configure Internet Explorer 4 or 5 to dial up the Internet on your modem, connect to a Web site and download any new content automatically while you are asleep. You get the fastest Internet connections and the Web pages are stored ready for you to view when you want. It all starts by dragging the icon to the left of the site address of the page you are interested in from the History window to the Desktop to create a shortcut to that Web site. Now right-click over the shortcut icon on the Desktop, and select **Subscribe** or, in this case, Make available offline, from the menu.

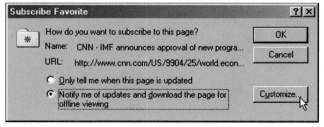

9 A window will now appear that gives you a couple of options. Make sure that the Notify Me Of Updates And Download The Page For Offline Viewing option is checked, and then click the **Customize** button.

10 This starts the **Subscription Wizard**, which makes configuring the subscription process easy. Your first choice is whether you want to download just the page selected or all the pages linked to it as well. Choosing the all pages linked option enables you to view the whole site offline, and all the links will work correctly. But it can mean a large file download and a lot of time spent online collecting the information, so make sure you really do need all the additional information before opting for this one. Make your choice and press Next.

11 You can get Internet Explorer to send you email to let you know the pages in question have changed and that the new content has been downloaded successfully. This is useful because it saves you from reading the pages only to find nothing has changed. Press Next when you have finished.

Store data offline

The amount of data that can be stored in your browser cache depends on the amount of space on your hard disk that you allocate. If you do a lot of Web browsing you will need to increase the cache size from Internet Options. If you find pages that you thought were stored offline are no longer available, it's time to increase your cache settings.

12 Configuring the download schedule is easy. Choose daily, weekly or monthly, check the box that says it's OK to dial up as needed. Select **Edit** to continue.

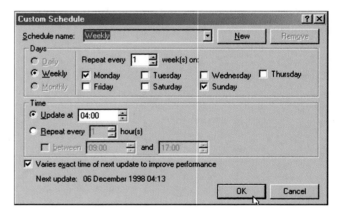

13 Select the day of the week and the time that you want the downloads. Internet Explorer can **vary the time** to avoid busy periods if it finds your specified time slows download too much. Select OK and then Next to continue.

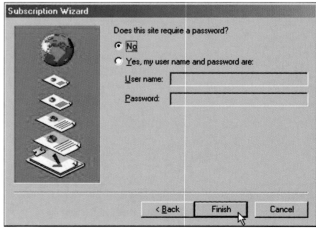

14 If the site you want to connect to is a closed one that requires a username and password, enter the details on the next screen. Select **Finish** to complete your subscription. This will take you back to the original subscription window, select OK, and it's all done. You can now surf the pages offline at your leisure, simply by entering the address in your browser or selecting the site from the Favorites folder.

Online support

If you have a problem with your hardware or software, there is bound to be a Web site where you can get help.

Support has become more expensive for computer companies. Many of them have decided to pass the cost on to customers or to offer premium support for those who are willing to pay a bit extra. They've also realized the power and convenience of using the Internet as a source for product information, advice, answers to frequently asked questions (known as FAQs) software updates and more. It's not the same as talking to a real person, and some of the sites are big enough to get lost in, but it beats listening to an engaged tone or hearing 'You are being held in a queue...'.

Microsoft

The Web site of the world's biggest software company is huge. Once you've visited a few times and bookmarked the places you think you'll need, you'll discover how valuable the site is. Microsoft routinely previews new products here (like Internet Explorer 5 and Outlook 98),

which you can download for free. There are free templates for Office users, a huge database of technical data, tips and tricks and a long list of country-specific sites. You can sign up for an email newsletter, which tells you when new stuff appears.

Compaq

The Compaq Web site is heavy on product information and news. There's a decent Presario section — Compaq's home PC — which has a list of known problems and their solutions. If that solution needs a piece of software from another vendor, there's usually a direct link. There's a list of software upgrades for such things as modems, graphics and fax cards that you can download, as well as a jargon buster, hints and tips and a friendly, interactive intro to the Presario PC. The site offers an email product information service, there's news of special offers, and, in the UK, there's a callback service.

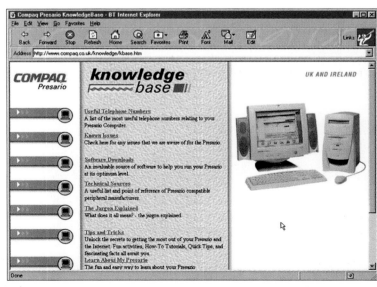

The Compaq site has helpful information, answers, and technical tips.

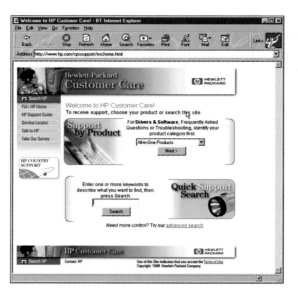

There's lots of help available at the Hewlett Packard site. The only problem is where to start.

Hewlett Packard

HP offers so much it's difficult to know where to start: Customer Care, the Support Advisor, one of the CD-ROM subscriptions, the Electronic Support Centre? There's even a faxback service. Your best bet is to click around until you find the most appropriate page. Visit the software driver section where you can download updates to various utilities.

Creative Labs

Sound cards are the bane of peoples' lives. Fortunately, the solution is often an easy one — you need the latest set of drivers. Creative Labs is clued into this,

Drivers HeadQuarters is the first port of call for software updates.

Company search tip

Don't know the address of the company Web site you're looking for? Try typing www.nameofcompany.com into the address box. If the site offers a free product update service by email, sign up for it. Then you won't have to keep going back to the site; it will tell you when anything new appears.

so you'll find directions on how to find the latest drivers on the opening page of the site. There's the usual mix of product information, but it's worth looking at the demos and free software section if you're a musician, because you'll sometimes find some useful free synthesizer sounds.

Drivers HeadQuarters

This is a super site that gathers the latest information about thousands of drivers from different PC companies. It's free, and all you pay for is the time it takes to download something. Here you'll find software updates for video adapters, CD-ROM drives, printers, modems, sound cards, scanners and more. Click on the category you want and you'll be taken to a list of the drivers currently on the site. Next to each one is the product name, a description and a link to the site where you can download it. It also features something called the Driver Detective, a free program that will zip through your system and see what versions of drivers you currently have.

Where to go

WEBSITES

- **Microsoft**
  www.microsoft.com
- **Compaq**
  www.compaq.com
- **Hewlett Packard**
  www.hp.com
- **Creative Labs**
  www.creaf.com/
- **Drivers HeadQuarters**
  www.drivershq.com

All sites were active at the time of going to press.

Message in a bottle

If you run into trouble using Windows, there are millions of other users online who would be happy to help you.

The biggest problem for the home PC user is knowing where to go for help. A knowledgeable friend can be a huge asset. But if you don't know any PC experts, or you don't want to annoy your pals by constantly asking questions, there are other ways to get help. The Net is a link to millions of Windows users. If you have a query, someone out there knows the answer.

There are several sources of help you can try. Online services like AOL, CompuServe and CIX are good places to ask questions if you have access to them. If you don't, Internet news is a great resource, and the Web itself is a mine of information. It's frustrating if you have a problem with your PC and don't know what to do. If you're on the Net, you're never alone.

Getting help from other users

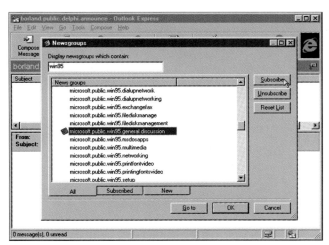

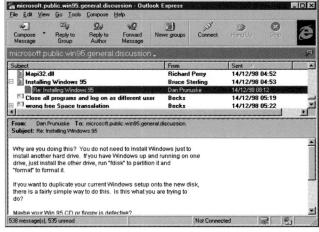

1 **Newsgroups** are the most popular discussion forums on the Internet and they are some of the best places to go to seek help and advice. If you have an Internet connection, your ISP should provide access to a news server. To read and post messages in newsgroups you can use Microsoft Outlook Express.

There are thousands of newsgroups. In order to participate in a newsgroup, you must subscribe to it. To choose the best ones to subscribe to, look at the newsgroup list (Tools, Newsgroups). Type the subject you're interested in and Outlook Express will filter the list so that only the groups with that subject in their name are displayed.

Newsgroups devoted to discussion of Windows 95 or 98 usually have names that contain win95 or win98. The microsoft.public newsgroups are the premier forums for getting help with problems because they are monitored by Microsoft. There are newsgroups for specific topics, such as disk management or printing, so you should subscribe to the most appropriate one for your problem.

2 Most of the newsgroups devoted to Windows issues are busy, so when you connect to the news server it's best to download only the **message headers**, not all the messages. Right-click the newsgroup name and select Mark for Retrieval, New Headers. When this action has completed, you will have a list showing the subject headings of each message, which will provide a clue to the question that was asked. To see the text of a message, just select it from the list and Outlook Express will download the message body.

It's considered bad form to ask a question without first checking to see if the same question has been asked in the recent past, so spend a few minutes browsing the list of headers. Messages that have replies to them are shown with a plus sign alongside. Quite often these replies will be useful answers.

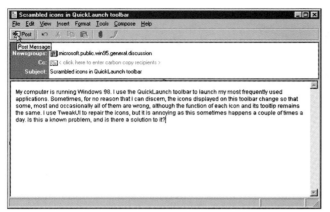

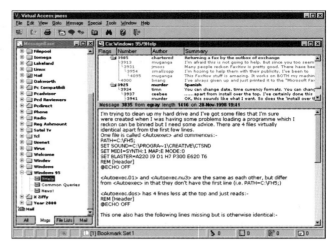

3 If you can't see any messages that answer your question, you'll have to post a message yourself. It's much like sending an email. Click the **Compose Message** button to open a window into which you can type your message. When you have finished, click the Post button to send it.

Because the newsgroups are so busy, you must do everything you can to help the person who has the answer to your question find your message. First, choose the most appropriate newsgroup to post your message. Make the subject header (which is all anyone who downloads headers only will read) a succinct description of your problem. Subject headers like Windows Problem or Help Needed aren't very useful. Keep to the point in the message body. Ask your question or describe your problem as clearly as you can. You should also make sure you provide any technical information that might be relevant, such as the version of Windows, the type of graphics card, how much memory your computer has, what other programs are running when the problem occurs and so on.

5 If you subscribe to AOL or CompuServe, these services have their own **online forums** that are available only to subscribers. Because the number of participants is restricted, there is a better chance that your question will be read and answered than in some of the busier Internet newsgroups. If you want to see what topics have been discussed before, you won't have to plough through quite so many messages.

Though less well known than the other two services, CIX is a valuable resource for computer users in the UK because it is the only online service that is UK-specific. With only around 15,000 subscribers, it has more of a community feel and offers a better chance that you will receive the help you want. CIX is different in that the software used to access its conferences (which are similar to Internet newsgroups) is designed to be used offline, so you won't run up a large phone bill while participating. For more information about CIX in the UK, call 0181 255 5000.

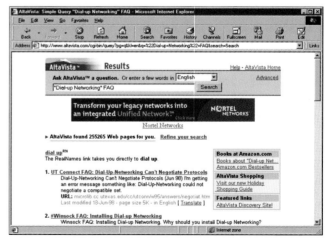

4 One of the disadvantages of Internet news is that messages aren't held on the news server for very long. You must check back regularly with the newsgroup to see if your question has been answered. One of the most valuable Internet resources is **DejaNews**. It's a searchable database of Internet news messages and a great way to find out if your question has ever previously been asked or answered.

To access DejaNews open up your Web browser and go to www.dejanews.com. In the search field enter some keywords that you would expect to see in messages related to your problem. Click Find. DejaNews will present you with a list of messages containing the words you specified. From the subject headers, you should be able to get an idea of how relevant they are. To read the full messages, just click on the hyperlinks.

6 Web sites are another invaluable source of help and information. **FAQs** are compilations of frequently asked questions (and answers) relating to a particular topic, usually created by individuals with a particular interest in that topic. A simple way to locate them is to include the keyword FAQ in your query when using a Web search engine like AltaVista. If you're interested in productivity tips and shortcuts rather than problem solutions, try searching for hints and tips instead.

Visit the Web site of your favourite computer magazine. Most magazine sites carry a wealth of information, including how-to articles and advice from the readers' help pages. Some sites even have online message boards where you can post your questions in the hope of receiving a reply.

Upgrading

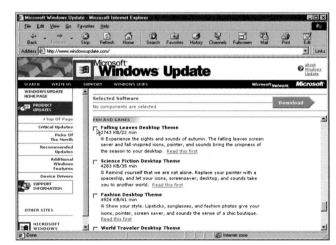

Download and install the latest Windows upgrades from the Internet.

In a perfect world, everything you bought would be fault free and run flawlessly for as long as you wanted to use it. But things aren't like that, and computers are no exception.

Software is complex and difficult to test exhaustively. Faults or bugs can occur, which can be a serious inconvenience. New hardware may appear, and existing software may not work properly with it. To remedy the problem an upgrade may be needed.

Because Windows is such a complex piece of software, upgrades are constantly being made to it. Microsoft has a Web site with the sole purpose of making upgrades available for download. Software that is developed by other manufacturers may also be upgraded from time to time. To keep your system running well, you should check for and install the latest upgrades.

Installing the latest upgrades

1 Updates for all current versions of Microsoft Windows are available from the **Microsoft Windows Update** Web site at www.windowsupdate.com. You can access the site directly from your Web browser or, if you are using Windows 98, by selecting Windows Update from the Start menu.

Besides updates for the Windows software on your computer, the Microsoft Windows Update site contains technical support information, such as on Frequently Asked Questions (FAQs) and Known Issues pages. It is worth browsing through this information because it can help you decide whether or not it is worth downloading and installing a particular upgrade. Some updates may solve problems that you will never encounter or fix Windows accessories that you never use. To see what updates are available for your computer, click on the Product Updates link.

2 Microsoft Windows Update relies on an active component that compares what software components are installed on your PC with what updates are available on the Web site. When you click on **Product Updates** this component is activated, and builds a list of updates that are appropriate to install on your PC. This means that you don't have to work out whether an update applies to your version of Windows: if it's inappropriate to install it, you won't be offered the chance.

The list of updates is grouped under headings. Critical Updates are those that Microsoft considers important that you install on your PC. They include fixes for bugs that could cause programs to crash or which create security loopholes that could allow unauthorized people to access your files. Recommended Updates are those that fix less serious problems or offer improved performance. Additional Windows Features may add new functionality to existing features or they may be completely new. In the Fun and Games category of this section you'll find new Desktop themes to enliven your computer.

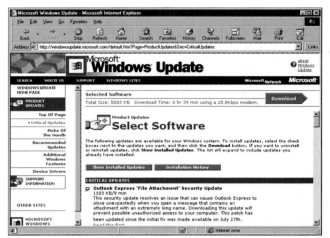

3 To select updates for installation, click the checkboxes next to the ones you want. At the top of the page you will see a tally of the total size of the updates you have selected with an estimate of the time it will take to download them. When you have chosen everything you want, click **Download**. This will start the download process. You will have to agree to an end-user licence, just as you do when installing software from disk. Upgrades from Microsoft Windows Update will be downloaded and installed automatically. If there are further steps that are specific to the item you have downloaded, they will be started automatically.

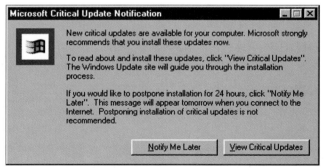

4 **Critical Updates** is a new Windows feature that you can download from the Windows Update site. It runs from the Windows Task Scheduler and checks, whenever you connect to the Internet, to see if there are any updates available in the Critical Updates category that haven't been installed on your PC.

If new critical updates are found, a warning like the one shown above will be displayed. If you don't want to bother about it at the moment, click Notify Me Later which will dismiss the warning for 24 hours. If you want to see what the new updates are, click View Critical Updates. This will take you to the Microsoft Windows Update site and show you the list of updates that are available. The new Critical Updates you need will already be selected, so all you have to do is click the Download button to download and install them.

Upgrade tip

Many of the problems solved by the Windows Critical Updates aren't really that serious for most home computer users. If you don't want to spend time downloading the updates and you haven't experienced any of the problems they are supposed to fix, don't worry about them.

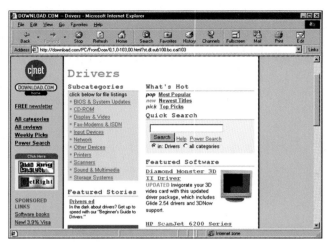

5 **Drivers** for the hardware in your computer may be available from the Windows Update site or they may be available from hardware vendors' sites. The Web site for your PC manufacturer is usually a good place to look. How the site is organized varies from one manufacturer to another, but the better sites have drivers organized by model of PC to make it easier to determine which ones are right for your computer.

The latest drivers are usually to be found on the Web site of the manufacturer of the hardware component — graphics card, printer, or whatever it is — that you need an update for. It is hard to find your way around many manufacturers' Web sites; as an alternative try one of the software archive sites like www.winfiles.com or www.download.com. These sites have links to all kinds of drivers, listed by type of hardware, making the one you want easy to find.

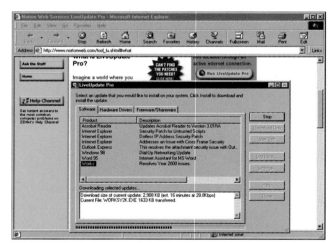

6 Drivers that you download yourself from Web sites must then be installed. If they come as an .exe file you must run it and follow the instructions. If they are in a .zip file you must unzip it and look for a Readme or similar file. This is a text file that tells you how to install the driver.

If you want an automated update system like Microsoft Windows Update that works for other software besides Windows, you need to buy a commercial product such as Norton Web Services or Cybermedia's Oil Change. These products consist of software that runs on your PC and works with your Web browser. When you run them, they connect to a special site maintained by the service provider that contains updates for a range of products. The software determines which updates are relevant for the products you own and lets you download and install them. You must pay a subscription fee to use a commercial update service, although the cost of the product will include a subscription for six months or a year.

13

Remote Access

You don't need to commute to the office five days a week to keep up with everything that's going on at work.

As communications get better and better, the need to travel decreases. Today, there is less and less need for office workers to make the daily trek to an office. They can move their PC and printer to their home and rely on the telephone network to connect to their office computer system. They become teleworkers, that is people who do their work in the usual way but depend on the telephone network to keep them in touch with their company.

Time saver

If you ever forget to take a disk of work home, with remote access you can dial the office PC and in five minutes retrieve the file you want to work on. It is a genuine time-saver and an aid to productivity.

You don't have to be a multinational company with a massive information technology budget to do this sort of thing. Remote access technology is of great use to self-employed workers as well. With a small budget, you could use a laptop at home or on the road to connect to your desktop computer to retrieve incoming faxes, email, and voice mail.

You will need

ESSENTIAL
Software Windows comes with Dial-Up Networking, which is enough software to enable remote access. If you want remote control, each PC must be running an additional third-party package, such as Symantec pcAnywhere or Traveling Software's LapLink Pro.
Hardware Two PCs, each of which must have a modem connected to a direct telephone line.

Remote access tips

● You can save time and money by sending large files in compressed form. They can then be decompressed or expanded at the other end. The best-known compression software is PKZip, which you can download from www.pkware.com/ pkzw 250.html although perhaps the best Windows 95 and 98 implementation is WinZip available at www.winzip.com.

● Try to keep the host PC as plain as possible as this will give the remote control software less work to do and will make the connection more responsive. So, for example, don't use any fancy screensavers. If the host computer is dedicated to remote use, think about turning the screen off and putting the mouse and keyboard away to stop people from accidentally switching it off. Most remote control software packages will let you the mouse and keyboard.

The equipment

Troubleshooting

When you are using a telephone line to connect to another computer, you haven't got an awful lot of bandwidth to play with and as a result the connection can seem a little sluggish. Most ordinary networks can easily manage data transfer rates of 1Mbps but you would be lucky to get 3Kbps out of even a modern modem.

There are a number of things you can do to speed up your connection. The first thing is to make sure your modem is correctly installed. It should also have the latest firmware — many modem makers post the latest firmware codes on their Web sites for you to download and install. You should check that your modem is running at the fastest possible speed. Open the Modem applet in Control Panel and click the Properties button. Check the Maximum Speed setting — if you have a V.34 or faster modem, this should be set to 115200bps. (This should be matched by the speed for your communication port - for more information, follow steps 4, 5 and 6 on pages 160-161.) Unfortunately, many modems are set to run at half this speed. Also, click the Connection tab and then the Advanced button. Make sure that the Use Flow Control option is checked and that Hardware (RTS/CTS) is selected. This makes sure that flow of data is being managed correctly. The quality of your phone line can also make a big difference to connect speeds. If you have a particularly noisy line, you should get your phone company to sort it out.

All you need to set up a remote connection is two modems and the software that comes with Windows.

A great thing about remote connectivity is that it is not expensive. The only hardware you need is two modems. You don't need any new software at all if you use Windows' Dial-Up Networking. If you want to explore remote control, you will have to buy something like pcAnywhere or LapLink and you need a separate copy for each end.

When buying modems, look for well-known brands as these tend to be more reliable and better supported. If you're buying new, you should get 56Kbps V.90 modems, even though they won't

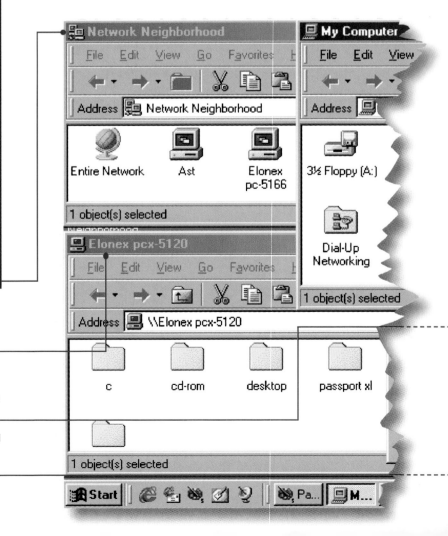

Network Neighborhood lists all the shared drives available. Here the computer can see two PCs — itself and the host computer.

The host computer shows all the shared items that you can access. It looks just like a normal Windows Explorer view.

This is a drive on the host computer that is mapped as local drive E:.

The connection information shows the duration of the call, the speed of the connection and the amount of data sent and received.

deliver their fastest speeds when used to connect to other PCs. This is because they can only connect at 56Kbps to Internet service providers. When they connect to other modems, their top speed is a mere 33.6Kbps. Even if they could connect at 56Kbps it would not be a great advantage: V.90 modems can only receive at 56Kbps and transmit at 33.6Kbps.

But if you're connecting to an office network that has a permanent Internet connection, two possibilities arise. First, you can connect to your office via the Internet. This means that you can effectively make long-distance calls for the price of a local call. Second, it means that, because you'll be connecting via an ISP, you'll be able to take advantage of the 56Kbps connect speeds.

Which software?

Both Windows 95 and Windows 98 feature **Dial-Up Networking** as standard, which allows a remote PC to access another PC or PC network. Both operating systems also include **Dial-Up Server**, which allows a PC to accept incoming calls from a remote PC trying to connect to it. If all you're after is remote access, there's no need to buy any extra software.

If you want remote control capabilities then you have to buy extra software. Don't forget that you may have to buy two copies as you'll need one copy installed and running at each end, although one or two include a two PC license. Most packages offer remote access as well as remote control plus a number of other features, such as remote printing and connecting via the Internet.

Remote control software has been around for a while, but the latest 32-bit Windows-compatible packages have made great progress in terms of ease of use, features, and versatility. There is a reasonably wide range of remote access packages available. These include **Close-Up 6.5**, **Microcom Carbon Copy 32 4.0**, **Artisoft CoSession Remote 7.0**, **Traveling Software LapLink Pro**, **Symantec pcAnywhere32 for Windows 95 8.0**, **Stac ReachOut 7.0** and **CA ControlIT 4.5**.

No single remote control package offers a perfect mix of power, ease of use and speed. But on balance two products stand out from the crowd: LapLink Pro and Carbon Copy 32 4.0. Another excellent choice is pcAnywhere 32. It's arguably the fullest featured remote access program with above average overall performance.

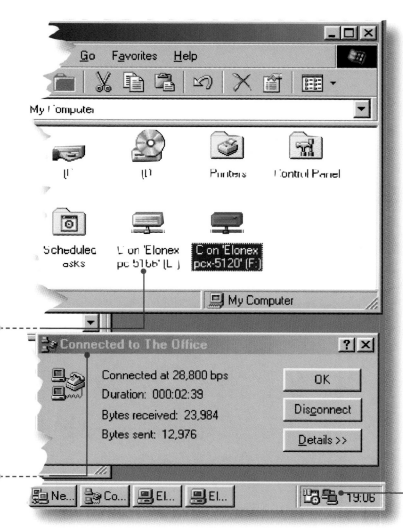

The connection status screens flash whenever data is sent and received.

Accessing your PC

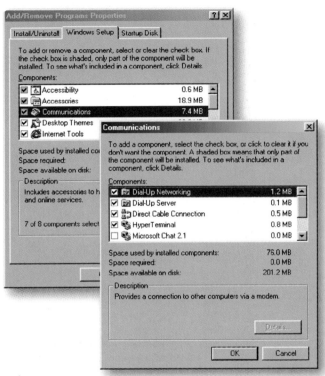

Connect to the office computer over the telephone network using Windows Dial-Up Networking.

The best way to connect two computers together via a telephone is to use the standard tools that come with Windows: Dial-Up Networking and Dial-Up Server. Armed with just a modem at each end and with this software installed, a PC will be able to access another PC as though it were directly connected to it by a network cable.

Because of modem speeds, the performance won't be as fast as a connection by cable, but you'll be able to do all the things you could if you were actually at the other PC. This technique of connecting is very useful for staff who spend a lot of time out of the office. Getting Windows remote access up and running is relatively simple.

1 At the host PC, install Dial-Up Networking and Dial-Up Server. Load the Add/Remove Programs applet in Control Panel and select the Windows Setup tab. Select **Communications** and click the Details button. Check the Dial-Up Networking and Dial-Up Server options. Click OK, then Apply.

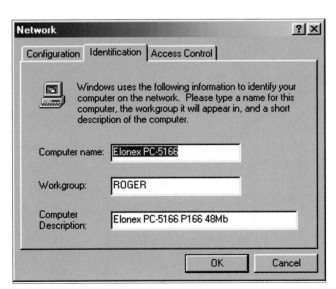

2 Load the **Network** applet in Control Panel. Make sure the NetBEUI protocol is installed in the list of installed network components. If it isn't, add it. Note the workgroup name by the Identification tab. Check that File and Printer sharing is enabled.

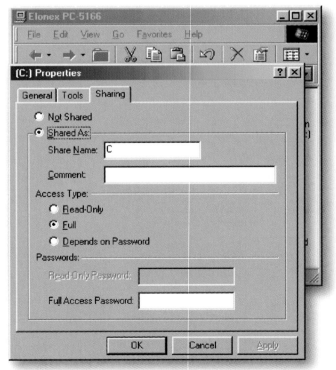

3 The next job is to share the drives or folders you want to be remotely accessible. Right-click a drive and select **Sharing** from the pop-up menu. Click Shared As and give it a share name. If you're sharing Drive C:, for example, you could call it C:. Once shared, a hand is added to the drive's icon.

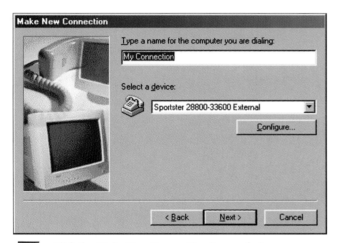

4 Open the **Dial-Up Networking** folder, click Connections and then Dial-Up Server. Click Allow Caller Access and set the password, if required.

5 Click the **Make New Connection** icon and give your connection a name, such as The Office. Click Next and enter the phone number of the modem at the other end. Click Next then Finish.

6 Right-click the new icon in Dial-Up Networking, select Properties and then click the **Server Types** tab. Select the Type of Dial-Up Server tab and from the drop-down list that appears choose Windows For Workgroups And Windows NT 3.1. Next click on OK.

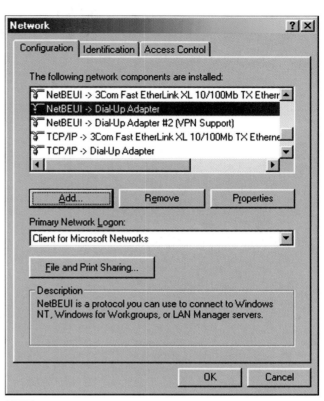

7 Load the **Network** applet in Control Panel and make sure that the workgroup name of this computer is identical to the one you're connecting to. If they differ, you won't connect. You're now ready to dial the other computer.

8 To make a **connection**, double-click the new icon in Dial-Up Networking, enter the user name and password, which is important if passwording has been activated at the other end. Your modem will now dial out and connect to the other modem. Once you've made a connection and logged in successfully, open Network Neighborhood. A little torch icon detects the network drives, and your modem lights should flash as data is received. The host PC should eventually be detected. Double-click to open the shared drives. You can, if required, 'map a drive letter'. This allows you to access a drive, directory or resource on a network as though it were local to your computer.

You can now use applications on your PC to access data files on the host PC at the other end of the line; Or you can use Explorer to copy a file from the host to your PC.

Access vs control

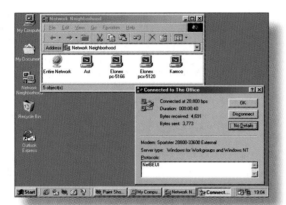

Depending on the network protocol used and network permissions, when you connect to a host computer you may also be able to access any networks the host is connected to. This will give you access to disk drives on other PCs as well.

Access tips

● If you cannot use remote control software for some reason and have to use remote access instead, you can reduce the amount of data being transferred to make your connection more responsive. The first thing you should bear in mind is that you should never try running an application over the phone line. Programs such as Word or Excel can take hours to load. Stick to transferring data and open it up using the applications on your local hard disk.

● Although it's possible to work on data stored on the host computer, this will be slow. It's a much better idea to copy the data to your local hard disk then copy it back when you have completed your work on it.

● If you have to copy a file, make sure that you are using a package like LapLink and you will only have to download the complete file once. The next time you copy the file, LapLink analyzes the original and your copy of the file and sends only the data that have changed. Alternatively, you could get someone at the other end to compress the data files to make them smaller and hence quicker to transfer.

● Another thing to avoid is browsing directories. If the computer at the other end has many hundreds of files in a folder, it can take several minutes for that directory listing to be transferred, so try and avoid random browsing.

Choose between remote access and remote control, depending on what you need to do with your remote PC.

Remote access and remote control sound similar. They perform similar functions but they are, in fact, very different. Depending on precisely what you intend to do over the phone, one or the other will be better suited to your needs. But don't worry too much. If you buy remote control software, the odds are that it will offer remote access as well.

Long-distance access

Remote access is like a long-distance network connection. It is as if you are connected to your office network, except that instead of your PC being linked to the network by a network cable, you use a phone line. Using remote access you can do everything you can do in the office: open files, copy files, print documents, send email, and so on.

  Typically you would copy data files from the office network to your remote PC, disconnect and then work on them with the applications on your remote PC. When you have finished, you reconnect and send the updated files back to the office. Access packages usually have a file synchronization feature to make sure the files on the PCs at both ends reflect recent changes.

  To cut down transfer times, most access programs use compression techniques. They save time by comparing the versions of a file on both ends and transmitting only the differences. This can make a huge difference when working on large files that change frequently, such as databases.

Remote control

Remote access works well with small data files, but to transfer large data files or to use an application not installed on your remote PC, you need remote control. When you launch a remote control session on a remote PC, your home or office PC's Desktop appears on the remote PC. It feels as if your screen, keyboard and mouse are connected to the PC at the other end of the phone line. You can run your office system's programs, load its data files and do almost anything that you could if you were in the

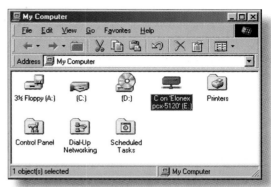

If you **map** a remote network drive it will appear as a normal disk drive, like your drive C:, in My Computer. Mapped drives are distinguished by a slightly different icon, with a network cable under them to signify a network connection.

office. The only data sent across the link is the office PC's display information and your local PC's keyboard and mouse input. The actual data files don't travel down the wire, so it's just as easy to work with mammoth files as small ones.

Pros and cons of control

Remote control applications offer various features, including a chat screen so that users of the client and host can discuss what the client is doing. There's an observation mode to allow remote users to watch a host user work without taking control, such as watching someone make changes to an interior design plan. And there is a shared work mode so two parties can jointly input on a project. Some even let you record sessions, to use as training videos.

But remote control has limitations, too. Sending a host computer's display across the phone network and replicating it on a remote computer is a slow affair, no matter how fast the two systems are. As the application runs on the host PC, a relatively simple computer is adequate at the remote end for access to the standard office programs. But the drawback is that it ties up a desktop computer in the office.

Browse with the Web

As well as using the Net for remote connections, several remote access packages can use Web browsers as client terminals, including Carbon Copy 32 and ReachOut 7.0. Microcom's Web site offers a free Netscape Navigator plug-in and Internet Explorer ActiveX control for remotely controlling a distant computer over the Internet from within your Web browser.

Upgrade tip

Even if you have Windows 98, there's one upgrade you should definitely get if you intend to do a lot of remote access: the latest release of Dial-Up Networking, version 1.3. This provides additional features for Windows 95 Dial-Up Networking that improve the performance, reliability and security of communications. There are versions for Windows 95 and Windows 98. The Windows 95 version can be downloaded from www.microsoft.com/ntserver/nts/downloads/recommended/dun13win95/default.asp and the Windows 98 is at www.microsoft.com/ntserver/nts/downloads/recommended/dun13win98.asp.

Private networks

It's not too hard to connect to other networks via the Internet, but you have to use public phone lines, so your connection is relatively insecure and eavesdropping is possible. However, it is possible to create your own virtual private network or VPN. Such systems use encryption and other security techniques to ensure that only authorized users can access the network and that the data cannot be intercepted.

Control your PC

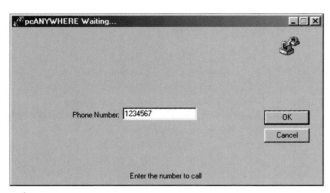

1 This example uses **Symantec pcAnywhere** as the remote control software. Your first job is to install the package on both computers. Installation is very straightforward. At the host PC, click the Be A Host PC button. Select the desired connection method, either directly over a network or by modem. In this case the modem is used. pcAnywhere is then minimized to show the Taskbar waiting for an incoming phone call.

Install a remote control package to work on your PC from long distance.

If you need to remotely access huge data files or run applications that you don't have installed on your home PC, you need to buy a remote control package. These are typically very flexible packages that offer remote access as well as remote control. Most also include some

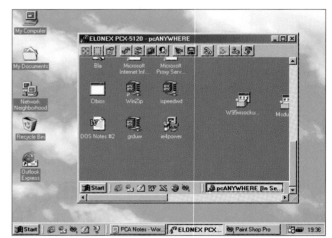

2 At the remote PC, load pcAnywhere and to connect to the host, click on the large **Remote Control** button. Select the connection method by clicking on the modem icon.

3 Next you have to enter the **phone number** of the host PC at the office and click OK. pcAnywhere then dials out. The other modem answers, the modems negotiate and a connection is established. You haven't set up any security, so there are no names or passwords to enter. It's possible to set up the host so that it calls you back, thus picking up the cost of the call.

Remote control tip

If you're using a notebook with a 640 x 480 screen to remote control a host computer with a screen running at 1,024 x 768, it's going to be a little awkward. You have two choices: you can either run the host screen in a little window and rely on the scroll bars to get you around, or you can scale down the bigger screen to fit on your screen. This is a neat trick but it can make the host computer look a little weird. So, to make life easy, why not pick a lower resolution on the host computer — say 640 x 480 or 800 x 600. To reduce the amount of screen data sent from the host computer and speed up the connection, drop the color depth from 16.7 million colours to 256.

useful features, such as automated file synchronization, good security options and file encryption and chat or speech modes. Chat modes enable two-way communication with a person at the other end — a feature that makes remote control packages very useful if you have to offer technical support. Some even allow you to remotely control a computer from any Web browser, which means that you could go to any cyber café in the world and still be able to remotely control your home or office computer.

5 When you are in control, you can work on the host PC as if you were sitting in front of it. You can **run applications** such as Word, print documents, even dial out through another modem to access the Internet. It might be a bit slow, but it's still very usable.

4 Once in control of the host PC, pcAnywhere removes any wallpaper backgrounds on the host and displays its **Desktop** in a window on the remote PC's Desktop. It is possible to run it full screen, so that you can't see your own Desktop, or scaled in a window. But when it has to scale down dramatically, because of wildly mismatched resolutions between the two PCs, the result can look rough.

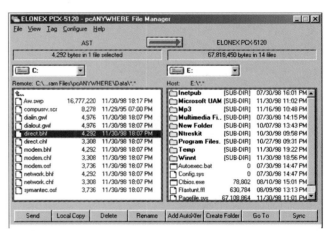

6 You can also perform file transfers. Click on the **File Transfer** button to bring up a very basic file manager, which lets you select the source and destination drives and folders on both machines. Then hit the red arrow to initiate a file transfer. You can use the Sync feature to make a specific folder identical at both ends on both PCs.

Jargon buster

Protocol An agreed format for transmitting data between two computer devices. The term is not confined to networking. Protocols can be used by serial communications for modems and to communicate with a printer. There are several networking protocols. TCP/IP is used when connecting to the Internet, IPX is used to connect to NetWare networks and NetBEUI is used to connect to peer-to-peer networks, such as Windows for Workgroups.

From a user's point of view, the only interesting aspect about protocols is that your computer or device must support the right ones if you want to communicate with other computers.

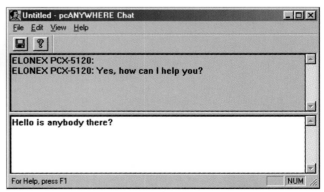

7 You can also **chat** with someone at the other end by typing in messages. It's a bit like using IRC on the Internet. If you both have sound cards and microphones you can even speak to each other over the connection.

Windows CE

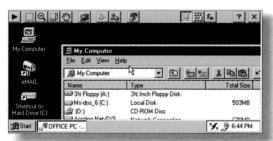

pcAnywhere CE works well, but the size of Windows CE handhelds makes the going hard.

Electrical tip

When using a modem with a Windows CE handheld PC always try to run the PDA off an electrical outlet, using the transformer. The battery life of Windows CE devices is never great and modems consume a lot of power. If you try and use a modem and you're relying on battery power, the batteries can be exhausted in less than 20 minutes.

You can access and control your home or office PC with a handheld PDA and a PC Card modem.

Incredible though it may seem, it is possible to remotely access or control a desktop PC with a handheld Windows CE PDA (personal digital assistant). All you need to add to your handheld PC is a PC Card modem and a copy of pcAnywhere CE. This is a pocket version of Symantec's product, shoehorned to run within the tight constraints of Windows CE. It's available in two versions, with host and remote modules or just the remote module.

Several connections

Installation is performed on the desktop PC while the PDA is linked to it. Several connection options are possible. You can either make the connection directly via a serial-cable session, or you can use a dial-in connection using a PC Card modem. Either way the software is easy to configure and use. To define a connection you simply tell the software what connection method you want to use, then set up a log-in name and password. The interface is like the full-size version of pcAnywhere. Each type of connection has an icon with its own properties, allowing multiple types of connections to multiple pcAnywhere hosts, but not simultaneously.

Hard to control

Since typical Windows CE handhelds have a screen no bigger than an envelope, controlling a remote screen many times its size is not without problems. You can minimize the problem by making sure that the host PC has a modest resolution, certainly not more than 800 x 600, and preferably less.

The problem is eased slightly if you used a PDA with a larger screen, such as Hewlett Packard's 360LX. It is possible to shrink the host display to fit the narrow confines of a PDA display, but don't expect icon labels or menus to be readable. A better solution is to use the scroll bars or pcAnywhere's Scroll option, which lets you scroll by dragging the pen. You have to do a lot of scrolling if you want to run any normal Windows applications on a PDA.

Glossary
A Jargon-Busting Guide

Account
If you're connected to a network or the Internet, you'll have a personal account, with your own user name and password to let you access the system and send email.

Acrobat
A file format developed by Adobe to contain complex formatting, images, and links. Acrobat documents can be displayed on a variety of platforms using a free viewer.

ActiveX
Technology developed by Microsoft to share information between applications. ActiveX controls can be embedded in Web pages, in the same way as Java applets, but unlike the latter only work on PCs.

Active window
The part of the screen currently being used, or "receiving the focus" when you type. The title bar, the top strip of the window, will usually be a different colour from that of inactive windows.

Adapter card
Printed circuit board that plugs into a PC expansion bus to communicate with other items of hardware. A display adapter, for example, connects the PC to the monitor.

Address
(1) A number that identifies a location in memory or on disk of one byte (8 bits) of data. (2) A name that identifies a destination on the Internet, such as a Web site or a mailbox.

Address book
Software with which you can list addresses. It will autodial a phone number and start a letter or email with the right address automatically filled in.

Analog
A signal that varies continuously rather than being composed of discrete steps. Sound waves and clocks with hands are analogue. Any equipment with an LED display is digital.

Animation
Moving images that can be created on a Web page using various applications, such as Macromedia Flash.

Anti-aliasing
A technique used to reduce the jagged effect of objects on screen, which is particularly noticeable when pictures are magnified. It blends the edges with dots of intermediate colors, giving smoother looking text and curves.

Anti-virus software
Software that hunts out and removes viruses on your PC. Most anti-virus software can be set to check the PC each time you switch on, but watch out for virus attacks from infected files copied on to the PC from elsewhere. (*See also Virus checker*.)

AOL
Abbreviation for America OnLine. An online service that provides a multitude of services in addition to Internet access.

Applet
Refers to small programs, such as the Windows Calculator or Character Map. Sometimes used to denote programs that can be run only from within other programs. Also refers to programs embedded in a Web page. (*See also Java*.)

Application
A program that produces useful output, such as a word processor, spreadsheet, or drawing program, rather than a utility (or applet) that serves to maintain or enhance the PC.

ASCII
Abbreviation for American Standard Code for Information Interchange. This refers to "plain text," which contains all the numbers and letters but no accented or special characters. This restriction means each character can be expressed in 7 bits instead of 8. Standard Internet mail is transmitted only in 7 bit format.

ASCII art
Illustration using ASCII characters and spaces. the smiley face :-) is an example.

Aspect ratio
The relative height and width of an image. Preserving the aspect ratio when resizing a graphic means it will remain in proportion.

Attachment
A file that is attached to an email message for electronic transfer. As Internet email can handle only 7 bit traffic, and application or graphic files are 8 bit, the mailing software encodes the file into a 7 bit form before adding it as plain text to the message. If you see a block of apparent gibberish at the bottom of an email message, that is almost certainly an attachment. Binhex, MIME, and UUE are all common standards of encoding.

Audio file
File containing digital sample data from a sound. In Windows, audio files normally have a .wav extension and are played back using Sound Recorder in the Accessories group.

Authoring software
Applications designed to create multimedia publications, presentations, or demonstrations, with sound, images, video, and hypertext. Macromedia Director and Asymetrix Toolbook are two well-known authoring products.

AVI
Abbreviation for Audio/Video Interleaved. A standard for storing synchronized sound and video in a single file. AVI files can be played using the Windows Media Player applet.

Backbone
The means by which the Internet service provider (ISP) is connected to the Internet. If you imagine the ISP as the size of a drainpipe, the backbone pipes are the size of a railway tunnel in comparison.

Background
(1) The picture or pattern used behind the icons and windows on your Desktop; also called Wallpaper. (2) A task that the PC performs while you carry on doing something else. For example, many word processors will check spelling and paginate a document as you type. (3) A repeated pattern of small graphic files that forms the background to a Web page.

Background printing
A system-wide background task. When you choose the Print command in an application, the job is sent to the Windows Print Manager, which queues up print jobs and carries them out as you continue working.

Bandwidth
The amount of data that can be transmitted in a given time. The term is used in the context of PC internals or peripherals, and, more usually, in relation to the Internet. If a Web site is running out of bandwidth, it becomes slow to access because too many people are trying to connect at the same time.

Banner ad
The small, discreet panels, often seen at the top of Web pages, advertising goods and services. Usually these are interactive: a mouse click takes you to the advertiser's own Web site.

Baud or baud rate
This describes the number of signal changes per second that occur in data transferred in a communications system such as the Internet. This is not the same as the quantity of data sent every second. (*See Bits per second.*)

BBS
Abbreviation for Bulletin Board System. This is an electronic messaging and file download system available free or by subscription. Online services that also offer Internet access are taking over, but BBSs are still available. Some are maintained by computer companies for downloading drivers and upgrades.

Beta software
An interim version of a new or upgraded program sent out by developers to beta testers outside the company. The latter use the software in real-world situations and report back about problems. This gives the developers a chance to correct these before the final version of the software is released.

Bigfoot
An Internet-based directory for locating names.

Binflex
An email attachment coding system for users of Apple Macintosh computers.

Bitmap
A bitmap image is made up of tiny dots or pixels. As you zoom in, the dots grow larger.

Bits per second (bps)
The number of single bits of data that can be sent every second over a network or a communications system such as the Internet. When checking the specification of a modem, make sure it is describing bits per second and not baud rate.

Blinking
A way of reducing the cost of using online services. The process of blinking involves connecting to a service for just long enough to send a pre-written message and to retrieve incoming data.

.bmp
The filename extension given to files that store bitmap image data. If you use the Paint utility in Windows, you can save or open BMP files created in any other paint program.

Bookmark
A code inserted in a document, multimedia title, or on a Web

page, so you can move straight back to that point at a later date. Software keeps a list of the bookmarks you have inserted and their position.

Briefcase utility

A program that allows you to keep files up to date if you use a notebook computer away from home. When you return, connect the notebook to your PC and the briefcase utility will update the files on each machine.

Browser

A program used for viewing pages on the World Wide Web. Netscape Navigator and Microsoft Internet Explorer are the most popular browsers, but there are others. Many include extra features for using email, taking part in newsgroups, and sending or receiving files. Browsers are all-purpose tools for every type of Internet activity.

Buffer

An area in memory that's used for temporarily storing information. For example, if you send a file to print before you have switched the printer on, the data is stored in a print buffer until the printer is ready.

Bulletin Board Service (BBS)

Bulletin boards contain free software and forums where you can discuss topics with others. More sophisticated systems have links to other bulletin boards and the Internet. To access a bulletin board, you need a modem and communications software.

Cache

A section of high-speed memory that temporarily stores data before it is used by the PC's processor, increasing the speed at which data is read from a hard disk.

CAD

Abbreviation for Computer Aided Design. Software that allows designers and architects to draw precise blueprints on screen and view them in 3D to see how the design will appear before anything is manufactured.

Callback

Security system used to reduce the risk of unauthorized users connecting to your PC if you have installed dial-in networking (part of Windows 95 and 98.)

Capture

(1) If you want to store the image that is currently displayed on the screen in a file, you can 'capture' it. In Windows, you can save the current screen as a graphics image by pressing the Print Screen key on the keyboard. (2) If your PC is on a network that shares one printer and you want to print, you can 'capture' the printer using the Printer icon in the Control Panel group.

Carbon copies

Email programs such as Outlook Express and Eudora allow you to keep or forward copies of emails, known as carbon copies.

Carrier (signal)

A continuous, steady sound tone that is used by a modem to send data along a telephone wire. The modem changes the frequency of the carrier — the tone — to represent different characters.

CD-R

Abbreviation for CD-Recordable, a type of CD drive and disc that can be recorded on.

CD-RW

Abbreviation for CD ReWritable. An extension of the CD-R format. CD-RW discs can be re-recorded.

Cell

(1) A single frame in an animation. (2) The boxes that hold data or calculations in a spreadsheet.

Censorship

Internet Explorer's Content Advisor option allows you to control the level of sexual content and violence that may be downloaded into your browser. However, the effectiveness of this depends on page owners giving their sites a rating, so normal supervision is the best all-round approach.

Channel

(1) One layer of an image that can be worked on separately. (2) A method of identifying each instrument in a MIDI orchestra. There are 16 channels and an instrument can be assigned to each. (3) In Microsoft's Internet Explorer 4, channels allow you to turn your computer into a virtual tuner by accessing and updating the content of a particular Web site's channel either online (whenever the Web site is updated) or offline (downloading the updated content at specific times that you choose.)

Chat

The facility of being able to talk to people over the Internet instantly, usually by typing in text, but also, if you have a microphone and appropriate software, by speaking. Internet sites where like-minded people can share their interests are known as chat rooms.

Checkbox

Small boxes that give you a set of options. To select an option, move the pointer on to the check box and click once; the box will now have a cross in it. If you don't want the option, click a second time and the cross will be deleted.

Chip

A small thin piece of silicon crystal onto which is etched a tiny circuit with hundreds of thousands of components. These components will do simple mathematical operations, such as adding and subtracting numbers (in a processor chip) or storing numbers (in a memory chip.)

Client/server

A way of organizing computer networks. The PC that you use is called the client. It sends instructions to a powerful computer called the server. The server processes the instructions and sends an answer back to the client.

Clip art

A collection of ready-made, public-domain images, borders, and icons for use in your own presentations or desktop published documents, sometimes supplied with a software program.

Clipboard

An area of memory that is used for temporary storage of data, for example when you cut some text to paste it elsewhere. In Windows, the Clipboard can store any type of data — text, audio, and images.

COM1

Name used in PCs to represent the first serial port. If you plug an external modem into the first serial port, you are connecting it to COM1. There are usually two serial ports (COM1 and COM2) in a PC, although it can support four. Some PCs have a mouse plugged into the first serial port and the modem plugged into the second port.

Communications software

A software program that works with a modem to send and receive information over a phone line to and from other computers and online services.

Compression

To reduce the size of a large file by encoding the data. Compression software programs can reduce the size of files but you have to use decompression software to read the files again.

CompuServe

An online service that can be accessed via phone lines with a modem. CompuServe offers its subscribers a range of services, including email, information services, and databases.

Computer names

In Windows, each computer that is connected to a network is given an identifying name. Double click on the NN icon on your Desktop for a list of other computers on the network.

Cookie

A small text-only file sent by a Web server to your Web browser that records your movement on a Web site and any preferences or information you may have entered such as log-in or registration information.

Crash

This is what happens when your computer freezes up and won't respond. The only way to get out of this is to switch off or reset (using the reset button or by pressing Ctrl-Alt-Del at the same time.) Unfortunately, you will lose anything you've input since you last saved your work, so make sure that you save your work regularly.

Cyber cafés

These combine a coffee shop with computers to access the Internet. They are useful if you want to try out the Internet to see if you like it without having to buy a modem and open an ISP account.

Database

Software that lets you enter information into a file so that it can be organized and searched. For example, a database could contain names and addresses. Each separate entry is called a record, and each individual part of a record is called a field.

Dedicated

A PC or printer that is only used for one particular job, such as storing data.

Default

Options that are used if no others are specified. For example, if you run a word processor and start typing a letter, it will use the default typeface, paper size and margins. You can always change the default settings.

Demo

A trial version of software. It shows the main features but has been crippled in some way. Sometimes you cannot save the work, or it will only work for a few weeks. (See Shareware.)

DHTML

Abbreviation for Dynamic HyperText Markup Language. This allows you to create Web pages that respond dynamically to user input. DHTML coding can bring a page alive when the user is browsing it by, for example, changing the color of header text when the pointer moves over it.

Dialer
Any separate utility program or a feature of a larger program that dials telephone numbers for you using a modem.

Dial-up connection
The process of connecting to another computer via a telephone line. A dial-up connection is the most common method of accessing the Internet via an Internet service provider.

Digital
Numbers and signals that can be processed by a computer. PCs cannot deal with analogue signals so converters are necessary. For example, a sound card contains an analogue to digital converter to adapt the sound signal from a microphone into numbers representing volume and tone.

Direct cable connection
A utility or small program that lets you link two computers together using a serial cable plugged into each serial port. The two computers can exchange files and share a printer.

Directory
Another name for a folder. A directory can contain files, other directories, or a mixture of both. (See Folder.)

DirectX
A collection of APIs (Application Programming Interfaces) that programmers and developers can use to write games and multimedia applications.

Disk tools
A set of software programs that help you monitor the performance of your hard disk, maintain it in good condition, and ensure that it's storing data efficiently.

Domain
(1) Groups of users or resources on a network. (2) Sections of the Internet, identified in the site name, for example .com (commercial or company).

Drive letters
A PC usually has two, three, or four disk drives. There's one floppy-disk drive A: and one hard-disk drive C:. If you have a second floppy-disk drive, this is called B:, and a CD-ROM drive is D:. More advanced PC configurations use additional drive letters to identify areas on a network, for example.

Driver
A piece of software that translates the instructions from Windows into a form that can

be understood by a peripheral piece of equipment such as a printer.

DVD
Abbreviation for Digital Versatile Disc. A CD format that can store seven times as much as an ordinary CD-ROM (4.7Gb) and future versions will be able to store 17Gb. Its main attraction is to play movies and advanced multimedia titles.

E-commerce
Business conducted on the Internet.

EDI
Abbreviation for Electronic Data Interchange. The transfer of data between companies and institutions using networks, such as the Internet. It is a popular way for companies to do business.

Electronic mail (email)
A way of sending and receiving messages on a network. If you are connected to the Internet, you can send messages to any other user who is also connected to the Internet, provided you both have the necessary software.

Encryption
The conversion of data into a secret code. Files are encrypted using a password and must be unscrambled using the same password. Encrypted files may be opened without a password but their contents will be meaningless.

Esc key
A key in the top left corner of a keyboard that is used to cancel an action. In Windows, pressing Esc is the same as selecting the Cancel button. If you press Alt+Esc, you will move between active program windows.

Ethernet
A cabling standard used for networking. Ethernet defines the type of cable, signal, and language used if you connect several computers. It's the most common standard used when creating an office network. The others are Token Ring and ARCnet.

Eudora
A popular software program for sending and receiving email.

Exchange
A program supplied with Windows to manage your communications. Exchange can control a fax modem, send and receive emails, and send and receive messages to users on the Net. (See Windows Messaging.)

.exe file
The three-letter filename extension – short for executable

– that indicates a file is a program that can be run without using another application.

Expansion card
A set of electronic components on a plastic card that expands the functions of your PC. For example, if you want to connect your PC to a network, you will need to add a network expansion card. If you want to fit external speakers to your PC, you will need to add a sound card.

Expansion slot
An electrical connector fitted to the motherboard that allows the electrical signals from the computer's expansion bus to be read by the expansion card.

Explorer
A program supplied with Windows to help you manage all the files stored on a disk.

Export
To convert a file so that it can be read by a different program. For example, if you have written a letter in Microsoft Word and want to give it to a friend who uses WordPerfect for Windows, you need to export the Word document to a WordPerfect format file using the File/Save As option in Word.

Extension
The three-letter code at the end of a file name that indicates the type or format of the file. For example, a filename might be Letter1 with the extension .doc. The three-letter extension, .doc, shows the file is a document. Similarly, .bmp means a bitmap file, .exe means an executable program file, and so on.

E-zines
Web-based magazines.

FAQ
Abbreviation for Frequently Asked Questions. A FAQ (pronounced fak) is a document that answers questions on specific topics. FAQs are posted on the Net to save technical support staff from having to deal with the same questions repeatedly.

Fax
A PC can send and receive fax messages, just like a fax machine, provided you have a fax modem and the appropriate software.

Fax on demand
A facility that allows the machine to respond automatically when a caller requests that a particular fax be sent to them. For fax on demand (or fax back) you must have a voicemail program.

File transfer
To send a file from one computer to another over a serial connection, such as a modem link or cable, between a desktop and laptop PC.

Filename
A name (with no spaces) that identifies a file stored on disk.

Filtering
In the context of email programs such as Outlook Express, filtering allows you to define rules which are applied to email as it arrives in order to filter out unwanted items.

Folder
An organized list of files on a disk. Folders are a way of subdividing a hard disk to make files easier to find. A folder can contain files, further folders, or a mixture of both.

Forums
Chat areas on the Internet, provided by AOL, CompuServe, and MSN.

FPS
Abbreviation for Frames Per Second. The number of frames in a video sequence that can be displayed each second. To give the impression of full-motion video, your PC needs to display 25 frames per second.

Frames
Windows that can be displayed within a single Web page at the same time. For example, you may have an index frame at the top of the page which stays in view while you browse other parts of the same site in a separate frame that takes up the rest of the page.

Freeware
Fully functioning free software that can be downloaded off the Internet.

FTP
Abbreviation for File Transfer Protocol. A method of transferring files from one computer to another over the Internet.

Full-duplex
This means your sound card can record and play back audio simultaneously so, providing you have speakers and a microphone, you can have a proper conversation. Half-duplex sound cards let only one person speak at a time.

.gif file
Abbreviation for Graphics Interface Format. This is a commonly used format for storing images and bitmapped color graphics, now one of the most popular formats for images stored on the Internet.

Graphics card
The electronic circuit that produces the picture you see on a computer monitor. Usually a separate card plugs into one of the expansion sockets inside a PC, but some manufacturers build the graphics circuit into the motherboard. It is also known as a graphics adapter, graphics accelerator, video adapter, and display adapter.

Graphics file
A file that contains data which describes an image. Web browsers generally recognize only .gif and .jpg graphics.

Handshaking
Signals sent between two communication devices, such as two modems, to establish how they should send and receive data.

Hang
A term that means a computer has stopped responding because of a fault.

Hayes-compatible
Hayes is a manufacturer of modems that let you send data over the phone. The company standardized the software commands that allow a PC to control a modem. These are also known as the AT command set.

History
A feature of some applications that keeps a log of the actions you have carried out, the places within a hypertext document you have visited, or the sites on the Net you have explored.

Hit
A unit of measurement of Web page activity. One hit equals one page visit, so a single visitor may generate dozens of hits as they wander around your site.

Home key
A key on a computer's keyboard in the group above the four cursor control keys. It will move the cursor to the start of the current line. Some word processing programs will move the cursor to the start of the document if you press the Home key twice.

Home page
The first page on a Web site. It is often also used as an alternative term for a personal Web site, referring to the entire thing as a home page.

Hotkey
A keystroke, or combination of strokes, that carries out a command without recourse to the menus and mouse. It is also known as a keyboard shortcut combination. For example, F1 summons help and Control+S saves your work in most applications.

Hotspot
In a multimedia title, an area of an image or text that does something if you click on it. You can tell that there is a hotspot in an image because the mouse pointer changes shape from an arrow to a hand.

HTML
Abbreviation for HyperText Markup Language. A series of special codes that define typeface and style and allow hypertext links to other part of the document or to other documents. A document coded in HTML can be displayed on any viewer software that understands HTML, such as Mosaic or Netscape Navigator.

HyperTerminal
A communications program that is included with Windows and allows you to call a remote computer via a modem and transfer files. It is useful to access bulletin boards or other online services.

Hypertext
A way of organizing information in multimedia titles. Certain words in the text include a link (or hyperlink) to another part of the document. In order to move there, click on the word.

Icon
A small picture that identifies a command or file. In Windows, each application you install has its own icon and its data files often use the same one.

Image editor
Software that lets you edit, change, or paint new parts of an image. Windows has a basic image editor called Paint.

InBox
A facility to store your email and fax messages. Double-click on the InBox to send messages or read new ones.

Input
To put information into a computer. When you type text on your keyboard, you are inputting data into the computer. Other examples are using a scanner or using a mouse to draw on screen.

INS key
A key on a PC that switches the typing mode between insert and overwrite.

Interface
More properly known as graphical user interface (or GUI, pronounced gooey), this is the link between an operating system or program and the person using it, a method of representing files, folders and functions with icons.

Internet (Net)
An international network that links thousands of computers using telephone and cable links. Users connect via a modem to server computers called Internet Service Providers, which are like local phone exchanges. You can send email and transfer files over the Internet around the world for the price of a local phone call. To get onto the Internet, you need a modem and an account with an Internet Service Provider.

Internet Relay Chat (IRC)
An Internet-based system allowing like-minded people to chat to each other using an IRC program.

Internet Service Provider (ISP)
A company that, for a fee, allows you to dial up its computers to gain access to the Internet. Fees are usually payable monthly in advance and it is generally less expensive to sign up for unlimited access at a fixed fee, rather than be billed for time online.

Internet telephony
An Internet phone allows you to talk to anyone anywhere in the world, for the price of a local call.

Internet Explorer
Microsoft's browser, used to access and view Web pages.

IP address
The numerical code that identifies the address of your computer and its ISP; a set of four numbers separated by dots.

Java
A programming language used on the Web. Small programmes called Java applets can be downloaded from a Web site and run on your PC by a Java-compatible Web browser, such as Netscape Navigator or Microsoft Internet Explorer. Java provides more facilities than are available through HTML. (*See HTML.*)

JPEG
Abbreviation for Joint Photographic Experts Group. This is a standard you may come across if you use graphic images. JPEG is a complex way of storing images in a compressed format so they take up less disk space.

.jpg
File extension used for files compressed in the JPEG format.

Junk email
Unsolicited email. This may be deleted or filtered out using your email program's filtering rules.

K56flex
Technology for boosting the receive rate of modems from 33.6Kbps to 56 Kbps over ordinary phone lines.

LCD screen
Abbreviation for Liquid Crystal Display screen, used for portable PCs.

LDAP
Abbreviation for Lightweight Directory Access Protocol, the method used to search the databases of Internet people-finding services.

LinkExchange
The best-known free banner exchange scheme allowing you to place a banner ad for your site on any of the hundreds of thousands of Web pages that are registered with LinkExchange. In return, your Web pages must display a participating site banner.

Local area network
A communications network linking several computers within an office or building so that you can exchange files or messages with other users or send files to a printer.

LocalTalk
The standard used by Apple to connect Macintosh computers together in a local area network. To connect your PC to a Mac network, you need to get a LocalTalk network adapter and software.

Lookup
One computer requesting information from a directory held on another computer.

Macintosh (Mac)
A range of personal computers made by Apple computers that use a different architecture, processor, and operating system from PCs. Some Macs can run PC programs.

Mailing lists
These enable email-based discussion. The Liszt Web site at www.liszt.com allows you to select a category.

Mapping drives/ printers
A way of accessing printers or files on the hard disks of other computers in a local area network. Assign a drive letter to the file/printer you want. This is called mapping a network drive.

Media
(1) A vague term used to mean something that will store or carry information. It generally refers to floppy disks or CD-ROM discs. (2) Information used within a multimedia presentation which could be sound, graphics or video.

Microsoft Frontpage
A Web page editor that allows you to create Web sites using templates for pages such as a search facility, a frequently asked questions (FAQ) page, feedback forms, and more.

Microsoft Network (MSN)
An online service that provides information, links to the Internet, and email.

MIDI file
A file that contains musical notes and sound information that can be sent via a MIDI (Musical Instrument Digital Interface) card. MIDI files can also contain information that describes the type of sound played as well as the note.

MIME
Abbreviation for Multipurpose Internet Mail Extensions, the most common system used by email applications to allow the automatic posting and display of email attachments.

Motherboard
The main circuit board in a computer. If you open your PC you'll see the motherboard at the bottom of the case. It's normally varnished green to protect the tiny connections and has the main electronic components and connectors soldered onto it.

Modem
A device to convert electronic signals from your PC into sound signals that can be transmitted by phone. To receive information the modem works in reverse and converts the sound signals back into digital electronic signals. Modems are used to connect to the Internet and for sending and receiving faxes.

MPEG
Abbreviation for Moving Picture Experts Group. The term also refers to the video compression systems which provide higher-quality video than Video for Windows.

Multimedia
The combination of text, images, video, sound, and animation within an application.

Multi-tasking
The ability of Windows to run several programs at once. The trick is that Windows switches very rapidly between tasks, giving you the impression that they are running in parallel.

Netiquette
Rules of courtesy that apply when dealing with other people on the Internet.

Netscape Navigator
A popular browser for accessing and viewing Web pages. It comes as part of Netscape's Communicator Suite.

Network
A way of connecting several computers and printers so that they can share data. To set up a network, each computer needs a network interface card and a cable. If linked to a network, you'll be able to send files and messages to other users.

Network drive
A disk drive you can access that is located on another computer on the network.

Network Neighborhood (NN)
An icon that appears on the Desktop if you are connected to a network. Double-click on NN and you'll see all the computers linked to the network.

Network protocol
A language that allows computers to communicate over a network. If a computer uses the wrong protocol, other computers will not be able to understand it. As well as using the right protocol, your computer must be set up to know its Internet address as well as the name and password to use to connect to your Internet service provider.

Network server
A dedicated computer used to support office networks.

Newsgroups
A feature of the Net that uses Usenet to allow interactive access to special interest groups.

Notebook computer
Small portable computer that is usually lighter than a laptop and has a smaller LCD screen and keyboard.

Null modem cable
Special cable that lets you link two PCs via their serial ports.

Object linking and embedding (OLE)
A system that lets you cut and paste data from one application to another, retaining the formatting and controls.

OCR
Abbreviation for Optical Character Recognition. Software to convert printed text into characters you can change on screen with a word processor.

Office suites
A complete package of software programs such as word processor, spreadsheet, database, graphics editor, and desktop publishing.

Offline browsing
Using your browser offline, drawing on pages that have previously been downloaded into the browser's cache. (See Cache.)

Offline reader (OLR)
Software that collects all messages fed into an offline database (from a discussion group, for example.) Read and reply offline, then connect again and send them back.

Online
(1) A modem that is connected to another modem via a telephone line and is currently transferring information. (2) A printer that is ready and waiting to print.

Online Service Provider (OSP)
A company that connects you to the Internet and provides its own commercial services.

Open
(1) To access a file and read its contents using an application. Most Windows applications will read a file via the File/Open menu option. (2) To look inside a folder to view the list of files or sub-folders stored in it. Open a folder with a double-click.

Operating system
The software that controls the actions of the different parts of your PC. In most PCs, Windows manages the screen, keyboard, disks, and printers.

Outlook Express
Microsoft's email program that comes bundled with Internet Explorer 4 and 5, and with Windows 98.

Paintbrush/Paint
Application supplied with Windows that lets you create or edit bitmap images.

Palmtop computer
Tiny hand-held computer.

Parallel port
A socket at the back of your PC that lets you connect it to a printer. A parallel port sends data to the printer over eight parallel wires.

Password
A secret code associated with your user name, which confirms your identity. If you subscribe to an online service you will have a public user name and number and a secret password that only you know.

Patch
A small program that will fix an error in a larger program.

Path
A series of directories or folders that locate a particular file.

PCI
Abbreviation for Peripheral Component Interconnect. A high-speed connection on the motherboard of your computer that can be used by components that need to exchange large chunks of data fast.

.pcx file
Method of storing a graphics file. The standard is widely used and is a good way of moving files between paint programs.

Phone dialer
Utility supplied with Windows that allows you to dial phone numbers from your computer. You need a modem and to be connected to the phone network, plus a normal telephone handset to use once you have dialed the number.

PING
A program that tests the nodes on a network or Internet link to ensure they are working correctly. If you use the Internet, you might see a message saying PING Tested. This means your ISP has tested its connections to other computers.

Platform
The type of hardware or the combination of hardware and system software that make up a particular range of computers. The PC-compatible platform usually means a computer that has an Intel-compatible processor running Windows. When you buy a new piece of software, the box lists the type of platform that the software requires to run it.

Platform independence
This describes programs that can work with different types of incompatible hardware.

Plug and play
A hardware and software development which means that when you plug a new adapter card — or a disk controller, network adapter or graphics adapter — into your computer, you don't have to configure it or set any switches. Windows will automatically configure and set up the new adapter.

Polling
A system to allow a fax machine to retrieve documents from one or more other machines while unsupervised.

POP
Abbreviation for Point of Presence. A telephone access number for a service provider that you can use to connect to the Internet. Most service providers have dozens of POPs across the country so you can connect to the Net with a local-rate call.

Port

Communications channel that allows a computer to exchange data with a peripheral. On the back of your computer, you'll see a range of connectors. They are all ports between your computer and peripherals.

PPP

Abbreviation for Point to Point Protocol. A set of commands that allows a PC to use the TCP/IP protocol over a phone connection. Normally, TCP/IP will work only over a network, but the PPP system fools it into working over a phone line. The TCP/IP protocol is the way in which computers talk to each other over the Internet. You must use the PPP system if you want to connect to the Internet using a modem.

Program

A self-contained set of software codes that is used to accomplish a particular task, such as word processing. A program file has an extension of .exe.

Properties

The attributes of a file or object. To view or edit all the properties of a file, select the file with a single click to highlight the name, and right-click once. This displays a menu of options. Select the Properties menu option and you will see the various properties for the object.

Protocol

A set of codes and signals that allows two different computers to communicate. A simple protocol ensures that data is correctly transferred from a PC to a printer along the printer cable. Other protocols ensure that a PC can communicate via the Internet or over a network. If you cannot get two PCs to exchange information, it's likely that they are using differenct protocols.

Public domain (PD)

Software that has no copying fee or restrictions. Public domain software is rare, as it means there is no copyright. More usual is freeware, in which the author retains copyright, but allows free distribution.

Push techology

This turns the Internet into a virtual TV in the way it delivers information. Instead of browsing the Web, you tune into a channel and whatever programs are on that channel are sent to your screen. By subscribing to, say, a news service, you can have news headlines delivered to your Desktop at regular intervals without having to go to a Web page to retrieve it.

Radio button

A circle displayed beside an option that has a dark center when selected. Radio buttons are a method of selecting one of a number of options. Only one radio button in a group can be selected at any one time. If you select another in the group, the first is deselected.

Real time

Processing time which is almost instant. This means the PC can solve a problem quickly and its result can influence the source of the data. For example, air traffic control PCs have to analyze the position of aircraft in a second so instructions can be issued and collisions avoided. If the PC was not working in real time, it would spend ten minutes calculating the action.

Remote access

To use your PC from another location with a phone link. You need two PCs, each with a modem, and special remote access software which is built into Windows. This allows you to dial one PC and access the files and folders on its hard disk.

Remote control

Far more powerful than remote access because it includes control over the applications on another PC. When you launch a remote control session on a remote PC, your home or office PC's Desktop appears on the remote PC and you can run your main one as if you were actually there.

Remote retrieval

Lets you call into your PC from another location to check your messages and faxes. Messages are played over the phone and faxes are redirected to a computer or fax machine near you.

Resource

A device which is available on a network or on a computer that can be used by an application or system software. This is a general term and can mean a disk drive on your PC or a printer connected to another computer on a network.

Right-click menu

A small menu that appears when you right-click the mouse. It is often used to select formatting or the properties of an object. In Windows, if you right-click over a blank part of the Desktop you can set the properties of the Desktop or create a new shortcut. If you right-click over a file or folder you can change its properties.

Safe mode

A special operating mode of Windows that is selected if a problem is detected when starting. Safe mode does not let you do anything except try to work out and fix the problem.

Scanner

A device that uses photo-electric cells to convert a drawing, photograph, or document into data that can be manipulated by a PC.

SCSI

Abbreviation for Small Computer Systems Interface. This is a high-speed parallel interface used to connect PCs to peripheral devices such as disk drives and scanners.

Search engine

An Internet-based search system which catalogues Web pages, allowing you to search for subjects, words, or phrases, or Internet addresses (URLs.) Two popular search engines are AltaVista and Excite.

Secure server

A safe method of exchanging credit card details between customers and shop on the Internet. The credit card information is encrypted so that if it were intercepted *en route*, it would be scrambled.

Send To command

A direct link to the email system running on your PC, such as Microsoft Exchange. Choose the Send To menu option and you can send a document as an email to another user on the network or you can send it as a fax to a fax machine.

Serial port

A connector and circuit used to convert data in a PC so that it can be transmitted in a single stream through an external cable.

Shareware

Software that is available free for you to sample. If you want to keep it, you are expected to pay a fee to the writer. Often confused with public-domain software that is completely free.

Shockwave

Multimedia content created using special software and viewed off a Web page by a Shockwave player plugged into your Web browser.

Shortcut

An icon placed on the Desktop in Windows that links to a file, folder or program stored on the disk. The shortcut has the same icon as the original file except for a tiny arrow in the bottom left-hand corner. The shortcut is not a duplicate of the original – it is a pointer to the original.

Signature

(1) An authentication code, such as a password, which you give prior to accessing a system or prior to the execution of a task to prove your identity.
(2) A sentence or paragraph used to end email messages and comments posted on the Internet.

Site management

The ability to look after your Web pages once you have created them, for example by checking that the hyperlinks to other sites are still working and updating time-sensitive data.

SLIP

Abbreviation for Serial Line Internet Protocol. A protocol that lets a PC communicate with the Net via a serial connection (modem and phone link) rather than a direct network connection.

Smileys

These are combinations of simple ASCII (plain text) symbols that can be used in emails, newsgroups, or chat rooms, to indicate simple emotions, e.g. :-) (I am happy) :-((I am sad.)

Sound card

An add-on device that plugs into an expansion slot inside your PC and generates analogue sound signals. The sound card generates sound from digital data, using either a digital to analogue converter or an FM synthesis chip.

Sound file

A file stored on disk that contains sound data. This can either be a digitized analogue sound signal or notes for a musical instrument digital interface (MIDI) instrument.

Sound Recorder

A Windows utility that lets you play back digitized sound files (the .wav standard) or record sound onto disk and carry out very basic editing once you have recorded the sound.

Spam

Junk email which can be sent to millions of people for little cost. Targeting methods are rarely used, resulting in all kinds of rubbish being sent.

Streaming audio

Instead of having to download an entire file before hearing a track, special software starts to play back the track as soon as possible, by downloading a file into a buffer, so that after a short delay it starts to play the music from there.

String

Any series of consecutive alpha-numeric characters or words

manipulated and treated as a single unit by the PC.

Suite
A collection of programs sold together. The best-known suites are for businesses and include word processing, presentation, spreadsheet, database, and communications programs. Suites are also available for use in specialist areas such as graphics creation, image manipulation, and Internet communications.

Surfers
People who spend some time wandering around the World Wide Web looking at Web sites.

Swap file
A file stored on the hard disk used as a temporary storage area for data held in RAM, to provide virtual memory.

System
A general term that refers to a computer, to a computer and its associated peripherals, or to the operating system software such as Windows.

TCP/IP
Abbreviation for Transmission Control Protocol/Interface Program. This is a set of standard commands used in networks and the Internet to allow computers to exchange information.

Telecommuting
Working at home on a computer that is linked by modem to a central office allowing messages and data to be transferred.

Teleconferencing
To link video, audio, and computer signals from different locations so that distant people can talk and see each other.

Template
A file containing text presented in a standard way, such as a memo or an invoice, into which specific details such as company addresses or prices can be inserted.

Thumbnail
A miniature graphic representation of an image.

.tiff
A standard file format used to store graphic images that can handle monochrome, grayscale, 8-bit or 24-bit color images.

Tile
To arrange a group of windows so that they are displayed side-by-side without overlapping.

UART
Abbreviation for Universal Asynchronous Receiver/Transmitter. A chip that

receives data from a modem whenever it arrives and stores it ready for access by your computer's processor and does the same thing for data going from the computer to the modem.

Undo
A function that lets you undo the task that you've just carried out. For example, it can undo a paste or a delete operation.

Unix
A multi-user, multi-tasking operating system developed by AT&T Bell Laboratories to run on almost any computer, from a PC to minicomputers and large mainframes.

Upgrade
To improve the performance or specification of your computer by adding more RAM, a larger hard disk or another kind of improvement. Software can also be upgraded.

URL
Abbreviation for Uniform Resource Locator. This is the Internet system used to standardize the way in which World Wide Web addresses are written. For example, the URL of the Microsoft home page is http://www.microsoft.com.

USB
Abbreviation for Universal Serial Bus, a communications bus for PCs that will eventually replace serial and parallel ports. It is fitted to new PCs and offers high data transfer rates. Up to 127 devices can be daisychained to a single USB port, in much the same way as seven devices can be linked to SCSI controllers.

Usenet
A section of the Internet that has forums, called newsgroups, in which you can comment on or add to other messages.

VDO Mail
A program designed to send and receive videomail.

Video adapter, board, controller
A board which plugs into an expansion socket in your PC and converts data into signals to drive a monitor.

Video capture board or card
An electronic board which plugs into an expansion socket in your PC and lets you display a TV picture.

Videoconferencing
Linking two or more PCs that can capture and display video and audio so that distant people can talk and see each other.

Video graphics card
An expansion card that fits into an expansion slot in your PC and allows it to display text and graphics.

Video mail
A way of sending and receiving email that includes real-time video capture by means of a Webcam.

Virtual
Something which does not actually exist except in an imaginary form in a computer.

Virtual memory
A large imaginary main memory which is made available to an operating system by storing unused parts of the virtual memory on disk and then transferring these parts into available main memory as and when they are required.

Virtual reality (VR)
A simulation of a real-life scene or environment by a PC which you can interact with and explore.

Virus checker
A piece of software used to check all files, including memory, on your computer for viruses. You should use virus checkers before opening email attachments.

Voicemail
Voicemail software answers your telephone for you. In conjunction with a modem with voice facilities, it will play a recorded greeting and record your callers' messages.

Wallpaper
In Windows, an image or pattern used as a background in a window. You can change the wallpaper from Control Panels.

WAVE or .wav file
In Windows, a standard method of storing an analog signal in digital form.

Webcam
A device that allows real-time video capture.

Webmaster
The person responsible for planning, design, maintenance, and marketing of Web pages.

Web browser
Used for accessing and viewing Web pages. The two most popular browsers are Microsoft's Internet Explorer and Netscape Navigator, which is part of Netscape's Communicator suite.

Web page
A single page of formatted text and graphics, coded as HTML, within a Web site.

White Pages
Any online directory that contains real-world information such as street addresses and telephone numbers, rather than just email details.

WhoWhere
An Internet-based directory for locating people.

Wild card
A symbol used when searching for files or data which represents all files. The wild card character "?" will match any single character in this position. The wild card character "or" means match any number of characters.

Windows Messaging
The updated version of Windows Exchange. It provides communications facilities for email, faxing, and networking.

WinFaxPro
The best-known fax software (from Symantec) including 200 cover-page designs, integration with Microsoft Exchange phonebooks, and more.

WinZip
A file compression tool that produces files with a .zip extension.

Wizard
A facility that provides interactive help and advice. Clicking on a button to activate a wizard starts up a question and answer procedure to find out what you want to do. Once the wizard has determined your needs, it will perform the task for you or let you do it yourself while it monitors the procedure.

World Wide Web (WWW)
Thousands of pages of formatted text and graphics (stored as HTML) that present a user-friendly graphical interface to the Internet.

Wysiwig
'What you see is what you get.' A word-processing or desktop publishing program where what you see on the screen is exactly the same as the image or text that will be printed.

Yahoo!
The biggest and best-known Internet search engine, which operates as a directory with Web sites sorted into categories.

.zip file
A file format used to save disk space. A single .zip file is used as a container for one or more compressed files. These must be expanded to their original size before they can be used.

Index